THE GALLIC WAR

GAIUS JULIUS CAESAR (?100–44 BC) was born into the senatorial aristocracy which controlled the operations of the Roman empire. Always a supporter of popular measures in the politics of the city, he became consul in 59 with the support of Pompey ('the Great'), but the alliance did not last, and the two men became first political and then military rivals. A ten-year proconsular command in the Roman province of Gaul brought him immense wealth as well as control of a huge and devoted army, both of which factors in 49 BC enabled him to challenge Pompey for supremacy at Rome. The civil war which resulted left him, after Pompey's defeat at Pharsalus and death in Egypt, in sole control of Rome's affairs; the perpetual dictatorship and extraordinary honours which followed marked a shift in the structures of Roman politics which, despite his assassination on the Ides of March 44, was to prove permanent, and which played its part in the change from Republic to Principate. The accounts which he wrote of his campaigns against the peoples of Gaul, Britain, and Germany (*The Gallic War*) and against Pompey (*The Civil War*) have been valued for centuries as classics of military practice and literary excellence.

CAROLYN HAMMOND read Literae Humaniores at St John's College, Oxford. In 1990 she was elected to a Research Fellowship at Downing College, Cambridge, where her work included studies of the battle narratives of Caesar and Livy. She was Curate at the Church of St Mary the Virgin, Gamlingay from 1997 to 2005, and is now Dean of Caius College, Cambridge.

OXFORD WORLD'S CLASSICS

JULIUS CAESAR

Seven Commentaries on The Gallic War

with an Eighth Commentary by

AULUS HIRTIUS

Translated with an Introduction and Notes by
CAROLYN HAMMOND

OXFORD
UNIVERSITY PRESS

OXFORD
UNIVERSITY PRESS

Great Clarendon Street, Oxford OX2 6DP

Oxford University Press is a department of the University of Oxford.
It furthers the University's objective of excellence in research, scholarship,
and education by publishing worldwide in

Oxford New York

Auckland Bangkok Buenos Aires Cape Town Chennai
Dar es Salaam Delhi Hong Kong Istanbul Karachi Kolkata
Kuala Lumpur Madrid Melbourne Mexico City Mumbai Nairobi
São Paulo Shanghai Singapore Taipei Tokyo Toronto

with an associated company in Berlin

Oxford is a registered trade mark of Oxford University Press
in the UK and in certain other countries

Published in the United States
by Oxford University Press Inc., New York

British Library Cataloguing in Publication Data

Data available

Library of Congress Cataloging in Publication Data

Caesar, Julius
[De bello Gallico, English]
Seven commentaries on the Gallic war / Julius Caesar; translated
by Carolyn Hammond. With an eighth commentary by Aulus Hirtius.
(Oxford world's classics)
Includes bibliographical references.
1. Gaul—History—Gallic Wars, 58–51 B.C. 2. Great Britain—
History—Roman period, 55 B.C.—14 A.D. 3. Caesar, Julius—Military
leadership. I. Hirtius, Aulus. De bello Ballico. Liber 8.
II. Title. III. Series.
DC62.C2813 1996 936.4—dc20 95–31674

ISBN 978–0–19–954026–6

13

Printed in Great Britain by
Clays Ltd, St Ives plc

ELIZABETHAE VERAE CAESAREANAE

You all do know this mantle: I remember
The first time ever Caesar put it on;
'Twas on a summer's evening, in his tent,
That day he overcame the Nervii:—

      (SHAKESPEARE, *Julius Caesar*, II. ii)

That civilization may not sink,
Its great battle lost,
Quiet the dog, tether the pony
To a distant post;
Our master Caesar is in the tent
Where the maps are spread,
His eyes fixed upon nothing,
A hand under his head.
Like a long-legged fly upon the stream
His mind moves upon silence.

      (W. B. YEATS, *Long-legged Fly*)

PREFACE

A new translation of *The Gallic War* does call for some explanation, not least because a number of versions are already available. Yet each generation needs its own translation of any classic text: the culture and mores of the translator's own time are bound to leave their mark. Besides, the subject-matter of *The Gallic War* is potentially distasteful, even immoral, for the modern reader. The drive to increase territorial holdings, high civilian as well as military casualties, and the predominance of economic motives for organized aggression—all these belong to an accepted norm of international activity in the ancient world, and hence need careful introduction and explanation as well as up-to-date translation. *The Gallic War*, moreover, is unique in kind. For as well as illustrating in depth the military practices and preoccupations of the first-century aristocratic Roman, it also provides a first-person *apologia pro suis rebus gestis* for the most famous Roman of them all, and an *apologia*, moreover, which its author intended to reflect on, and influence, the events of the civil war through which Republic gave way to Principate.

In making this translation, my thanks go to Philip Pattenden for his help with matters of time-reckoning, and to Grace Corne for her information on the use of woad as a dye. I have been indebted more times than I care to remember to the advice and assistance of Philip Rubery and Paul Millett.

CONTENTS

LIST OF ILLUSTRATIONS

INTRODUCTION

Caesar's Career

Gaius Julius Caesar, born about 100 BC, murdered by his supposed friends and colleagues on the Ides of March 44 BC, is one of the most famous protagonists on the stage of ancient history. The most important and detailed contemporary source for his life and political career, with the exception of his own extant writings, is Cicero, whose speeches and letters offer a wealth of information and reflection on Caesar. Much later, his life was celebrated by biographers: early in the second century AD Suetonius presented him as the first of the Roman emperors, while his Greek near-contemporary, Plutarch, compared Caesar with the most famous and successful general the Greeks and Romans had ever known—Alexander the Great. Indeed, it is from Plutarch's vision of Caesar that Shakespeare draws the inspiration, characterization, and information for his play about the Ides of March and its consequences.

The biographical style of both Suetonius and Plutarch is moral and anecdotal: Suetonius underlines the fact of his extraordinary achievements, but does not carry the theme of ambition through to the very end:

he may be judged to have misused power and deserved assassination. Not only did he receive excessive honours, such as a perpetual consulship, dictatorship, and prefecture of morals, the title of Imperator ['commander'] as a first name, the title of Father of his Country as a last name, a statue among the kings of Rome, and a throne on a platform at the theatre: he also allowed himself to be voted divine honours . . . (*The Divine Julius* (*DJ*) 76)

Caesar left certain of his friends with the impression that he had no desire to live longer, since he was no longer enjoying good health; and that it was on this account that he paid no heed to omens or to the warnings of his friends. (*DJ* 86)

Plutarch, on the other hand, makes Caesar's drive for preeminence the *leitmotiv* of his *Life* and a cause of both his rise to power and his downfall:

It is said that while Caesar was crossing the Alps and passing through a barbarian village of wretched appearance with only a few inhabitants, his companions laughed and said, 'Can it possibly be that even here there are ambitions for office, struggles for supremacy, and jealousies between powerful men?' But Caesar answered in all seriousness, 'I would rather be first among these men than second among the Romans' . . . Likewise, as he was reading about Alexander . . . he wept: when his friends wondered why, he told them, 'Do you not think it a reason for grieving that at my age Alexander was king over so many nations, while I as yet have achieved no glorious deed?' (*Caesar* 11)

Caesar died at the age of 56, having survived Pompey for little more than four years. But as for the power and sovereignty which he had struggled to achieve throughout his life, the only fruit he harvested from them was a title and a glory which aroused the envious hatred of his fellow-citizens. (*Caesar* 69)

This picture of Caesar's life and career as an interaction between extraordinary talent and destructive ambition has been influential, and is still persuasive. He was, after all, a man who rewrote history, and who did so in two quite different ways. In metaphorical terms, he rewrote history in that his career spanned, and in a sense even generated, the shift from Republic to Principate. Thus Caesar figures in the historical record as both destroyer of the Republic and founder of the Empire. In literal terms, on the other hand, he rewrote history in that he himself composed historical narratives, which he called 'memoirs' or 'commentaries' (*commentarii*) on two of the wars in which he was engaged. The last three commentaries are usually known as *The Civil War* (*CW*); the first seven, translated here together with an eighth by Caesar's lieutenant Hirtius, are known as *The Gallic War* (*GW*). 'Rewrote', of course, implies that not everything in the Gallic and civil wars happened precisely as he tells us.

It is essential to evaluate Caesar's writings in their proper setting by considering the social and political context of his career, and the force and range of the competitive ethos of the Roman aristocracy, to see how the acquisition of an empire helped to channel this ethos into expression on a world scale. The Julian family (*gens Julia*), was among the small group of Roman families known as 'patrician': these

patrician families constituted a caste entitled to certain political and religious privileges and duties. In most respects, however, the archaic distinction between patrician and plebeian
citizens had ceased to be significant by the first century. By
now the major political divide was between two groups less
clearly differentiated by birth, namely, the senatorial aristocracy (*nobiles*) and the people (with certain exceptions, the
terms *populus* and *plebs* are now used without distinction).
A third group, the *equites*, fed men like Marius and Cicero
into the senatorial aristocracy through the hierarchy of
magistracies.

In Caesar's day, then, neither being a patrician nor being
a *nobilis* was primarily a matter of ideological allegiance.
Certainly neither category entailed supporting suppression of
popular interests in favour of those of the élite: indeed, Caesar
made his way to the top by championing (or exploiting, depending on your point of view) the popular interest at Rome.
Contrary to the impression given by some of our sources for
Roman history, the majority of Roman citizens who made up
the electorate were by no means servile and submissive to the
dictates of aristocratic politicians. The Roman people had a
voice and agenda of its own, which often ran counter to the
Senate: politicians who wanted to succeed had to be seen to
please the people and protect its interests. Understanding this
point is essential to an accurate assessment of Caesar's career.

As for the Senate, it was a body of aristocrats which for-
mulated decisions and provided the magistrates to run the
city and its territories. But it had no powers to pass legislation on its own, and so it was dependent upon the goodwill
of the people to give legal force to its deliberations.

The Roman people in turn depended on magistrates to
execute its decisions, among them the unique institution called
the tribunes of the people (*tribuni plebis*), which played such
an important part in the troubles of the late Republic. The
ten tribunes were sacrosanct, and had the right of veto
(*intercessio*) against actions of other magistrates, including
other tribunes. They were even entitled to bring legislation
directly before the people, without reference to the Senate. In
133 BC Tiberius Gracchus used his position as tribune of the

people to bypass the Senate and introduce controversial new laws to the advantage of the people. He and many of his supporters were murdered by his senatorial opponents when he tried to stand for a second tribunate: ever since, some Roman aristocrats had been keen to follow his example in winning the people's support, though not to share his fate.

His brother Gaius Gracchus was the first to imitate and exploit what came to be seen as a 'popular' political model. He extended the range of popular political strategies to include not just laws for the distribution of corn to citizens, but also the increased influence and authority of the *equites* at the expense of the Senate. He was even credited with attempting to extend the franchise to the Latins, just as—much later—Caesar aimed to enfranchise the Transpadanes (a means of expanding his base of electoral support). Unlike his brother, Gaius did win a second tribunate, but in 121 the Senate reasserted itself: his supporters were executed without trial and the magistrate responsible tried and acquitted.

These unhappy precedents did not deter imitators. Men like Caesar and his contemporary Publius Clodius were only the last of a succession of politicians who mobilized the strength of the Roman people as a means of winning and perpetuating office during the later Republic. Of course, in so far as the Roman people *elected* their magistrates, *all* politicians needed to win popular favour. But not all politicians were prepared to signal support of the many at the expense (or so it might appear) of the few. Like Caesar, Clodius was born into a patrician family (the *gens Claudia*). But Clodius had himself co-opted into the *plebs*, because he wanted to become a tribune of the people, and the magistracy was not open to patricians. Although the same route to political advancement was open to Caesar, he did not take this option. He remained a patrician, and instead climbed the more conventional career ladder of magistracies: quaestor, aedile, praetor, propraetor, consul, proconsul. The other magistracy which he held, the dictatorship, was not part of the conventional career structure of the Roman aristocrat: but this ancient emergency magistracy, revived in the 80s by the dictator Cornelius Sulla, was to become a convenient and adaptable office by which Caesar could control Rome, without the squabbling inconvenience of an ambitious consular colleague.

Like other members of the Roman élite, Caesar began adult life as a citizen with military service, in Asia and Cilicia (80–78 BC). Such military service was a privilege as well as a duty of citizenship. Again like other Romans—notably Cicero in 70—he undertook a prosecution (of the consular Gnaeus Cornelius Dolabella) as a way of making his mark in the city. Advocacy was another privilege of the aristocratic citizen: an opportunity for winning friends and demonstrating allegiance and, crucially, of developing and displaying the oratorical skills on which a successful political career depended. According to Cicero, Caesar was a notable orator. In the *Brutus*, a rhetorical treatise written in 46 BC, probably while Caesar was wiping out the remnant of the Pompeian resistance in Africa, Cicero makes his friend and correspondent Atticus speak with warm praise of Caesar's ability:

Caesar . . . corrects corrupt and faulty habits with simple and accurate usage. Thus when he adds to his skilful choice of Latin words (this is indispensable for every freeborn Roman citizen, even if you are not an orator) rhetorical ornaments, then he seems—as it were—to be setting well-painted pictures to hang in a good light . . . I see no one for whom he must make way. He possesses a certain clarity in his manner of speaking which has nothing to do with preparation or practice: in voice, gesture and appearance his manner is, so to speak, grand and noble. (261)

When Suetonius discusses Caesar's oratory, he quotes a part of the *Brutus* passage. He also makes explicit the importance of the link between skill as a public speaker and political advancement, when he notes that: 'In both eloquence and military skill, Caesar either equalled the excellence of the best men or he surpassed it' (*DJ* 55).

Caesar became a quaestor (the lowest of the magistracies conferring membership of the Senate) in 69 BC. Two years later he was signalling both his support of Pompey (then Rome's most important commander and politician) and his 'popular' intentions by speaking in favour of the Gabinian and Manilian laws. These gave a special command to Pompey, among other things to curb the piracy which appeared to pose such a serious threat to Rome's food supply. Both of these laws were passed by tribunes of the people despite opposition from the Senate.

Pompey's military reputation has suffered severely as a result of the damaging portrait of him painted by Caesar in *The Civil War*; but this ought not to be allowed to obscure the spectacular nature of his political ascent—much more spectacular, in fact, and much more 'unconstitutional' than Caesar's more conventional early career. By the 60s Pompey was Rome's most important commander and politician. He had raised an army on his own initiative in 83 to support Sulla in the civil war, and in 82 was sent to Africa to defeat his enemies, first as Sulla's legate and then with an extraordinary command (the propraetorian *imperium*). Out of this came a triumph at the age of about 26, and the surname 'the Great' (*Magnus*)—perhaps an ironic or even malicious gift from the dictator, perhaps his own attempt to style himself after Alexander. All despite the fact that Pompey was not properly eligible to stand for even the lowest magistracy, the quaestorship, until he had reached the age of 30.

At about the age of 35, in 65 BC, Caesar was a mere curule aedile. This urban magistracy carried the obligation of holding games on public holidays—another means of winning popular support. Two years later, in 63 BC, Caesar became chief priest (*pontifex maximus*). This was not a magistracy but an influential religious position. Its importance may be gauged by the scandal caused when he defeated two senior and more distinguished senators to get it. Not implausibly, Suetonius attributes his success to bribery on a large scale: 'He counted up the sum of his debts, and in the morning set off for the election, reputedly saying to his mother as she kissed him goodbye that if he did not return as chief priest he would not return at all' (*DJ* 13). This was the year of the conspiracy of Catiline. It was also a year in which the issue of sacrosanctity of the people's tribunes was raised once more, this time through the prosecution of an old man called Rabirius, a prosecution behind which Caesar's hand was detected.

During 62, when he was praetor, the rites of the Bona Dea, a goddess worshipped only by women, were held at Caesar's house. The bizarre incident of Clodius being found there dressed as a woman prompted Caesar, so Cicero tells us, to send a messenger giving his second wife Pompeia the news that they were divorced—because, as Plutarch makes him say, 'Caesar's wife must be above suspicion' (*Caesar* 10: see also Cicero, *Letters to Atticus* 1.12, 13). He had married Pompeia in 67, two years after the death of his first wife Cornelia, whom he married in 84. The following year he went out to Further Spain (Hispania Ulterior) as *pro*praetor. Because there were too few regular annual magistrates to supply governors for the growing number of Rome's subject territories, it had become standard practice to extend a magistracy for a further period, usually of one year. The promagistracy could also be conferred without the holding of the regular magistracy, as happened in 61 when Caesar became proconsul of Further Spain, and successfully conducted his first military campaign, against the Lusitani, a people of western Spain who had been conquered by Pompey in the 70s. He stood for the consulship, the supreme magistracy held annually by two men, in 60 BC.

In 60 BC Pompey, Crassus, and Caesar formed an unofficial pact which has come to be known as the 'first triumvirate' (on the analogy of the triumvirate of Antony, Octavian, and Lepidus in 43). The historian Asinius Pollio survived the civil wars of 49–31 to write a history of Rome under Augustus, and chose the moment of this pact as the start of his account of those wars. Caesar, by contrast, ignores the pact and its renewal (see *GW* 3.2). Pompey had held the consulship in 70 BC with Crassus as his colleague: they were by now senior consulars, men of power and prestige. At the time they must have appeared to outrank Caesar. With their support, he was elected consul for 59: his colleague, Bibulus, was hostile and uncooperative. Nevertheless, Caesar could now ensure that Crassus, who was notoriously wealthy and had lent him large sums, was paid off. Until he returned to Rome at the end of 62 Pompey had been campaigning in the East, enriching both the state and himself. Now he needed his actions confirmed by the Senate, and his veteran soldiers suitably rewarded, and Caesar, who was well placed to ensure both, had Pompey's settlement of the East ratified, and set about a distribution of land to his veterans.

Succeeding in Roman politics was an expensive business, but a foreign war offered opportunities for enriching self and state (i.e. the Roman people) at the same time. No doubt Caesar would have been impressed by the example of Pompey's conquests in the East. So it was a matter of considerable importance what province (the word means both 'territory' and 'sphere of command') would be offered to him in 58 BC, when he would follow the usual route for ex-consuls of going abroad for a year or more as a proconsul. According to Suetonius, instead of naming a territory the Senate had decreed 'the woods and pastures' (*DJ* 19) as the proconsular province for 58. The reason for this unusual designation is not clear. Perhaps it was a temporary expedient, to allow time for the threat from Gaul to be assessed. In any case, Caesar was not satisfied, and mobilized the special powers of the tribunes to get what he wanted: the tribune Vatinius carried a law for Caesar which gave him Cisalpine Gaul and Illyricum as his province. The Senate had no say in this tribunician law, not even in the appointment of Caesar's subordinate officers (or 'legates': *legati*). Transalpine Gaul was soon added to his province, and the proconsulship was set to last for five years.

During his years in Gaul Caesar campaigned against both Gallic and German peoples, and breached the frontiers of the Rhine and English Channel. These achievements won him fame at home as well as—presumably—sufficient riches to pay off debts incurred in winning his magistracies (a crucial factor in the search for a 'suitable' proconsular province); both the fame and the wealth were to stand him in good stead at the end of 50 BC, by which time it was clear to everyone that civil war was looming. This was the moment when he must have written and published the seven books of *The Gallic War*. Caesar does not give us his own account of the final deterioration of relations between himself and Pompey: the eighth commentary was written after Caesar's death by his supporter and lieutenant Aulus Hirtius, and takes the story of the war from the end of 52 right up to the eve of civil war.

Rome's political consensus was breaking down. From 51 onwards, Caesar's enemies at Rome began trying to have him recalled and brought to trial. It was partly the need to avoid prosecution that made him so eager for the consulship of 48, for he could not be prosecuted during the term of his magistracy. Again, it was through tribunes of the people that Caesar tried to defend his interests at Rome—this time the younger Curio and Mark Antony, who tried to quash the attempt by Caesar's opponents to force him home without his army. But Curio and Antony failed. At the beginning of January the Senate, relying on Pompey to defend it, decreed that Caesar must dismiss his army and return, and put its own forces in Pompey's hands. Caesar crossed the Rubicon into Italy with his army, and the civil war began.

Caesar's first campaign of the civil war took place in Spain against Pompey's lieutenants (CW 1). Curio, fighting on Caesar's side (or, as Caesar would put it, 'for the Roman people'), was defeated and killed in Africa (CW 2). In 49 BC Caesar was elected dictator for the first time, but resigned the office on becoming consul for the second time, in 48. In that same year he defeated Pompey at the Battle of Pharsalus (CW 3), and Pompey fled to Egypt where he was murdered. Caesar spent most of 47 campaigning in the east, with an interlude for his famous liaison with Cleopatra.

The war continued until the Battle of Munda in 45 BC, when all opposition was wiped out, or so it appeared. Caesar held his third, fourth, and fifth consulships from 46 to 44 in succession: but by 44, when it seems he was edging towards a more glamorous—and dangerous—title, that of king (rex), his opponents had found another way to mark their enmity, and on 15 March they killed him.

Caesar's Army

The Roman army, like Caesar himself, is a famous character in history. Its reputation for ruthless efficiency and organization as a unit, and the reputation of the individual soldiers for courage, especially of the self-sacrificing kind, are unparalleled among both ancient and modern armies. Caesar generally assumes that his reader is well acquainted with all the necessary detailed information about the army's command-structure, equipment, and tactics. Thus, if his account is to make sense the minutiae of military organization must often be supplied from other sources.

The largest regular unit of the Roman army was the legion, with a nominal strength of 6,000 soldiers: since Marius' reorganization at the end of the second century BC even the poorest citizens were eligible for the privilege and duty of military service. These reforms also brought about the arrangement of the legion into cohorts rather than maniples ('handfuls' of men): ten cohorts per legion each containing 600 men, three maniples (each of 200 men) per cohort, two centuries per maniple. Even when the strength of the legion dropped well below 6,000 (perhaps because of battle casualties) the number of cohorts was kept at ten. Under Marius the eagle (*aquila*) had become the standard symbol for each legion, but the cohorts each had their own standards (*signa*) as well: these were used to signal the start of a march, manœuvre or battle.

Just as each legion had a number, according to when it was enrolled, so did each cohort (the more experienced soldiers were put in the first cohorts). There was no longer any obligation to serve from youth till the age of 46: legionaries typically served twenty years or sixteen campaigns before discharge. Some were volunteer re-enlisted veterans (*evocati*). All the soldiers in a legion by now carried the same equipment: they wore defensive body-armour made of leather and metal, and carried a shield (*scutum*) made of wood covered with leather and metal. The usual offensive weapons carried were the sword (*gladius*) and javelin (*pilum*). Military pay was low, and so the legionary expected profit to come from successful campaigns.

The auxiliary forces who accompanied the legions consisted of light-armed troops supplied by subject territories. They were often stationed on the wings in battle, though if the Roman commander had doubts about their loyalty he would sometimes place them in the centre to stop them running away. There might be as many auxiliaries as heavy (i.e. legionary) infantry in the armies of Caesar's day, including javelin-throwers (*iaculatores*), slingers (*funditores*), and archers (*sagittarii*).

By the first century BC the cavalry was also composed of allied and provincial foreigners. About 300 cavalry usually accompanied each legion, and these were divided into squadrons (*alae*), each of which subdivided into troops (*turmae*). The troops subdivided again into decurions (*decuriae*). They were mainly used for skirmishing, scouting, and pursuing routed enemies, but the mobility afforded by their being mounted made it easy for them to run away in times of danger, and they were thus treated as unreliable: Caesar never shows himself depending on them.

When on the march, the army was usually arranged in a column (*agmen*). Each legion had its own baggage: as well as the individual soldiers' packs (*sarcinae*), there was the heavy baggage (*impedimenta*), including siege-engines and equipment carried by pack animals or on waggons. On the march the army could typically cover about 15 miles in a day, though by forced marches (*magna itinera*) the distance might be considerably more. When deployed for battle, the ten cohorts of the legion formed up with four in the front line, then a line of three, and finally three more at the back (*triplex acies*): this enabled the commander to combine manœuvrability and depth of front facing the enemy.

The Roman camp in Republican times followed a uniform pattern (see diagram), with the same arrangement of gates (*portae*), transected by the same arrangement of roads (*via principalis; via quintana*), very much like a small town, with even a market-place (*forum*). The standard ancient description of a Roman camp is given by the second-century BC Greek historian Polybius (6.27–32: some of the details of his account are controversial). Those camps which were to be occupied throughout a winter or a campaigning season were strongly fortified: but they followed the same plan as the camp of an army on the march which was stopping only for

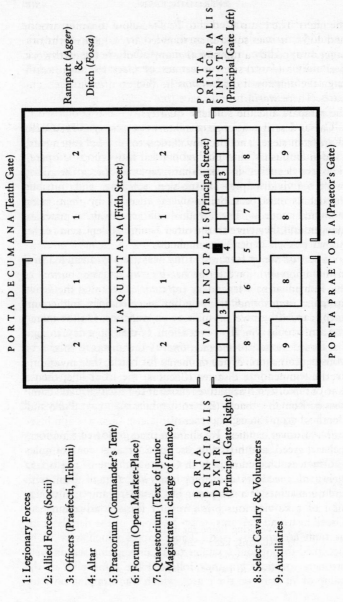

1: Legionary Forces

2: Allied Forces (Socii)

3: Officers (Praefecti, Tribuni)

4: Altar

5: Praetorium (Commander's Tent)

6: Forum (Open Market-Place)

7: Quaestorium (Text of Junior
Magistrate in charge of finance)

8: Select Cavalry & Volunteers

9: Auxiliaries

PORTA DECUMANA (Tenth Gate)

PORTA PRAETORIA (Praetor's Gate)

VIA QUINTANA (Fifth Street)

VIA PRINCIPALIS (Principal Street)

PORTA PRINCIPALIS SINISTRA (Principal Gate Left)

PORTA PRINCIPALIS DEXTRA (Principal Gate Right)

Rampart (Agger) & Ditch (Fossa)

FIG. 1 Plan of a Roman Camp

the night. The camp needed to be sited close to water, wood, and food; it was square, surrounded by a high earthwork (*agger*) topped by a rampart (*vallum*). Outside the earthwork was a ditch (*fossa*) some 9 feet across and 7 feet deep: earth from the digging of ditches was heaped up to form the ramparts. There was a broad space (*intervallum*) inside between the rampart and the soldiers' quarters.

Caesar describes a range of military operations in *The Gallic War*, from sieges and circumvallation to naval engagements, sudden ambushes, and pitched battles. Most of these operations are described in a few paragraphs at most. The result is often a vivid, impressionistic sketch of what went on; but the details must be supplied by the reader's imagination or from other sources. The technical military details he provides may often be sketchy: on the other hand, his depiction of the Roman soldiers under his command is one of the most prominent and distinctive features of his narrative, and has made a lasting impression on later generations for its contribution to the Roman army's legendary reputation. Nothing in Greek literature corresponds to the prominence of these soldiers or to their moral—as well as military—significance in the explanation of the action. The centurions have a special place in Caesar's depiction of the men under his command: their acts of conspicuous bravery at moments of crisis can be pivotal in averting impending disaster (Baculus, 3.5, 6.38; Petronius, 7.50) or in offering narrative reassurance to balance and compensate Roman setbacks (Balventius, Lucanius, 5.35; Pullo and Vorenus, 5.44; Fabius, 7.47; see also 6.40). In most Latin literature, however, soldiers are characterized more by aggression, lechery, greed, and boastfulness. For Suetonius, for example, lechery was a hallmark of both Caesar and his men: he offers plenty of anecdotes describing Caesar's sexual adventures, and quotes lines of a song sung at Caesar's triumph, in which his men take vicarious pride in their leader's achievements:

> We bring home the bald adulterer—
> Romans, keep your wives indoors;
> All the gold you borrowed, Caesar,
> Went to pay your Gallic whores.
>
> (*DJ* 51)

There is nothing to correspond with this in *The Gallic War*. Neither Caesar nor his men are described as having anything to do with the prostitutes who were a regular part of army life. Other negative characteristics such as aggression, greed, and boastfulness do surface, but only in particular contexts, intended to help the reader evaluate the progress of an action or anticipate its outcome. So, for example, if greed and aggression are predicated of Gauls or other enemies, they tend to signal moral and military inferiority to the Romans. If they are attached to Romans, it is usually because Caesar wants to explain a setback: thus, the aggression of the Romans at Gergovia (*GW* 7.47) is represented as over-enthusiasm, a creditable expression of courage which should have been controlled and exploited by the officers. It may seem surprising that aggression appears as a mainly negative characteristic, but throughout *The Gallic War* Caesar stresses the relationship between himself and his men as one of co-operation and above all *control*. Uncontrolled aggression poses a threat to strategic planning and careful tactics. The proof of this comes from the Gauls and Germans, whose random aggression is highlighted to form a contrast with the channelled, organized sort displayed by the Romans.

Greed is closely linked with aggression as a negative factor and a dangerous motivator of men: among the Gauls it usually signals defeat or weakens their moral position (e.g. 7.37). The part actually played by expectations of enrichment in the motivation of the Roman soldier is impossible to quantify. Certainly the historical sources tend to reflect a more positive version of the kind of inducements on offer than the simple desire for booty:

The Romans are good at inciting their young men to face danger . . . The commander calls a meeting of the army and makes those who have done some outstanding deed stand forward. First he praises each one for his courage and anything else in his earlier conduct which is worth mentioning. Then he distributes the rewards. (Polybius, 6.39)

Caesar lavished generous rewards, which showed that he was not piling up wealth from his wars for his private luxury or a life of ease: rather he laid it aside in trust as a prize for bravery which was open to all. (Plutarch, *Caesar* 17)

But even in Caesar's text there are hints that the safety and glory of Rome, and the hope of rewards for courage, were not always the primary motivating factor for the legionaries. In *GW* 6, when Caesar and his subordinates are trying to crush the Eburones, there is a possibility that greed will endanger the Romans: 'Great care was needed . . . to keep the individual soldiers safe . . . for the desire for plunder lured many of them farther afield, while the woods, with their strange and hidden paths, prevented them marching in close formation' (*GW* 6.34). Similarly, Caesar is prepared to mention the desire for plunder in negative terms, for example, at the siege of Avaricum, when the Romans' desire to avenge the deaths of fellow-citizens is so strong that it overcomes the desire for enrichment: 'Not one of our men gave a thought to booty. They were so severely provoked by the massacre at Cenabum and the effort they had put into the siege that they spared neither the elderly, nor the women, nor even the little children' (*GW* 7.28). Boasting is the most distinctive indicator of Gallic and German inferiority, perhaps because it is a feature strongly associated with commanders as much as with their men. Caesar, naturally, never describes himself boasting of past achievements or promising future ones beyond his ability to deliver, and this is in sharp contrast to the way he characterizes the German Ariovistus, or the Arvernian Vercingetorix. Ariovistus boasts that the Germans are invincible (*GW* 1.36), Vercingetorix of the ease with which the rebel Gauls will impede Roman advances (*GW* 7.14). In *The Gallic War*, when Caesar is the commander, the link between boasting and defeat would be unlikely to surface on the Roman side. But the expectation emerges from comparable narratives that Roman commanders who boast of their ability to win battles usually come to grief in a conspicuous manner: this is true of Minucius and Varro in the second Punic War (see Livy 22.14, 38), as it is true of Pompey—at least as Caesar describes him—at Pharsalus (*CW* 3.86).

Caesar's Targets

The opening sentences of *The Gallic War* give the reader a bare minimum of information about the peoples Caesar was to encounter. Not until the sixth commentary does he tell the reader in more detail about the Gauls and Germans (6.11–28). Even then, his account raises numerous difficulties: it is clear from various details that he is prepared to describe things which he has not observed in person. For example, he tells of an animal found in Germany which can only be the reindeer, but states that it has only one horn. Similarly, he claims that the elk has no joints in its legs, and recounts a method of trapping them based on that wholly erroneous fact (6.26–7). Often such problems can be solved by the explanation that he drew his information from a written source, rather than personal observation. But this solution raises problems of its own: because of independent evidence, it is obvious from such examples that he was reporting what he had not seen, while we have no distinct and separate sources by which to judge the accuracy of most of *The Gallic War*.

The name of the *Galli* had been a means of provoking fear among the Romans ever since they had invaded the city in 390 BC. Writing about thirty years after Caesar first entered Gaul, Livy gave an account of the Gallic sack, and included a discussion of Gallic customs which probably drew on the systematic ethnographical account by Posidonius, the influential first-century Greek philosopher (?135–50 BC). How far Caesar's ethnography was itself influenced by Posidonius is a moot point, but at any rate it is clear that Livy had also read *The Gallic War*, for he echoes its famous opening words (5.34): it is apparent from his description that Caesar's account of Gallic and German customs had already become a standard.

In contrast to the Gauls, the Germans had threatened the safety of Rome more recently. At the end of the second century the migrations of two Germanic peoples called the Cimbri and Teutoni (see e.g. *GW* 1.40) had caused a panic which was only quelled by the victories of Gaius Marius. As well as reorganizing the army, Marius led it to a succession of famous victories in Africa and Gaul; he also happened to have been married to Caesar's aunt, Julia. Livy gave detailed information about the Germans in Book 104 of his history, but this is now lost. Still extant, however, is an ethnographic study by Tacitus, the *Origin and Geography of the Germans*, or *Germania*, which probably drew heavily not only on Caesar but also on another lost work, the *German Wars* of Pliny the Elder. It too echoes the opening of *The Gallic War* (*Germania* 1).

Caesar—notoriously—divides Gaul into three parts: Belgic, Aquitanian, and Celtic Gaul. His fellow Romans would have referred to these regions all together as Hairy Gaul (Gallia Comata), perhaps because the inhabitants wore their hair long. A fourth region is usually referred to by Caesar as the Province (modern Provence). It was also known as Transalpine Gaul (Gaul-across-the-Alps) in contrast to Cisalpine Gaul (Gaul-this-side-of-the-Alps; also called Nearer Gaul), or as Gallia Togata (Toga-Wearing Gaul), in contrast to Gallia Comata. In the Italian peninsula the River Rubicon marked the boundary between the territory of Cisalpine Gaul and that of Rome. The Province was in a different category and had a different status from Hairy Gaul in 58 BC. It had come under permanent Roman control in the second century, following the development of Roman links with Marseilles (Massilia), and the establishment of a permanent fortified base at Aquae Sextiae (Aix-en-Provence, the site of Marius' victory against the Teutoni in 102 BC). The Province gave Romans an important land-route from north Italy to Spain, where Roman influence had been much longer established.

At the time of Caesar's intervention the lands and peoples beyond the Province remained for the most part in obscurity. The Allobroges, a people living in the north-east of the Province (and south-west of the Helvetii, who were to be Caesar's first target), won a brief prominence for their part in exposing Catiline's conspiracy in 63 BC: according to Cicero, Catiline had tried to recruit them as part of a rebellion against the Roman ruling aristocracy both within and outside the city. They demonstrated their loyalty to the Senate instead and won praise for their trouble in Cicero's *Third Catilinarian Oration*. But the speech also betrays the fear and suspicion which Gallic peoples more often excited than gratitude: 'Could it be that Lentulus and the other conspirators in the city were so demented as to entrust these crucial matters to unknown barbarians . . . ? And what of these men from Gaul, from a state barely pacified, the only nation both able and willing to make war upon the Roman people . . . ?' (3.22) Little more than a year later, in 61, the Allobroges made such attacks on the Province that it was deemed necessary to send a praetor, Gaius Pomptinus, to subdue them (according to the excerptor of Livy 103: cf. Cassius Dio, 37.47–9).

Away from the Mediterranean climate and geography of the Province, Hairy Gaul must have seemed a cold and unattractive place to the Romans. Caesar was not the first to describe the customs and civilization of the Gauls, but like his Greek predecessor Posidonius he takes Gallic inferiority for granted, and treats them as barbarians—their customs and practices are interesting, but they are unquestionably inferior in every way to their would-be conquerors. Writing in the time of Caesar's adopted son Augustus, the geographer Strabo describes the Gauls as simple, argumentative, volatile, and boastful, and writes that they react foolishly to victory, and are panic-stricken by defeat. He quotes Posidonius for the Gallic custom of decapitation of enemies (*Geography* 4). In general, the Greeks and Romans who wrote about Gaul, and who are our only source except for archaeological remains, tended to react in two different ways to what they saw there or what they heard about Gaul. Either they assimilated the customs and practices they found to Roman or Greek equivalents, or they reacted against them as alien and barbarian. In either case, the preconceptions and expectations of the writer tend to distort the evidence they provide.

The pattern of Gallic urbanization, with the development of fortified towns (*oppida*) as centres of government and economic activity, was becoming well established by the start of the first century BC. The Romans, however, who would be looking for signs of structured town-planning and monumental civic building, did not recognize these as marks of culture on a level with their own. Caesar tells us that the Greek alphabetic script was in use in Gaul for the recording of public and private accounts (*GW* 6.14), but the point is made in the context of the reluctance of the Druids (*Druides*) to commit their teachings to writing. The Romans saw no evidence of a literate culture on a par with their own. Tacitus, indeed, remarks of the Germans, whose civilization borders that of the Gauls, that their only historical records were provided by ancient songs (*Germania* 2). Moreover, Caesar's picture of the systems of government and public office of the various Gallic communities is clearly assimilated to Roman practice. He writes of 'states' (*civitates*), 'senates' (*senatus*), 'leading citizens' (*principes*; *primores*), 'magistrates' (*magistratus*), 'factions' (*factiones*), 'dependants' (*clientelae*), and the like. So also he identifies the various Gallic deities by assimilation to their Roman counterparts (*GW* 6.17). As far as Gallic religious practice is concerned, the emphasis remains firmly on fascinating barbarity: the most famous proof of which is the custom of Druidic human sacrifice described at *GW* 6.16. The Germans are set still further apart from a model of civilization as the Romans perceived it: their religious practices are more primitive, while their nomadic lifestyle, strong emphasis on physical endurance, and total preoccupation with warfare all set them at odds with the development of agriculture, private property, and fortified cities by which Romans would have evaluated progress.

Caesar's Writings

All that remains of Caesar's literary output is the collection of seven commentaries on his campaigns in Gaul and three commentaries on his war against Pompey. The reader must look to later authors to discover his remarkable range. Suetonius gives a summary of his writings beginning with his published speeches, some of which were still available in the biographer's own time. Among the other writings noted by Suetonius is a work in two volumes which he was said to have composed while travelling back from Transalpine Gaul to hold assizes in Cisalpine Gaul, the *On Analogy*. Suetonius does not mention the year, but it may have been 52 BC. It was dedicated to Cicero, another Roman stylistic theorist. 'Analogy' as a stylistic principle entailed the elimination of irregularities of grammar: it was contrasted with 'anomaly', the recognition that irregular usages could be valid through custom. The publication of this work at such a time was

surely meant to do more than prove his all-round erudition
and range of skills: choice of grammatical and verbal style
appears to have been a matter of political significance, and it
is possible that the literary style, as well as content, of the
Commentaries was intended to convey a political message.

Also in two volumes was his *Anticato*, written in 45 BC,
the year of his victory at Munda over Pompey's sons. This
was a reaction against the theme of the *Cato* which Cicero
composed to praise the arch-Republican, pro-Senatorial, anti-
Caesarean politician after he died at Utica in 46. Though
Caesar did admire the style of Cicero's composition, he could
not allow such hagiography to go unchallenged. Plutarch,
who mostly ignores Caesar's literary productions, does discuss the *Anticato*. He is surprised to find it hostile, for he
also records an anecdote according to which, on finding Cato
dead at Utica, Caesar said, 'I begrudge you your death, Cato:
for you have begrudged me the chance to spare your life'.
Plutarch is prompted to ask at this point, 'how could he have
spared Cato's life, given that he pours out such a torrent of
wrath on him dead?' (*Caesar* 54)—a telling comment on how
Caesar's policy of so-called clemency was re-invented and
developed in the later tradition.

Suetonius grouped a number of other works at the end
of his list, including some poetry, and an arrangement of
Caesar's letters to the Senate. Some of the letters which he
wrote to Cicero still survive (*Letters to Atticus* 9.6a, 7c, 13a,
14, 16; 10.8b). More-intimate letters, written in a cipher for
which Suetonius helpfully provides his reader with a key, have
not survived. His *Collection of Sayings* is referred to by Cicero
(*Letters to Friends* 9.16) under the title of *Apophthegms*:
along with other minor works, it was suppressed by Augustus.
Suetonius does not explain why, but implies that these works
were not of a standard to reflect well on a Caesar who was
by this time officially 'the Divine Julius'.

The ten *Commentaries* are Caesar's outstanding literary
achievement, and the seven commentaries which make up
The Gallic War are the most polished and perfect of the ten.
In contrast, the three commentaries on *The Civil War* are
uneven in texture and of widely varying length and disjointed

structure. All the same, *The Civil War* still reveals a superiority in terms of literary technique when compared with the continuations of Caesar's text by unknown hands (usually referred to as the *Alexandrian War*, *African War*, and *Spanish War*). Critical opinion has, on the whole, been in agreement as to the excellence of their Latinity: in this respect at least, the *Commentaries* are simple and straightforward. Where, however, both the historical evidence they appear to provide and the aim and purpose of their composition are concerned, there is no such critical consensus: rather, a sharp dichotomy persists between those scholars who accept the historical evidence of the bulk of the *Commentaries* at face value, and those who assess the material primarily in terms of its relationship to a hypothesized authorial intention. In particular, scholars who take a positive view of Caesar and his achievements have tended to credit him with simple, honest, factual narration of what happened in the wars in Gaul. This approach is typified by the studies of the English scholar T. Rice Holmes. On the other hand, those who incline to the type of Caesar as an ambitious, machinating tyrant more often perceive within the narrative signs of propagandist manipulation of the material for personal political advantage. This alternative approach is exemplified in the writings of the French scholar Michel Rambaud, who refers to Rice Holmes in characteristically polemical terms, criticising the 'crédulité de l'anglais qui, "scholar and gentleman", défend César, parce qu'un gentleman comme César ne pouvait pas mentir' (*L'Art de la déformation historique dans les commentaires de César*, 8).

In the end, a dichotomy between 'factual' and 'propagandist' interpretations is unlikely to do justice to the complexities of the text. For one thing, manipulation of a narrative to show oneself in the best possible light may appear to a modern reader to be deceptive and fraudulent, while an ancient counterpart might regard this as both natural and appropriate. For another, the simplicity of Caesar's narrative (as was suggested earlier) may be meant to indicate association with 'popular' political causes: it cannot be dismissed as just a device to beguile and deceive the reader into accepting the narrative at face value. Though this latter is undoubtedly also an effect of the narrative, it may not be a wholly intentional or primary one.

Cicero's remarks on the style of *The Gallic War* have been much quoted from Suetonius onwards, though they are frequently misunderstood as proof that Caesar did not intend his *Commentaries* as polished, finished, historical compositions. They come, like the discussion of Caesar's oratory, from a passage in the *Brutus* (262):

Brutus replied: His speeches certainly appear to me extremely praiseworthy. I have read a number of them, and also his *Commentaries* which he composed about his deeds.

Atticus answered: They are indeed praiseworthy; they are like nude statues, upright and full of charm, stripped of all the clothing of rhetorical ornament. But while he wanted others to have material ready-prepared to select from when they wished to write history, he did a favour to fools, who want to apply curling-tongs to his material, but he surely deterred men of sense from writing: for in history there is nothing more pleasing than clear and brilliant brevity.

'Brevity', when applied to either oratory or history, points to what is usually known as the 'plain style': this term 'plain style' refers to a particular mode of rhetorical expression, not to a lack of rhetorical devices in composition. The metaphor of sculptured nudes reinforces Cicero's point that the *Commentaries* display a studied, artistic simplicity, not just an incidental lack of stylistic and narrative complexity.

The question of the date of composition of *The Gallic War* may also help to establish to what extent the *Commentaries* may appropriately be categorized as either 'factual' or 'propagandist'. Following the statements of Aulus Hirtius in the eighth commentary, some have simply accepted that each book or commentary was composed at the end of the year of which it gives an account, and then sent back to Rome as an official campaign report (8.48). Others, more plausibly, have seen in the text as a whole a coherence which makes annual composition unlikely: and have further perceived in Caesar's self-portrait a deliberate preparation and justification of his position in 50 BC. The easiest—and most probable—compromise suggestion is that the outline of each commentary was sketched during or just after the campaigning season, and that these outlines were later written up into their present form.

Certain features of Caesar's narrative are particularly distinctive. These are not mere idiosyncrasies, though. Form and style can indicate the views of an ancient writer with the same clarity as content. So, to describe Rome's decline and decay Sallust and Tacitus choose a disjointed and abrupt style, while to write of Rome's destiny and the glorious birth of her empire Livy chooses a richly elaborate one. Caesar writes in a remarkably pure and simple Latin which perhaps aligns him with the purity and simplicity of an ideal Rome. One of the most unexpected features of the text is that it is entirely written in the third person (with the exception of a small number of authorial interventions). Thus, in describing the action Caesar always refers to himself in the form, 'Caesar did . . .', never 'I did . . .'. It has been claimed that he was writing according to the rules of a particular genre, and that these rules obliged him to write in the third person: but the evidence that a text like *The Gallic War* had any obvious formal predecessor is not easy to substantiate. The precise effect, moreover, of the third-person narrative is difficult to calculate: it certainly fosters an air of objectivity, an illusion of independence. At times, the linear, point-by-point baldness of the narrative is evocative of a report style, and this also contributes to that effect.

Other features of his style, though they point to the same end, are more difficult to describe and assess—not least because they lack an obvious English equivalent. For example, in the ancient world the composition of both prose and poetry was informed by an acute sensitivity to both the presence and the absence of rhythm. In poetry, rhythm was divided into various metres (dactylic, iambic, etc.), each with particular generic associations; in prose it was important to achieve a shape and balance by a disciplined use of rhythm, while not becoming so rhythmical that the end-product was practically poetry. This balance was achieved in part by the restriction of distinctive rhythm to the ends of sentence-units (*clausulae*). Caesar avoids rhythmic prose, because it would be inappropriate to history written in the plain style; moreover, successions of long syllables at the ends of clauses—a feature most historical stylists would have avoided—are common. Rhythmic and stylistic elaboration tends to come, if at all, with moments of fast-moving or emotive narrative. In any case, a translation cannot adequately reproduce rhythmic effects, except by substituting the closest equivalent features of English prose style, such as anaphora, alliteration, and balanced short clauses.

A stylistic feature which Caesar shares with the other historians of antiquity is the use of the historic present tense at moments of tension or drama, particularly during battles and other fast-moving action. This is also too alien to a modern English idiom to be comfortably translated. For example, the news of storm-damage to Caesar's fleet during the second expedition to Britain is narrated in the perfect tense, but this changes to a historic present as Caesar begins to take action: 'Riders *came* to Caesar from Quintus Atrius, and *reported* that a storm had arisen ... Caesar *orders* the legions and the cavalry to be recalled: he himself *returns* to the ships' (5.10–11). The switch from imperfect or perfect to historic present can be abrupt: the following example also has short clauses with the verb standing first (instead of at the end as is more usual in Classical Latin prose), another device which cannot always be comfortably reproduced:

Left behind with the garrison because he *was* ill was Publius Sextius Baculus. He *had been* one of Caesar's senior centurions ... and by now *had gone* five days without food. Baculus *was anxious* for his own safety and everyone else's, and *emerges* unarmed from his tent. He *sees* the enemy looming close ... he *seizes* weapons and at the gate he *takes his stand*. The centurions *follow* his lead [*Consequuntur centuriones*: the verb comes first in the Latin] and together they *hold off* the attack for a while ... (6.38)

One of the most famous and distinctive features of Greek and Roman historiography is the universal custom of composing speeches for characters at important moments. The habit is so alien to a modern documentary approach to historical composition that scholars are only now abandoning the idea that the speeches found in ancient historiography have some basis in fact or contain some kernel of truth. Caesar's fellow Roman historians all compose lengthy direct (*oratio recta*) speeches for their characters, which are meant to help explain the action for the reader. Caesar's practice is rather different. Throughout Books 1 to 3 of *The Gallic War* no character is given direct speech. Any speech which is reported stays in its indirect, reported (*oratio obliqua*) form: for example, 'Ariovistus spoke and said that he had crossed the Rhine...' (rather than, 'Ariovistus spoke and said, "I have crossed the Rhine..."'). The reason for this is not entirely clear. From Book 4 onwards the use of direct speech begins to increase, but although Romans are allowed to encourage their fellow-soldiers in brief direct speech, the longest direct speeches are all given to Gauls, with an emphasis on barbarity and deception. It is worth remembering that the longest direct speech in the *Commentaries* is given by Caesar to the Arvernian Critognatus, and advocates cannibalism (*GW* 7.77); and that in *The Gallic War* Caesar never gives himself a single word of direct speech. In fact the only time he does speak directly in the *Commentaries* is, significantly, as the Battle of Pharsalus is about to begin (*CW* 3.85).

In this translation, the style and simplicity of Caesar's Latin has been reproduced as faithfully as possible without resorting to unnatural English expression. A restricted vocabulary and repetitive sentence-structure ('Caesar did this ... then Caesar did that') would not always make appealing reading, but these features are true to the feel of the original Latin, and are never used by Caesar in such long stretches as to make the text monotonous. The effects of historic presents, rhythm, balanced word-patterns, and varied sentence-length have been rendered by appropriate English equivalents as much as possible, again while avoiding distorting the shape of the English. Indirect speech is not recast in its direct form, or vice versa. First-person verbs and adjectives keep the number of the Latin: so *demonstravimus* is translated by 'we explained' (*demonstravi* would be translated 'I explained'), and *exercitus noster* is left as 'our army' (it could mean 'my [Caesar's] army' or 'the army of us Romans'). Thus, the reader can assess for herself or himself the range of meaning of the Latin in this respect. Distances are given in English miles, not Latin *milia passuum*. Times (e.g. 'at the end of the third watch') have usually been translated literally and a note of explanation given, because Roman hours change in length according to the season. The names of most familiar geographical features have been given in their modern form—Rhine for *Rhenus*, Loire for *Liger*, 'Cevennes' for *mons Cevenna*—because such features have not greatly altered in size or direction since Caesar's day. Place-names, however, have been left in their Latin form: *Lutetia* is not the same as Paris nor *Massilia* the same as Marseilles, though they may stand at more or less the same locations.

The emphasis throughout this translation is on combining the need for accurate reproduction of the sense with readability; moreover, care has been taken to avoid misleading readers with anachronistic translations such as 'Empire/imperial' for *imperium*, or the use of the derogatory English versions of Latin words which are neither inherently, nor in terms of clear context, negative: use of the English word 'tribe' to translate the neutral Latin noun *civitas* wherever *civitas* refers to a Gallic people is a notorious example. Conversely, the derogatory sense of a term like *barbari* ('barbarians') has been retained, to show where and how Caesar uses denigration to underline the inferiority of the enemy. Finally, a word about headings at the beginning of each book. AUC stands for *ab urbe condita*, 'from the foundation of the city' (traditionally put by the Romans at 753 BC). All these headings and dates are for the reader's convenience only and do not form part of Caesar's original text (which of course also lacked the numbered paragraph divisions now inserted for ease of reference).

Caesar's Influence

It is perhaps suggestive that one major work devoted to the *Nachleben* of Caesar was written in 1925 and published in Berlin by a German Romantic scholar and translator of Shakespeare. Gundolf begins with an emphatic statement:

Today, when the need of the strong man is felt, and ... when, particularly in Germany, the guidance of the people is entrusted to any
striking talent in the military-economic field ... and ... rabid petty
bourgeois individuals are considered statesmen—we should like to
recall to the minds of those of hasty judgment the great man ...
Caesar. (*Caesar. Geschichte seines Ruhms*, English translation by
J. W. Hartmann, *The Mantle of Caesar*, London, 1929)

He goes on to claim that by presenting the life of a great man
the historian can invoke 'historical forces and their incarna-
tions: the nations and their leaders' ('die Völker und die Führer').

For one scholar, then, writing in the first half of this century, Caesar was a mythic figure, a symbol of successful
imperialism, and (by the end of the book) an embodiment of
Nietzschean ideals as 'the lordliest of men', a 'wish-saviour'.
In Germany after the First World War the resonances of the
life of a man who rose from political obscurity at a time of
internal strife and external threat, to extend the boundaries
of empire, to enrich the citizen body through conquest, and
then to impose a new political order and rule had an obvious
appeal and significance. But not every generation has inter-
preted Caesar in the same terms: and his very flexibility is
what in the end guarantees both lasting appeal and quasi-
mythic stature. One reason why this appeal continues strong
is that he has never been a purely *historical* figure: that ideas
about who he was and what he did have never been solely
dependent on a written tradition. In France in particular,
though also in Germany and England, folk-memory persisted
in attaching tales of Caesar's presence and influence to individual localities.

The historical element of the Caesar-tradition is based on
a number of sources. Contemporary or near-contemporary
ones include the *Commentaries* of Caesar himself and the
writings of Cicero and Sallust. Though no longer extant,
Pollio's *History*, and the books of Livy which treated the
years of his political ascendancy (103–116), undoubtedly also
left their mark on later Greek and Roman historians. Less
than fifty years after the Ides of March Ovid could depict
Caesar's apotheosis as the culmination of a historical shift
from chaos to order in his epic *Metamorphoses*; but Lucan's

epic poem on the civil war, the *Pharsalia* (AD 65?), gave a less honorific view, and Suetonius delighted in recounting stories of the vices of Caesar as well as of the other emperors. By the time Shakespeare wrote his *Julius Caesar*, an English translation of another later source was also available: Plutarch's *Parallel Lives of the Greeks and Romans*.

Early post-Classical references to Caesar range from the trivial to the historically aware. Augustine more than once compares Caesar and Cato in imitation of Sallust (Sallust, *Catiline* 53: cf. *Civ. Dei* 1.23; 5.12; 19.4). His view of Caesar is influenced by a conviction of divine destiny behind the Roman Empire (5.21). Two hundred years later, in his *Etymologiae* (9.3.12), Isidore of Seville drew on Pliny (*Natural History* 7.47) to explain the name 'Caesar' as indicating either that at his birth he was cut (Latin *caesum*) from his mother's womb or that he had flowing hair (Latin *caesaries*). In the thirteenth century Thomas Aquinas—using Caesar as symbolic of Rome's temporal power in a way which became a commonplace—argues that the murder of Caesar was justified because he took power by violence (*A Commentary on the Sentences of Peter Lombard* 2.44.2).

Not long after Aquinas, but with a very different approach, Dante invested Caesar's name with fresh glory and appeal. Instead of propagating the Suetonian-Plutarchan polarity between Caesar the great achiever and Caesar the man of destructive ambition, Dante presents Caesar as, in a sense, an earthly counterpart to God. In *Paradiso* (6.57–66) Caesar seizes the holy standard (*sacrosanto segno*) of Rome's destiny: this view of his high office and holy function is upheld in *On Monarchy* and the *Letters*. In contrast, as principal architects of the assassination on the Ides of March, Brutus and Cassius are, for Dante, traitors of the stature of Judas Iscariot—they hang in torment beside him in Hell (*Inferno* 34.61–9). Petrarch was less enthusiastic, no doubt because he had read his Cicero thoroughly. By writing a detailed account of Caesar's life based primarily on the *Commentaries* themselves, Petrarch established a historically informed picture of Caesar, the influence of which prevailed until the time of the German historian Theodor Mommsen (1817–1903).

Linguistic interest in Caesar's text was as strong as moral and historical interest in his life. The first edition of the *Commentaries* was published at Rome in 1469 by Bussi. At about this time another Italian, the humanist scholar Laurentius Valla, was quarrying Caesar's text for his six books on the elegance of the Latin language. A third focus of scholarship was on Caesar's value as a military theorist, and in 1559 the French humanist Ramus published his work on Caesar's excellence as a military commander—an acknowledged predecessor of Clausewitz's *vom Kriege* ('On war', 1833) in the nineteenth century. This prompted a number of imitations, including in England Captain Cruso's *The Complete Captain or An Abridgement of Cesars warres, with observation upon them*, published in 1640. Imitation, of course, was not confined to military or literary theory. Cesare Borgia is a famous practical imitator of his Classical namesake, albeit a less successful one. The achievements of both were praised by Machiavelli in *Il Principe* (7, 16), and in the *Discorsi* he repeatedly turns to Caesar as an exemplar of specifically military excellence.

In France the essayist Montaigne reflected—sometimes at length—on the power of Caesar's presence and his excellence as a general:

Caesar, in my opinion, deserves particular study, not only for the knowledge of history, but for himself too . . . I read him with rather more reverence and respect than one feels in reading human works . . . Except for the false colours with which he tries to cover his evil purpose and the filth of his destructive ambition, I think the only thing which can be said against him is that he speaks too sparingly of himself. For he could not have done so many great things without having had a much greater share in them than he lays claim to. (2.10, 'Des livres')

Elsewhere he commends Caesar's writings in practical terms, 'these should be the breviary of every man of war, as the true and sovereign model of the art of war' (2.34, 'Observations sur les moyens de faire de guerre de Julius Cæsar'). According to Gundolf, Montaigne was perhaps the first scholar to use the *Commentaries* as studies of character (*Seelenkunde*).

In the seventeenth century this interest in Caesar as a model for statesmanship, literary composition, and command continued. Shakespeare's version of his end, frequently studied in depth, needs no comment here. The writings of Francis Bacon on Caesar are perhaps less familiar. His *Imago Civilis Julii Caesaris*, found among his papers and published posthumously, reflects on Caesar's concern for personal advancement rather than the common good, and ends with the paradox that he was destroyed by his own popularity (*Opuscula Posthuma* 1658: an English translation was added to the second edition in 1661). The *Apophthegms* (1625) made complimentary reference to Caesar's lost book on that subject, as did the *Advancement of Learning* (1605).

For Milton, tyranny and kingship were the important issues, and he acknowledged a reluctant admiration: 'Indeed if ever any tyrant were to be spared, I would wish it to be he: for although he rushed a kingship upon the republic somewhat too violently, yet he was perhaps most worthy of kingship' (*A Defence of the People of England* (1658), ch. 5). There are hints of a similar reluctant admiration in Hobbes: he argues that the flattery and reputation of an ambitious man may have particularly dangerous consequences in a popular government: 'By this means it was, that *Julius Caesar*, who was set up by the People against the Senate, having won to himselfe the affections of his Army, made himselfe Master, both of Senate and People' (*Leviathan* (1651), ch. 30). Such actions Hobbes denounces as 'plain Rebellion', comparable with 'the effects of Witchcraft'. But the points he focuses on, namely, Caesar's care to maintain a good relationship with the people and his concern for his reputation, are precisely those which emerge with such deliberate force and clarity from the *Commentaries*.

In Louis XIV's France, others had their contribution to make. Not only drama such as Corneille's *La mort de Pompée*, either; it had become fashionable to echo ancient rhetorical commonplaces by means of elaborate comparison of Alexander and Caesar. La Rochefoucauld gave Caesar the preference (*Réflexions diverses* 14: 'Des modèles de la nature et de la fortune'). La Bruyère characterized Alexander as a mere hero,

Caesar as a great man (*Les Caractères, ou les moeurs de ce siècle*, ch. 2: 'Peut-être qu'Alexander n'était qu'un héros, et que César était un grand-homme').

The eighteenth century saw further change and development in Caesar's image and legend. Montesquieu (1689–1755) admired some of Caesar's achievements, but gave Alexander the preference for the economic advantages which his conquests procured (*De l'esprit des lois* 2.14, 1748). In any case, his Ciceronian attitude was fundamentally at odds with the ethos of Caesar's last years. This view is more forcefully restated by Rousseau, for whom Caesar is a tyrant and to be damned as such. Voltaire's writings, for example *La Mort de César* and *Triumvirate*, contain elements of these themes, and he also returned to the old Sallustian comparison between Caesar and Cato. Of similar mind, respecting the man but not all his actions, was Voltaire's admirer and correspondent Frederick the Great of Prussia. Frederick both compared himself and was compared by others—including Voltaire—with Caesar. The parallel, not surprisingly, was most keenly and positively felt in the military sphere.

The most famous of Caesar's self-proclaimed military successors is Napoleon Bonaparte. His admiration led him to demand of Goethe the writing of a drama about Caesar, but the work never materialized, despite the fact that Goethe had eulogized Caesar as 'Inbegriff aller menschlichen Größe' ('incarnation of all human greatness'). The positive aspect was once more in the ascendant: a fact confirmed by the enthusiasm of Johannes von Müller, who was appointed Napoleon's historiographer from 1804. This is perhaps slightly unexpected in a Swiss recording the Helvetian war of *GW* 1 (in his *Geschichte der schweizerischen Eidgenossenschaft*, 5 vols., 2nd edn., 1826). Napoleon saw in Caesar an example, a parallel, a forerunner of his own achievements: he himself wrote a *Précis des Guerres de César*, commenting upon Caesar's text. The example was followed by his nephew Napoleon III, who wrote an *Histoire de Jules César* with self-justificatory intentions (1865–6).

The range of purposes for which the name and life of Caesar can be utilized seems to be limitless: he is both democrat and autocrat, soldier and man of letters, destroyer and achiever. In the twentieth century his life has once again attracted the interest of dramatists (Shaw's *Caesar and Cleopatra*, 1901; Thornton Wilder's *The Ides of March*, 1948). His value as a political symbol, however, has been less prominent: empire-builders like Mussolini would naturally look more towards Caesar's successor Augustus as a model for their schemes. Whatever the realities of its own territorial aggression, moreover, the Soviet Union found its heroes in men like Spartacus who resisted Rome's dominion; while Hitler's links with Caesar are more by negative implication—both during and after the war, French writers came to see in Caesar's adversary Vercingetorix (see *GW 7*) the model for the Resistance movement, hence casting Caesar in the Hitlerian role of imperialist invader.

In a world where military expertise is no longer a *sine qua non* of the governing élite, Caesar's writings do not attract the same degree of attention as either his personal life or his political actions (except, naturally, among specialist scholars). Rather, they have been relegated to the position of introductory reading for those learning the Latin language. Noël Coward could use the subject of 'how Caesar conquered Gaul' as symbolic of the unsophisticated education of an English gentleman (in 'The Stately Homes of England'). It is hardly surprising that after two world wars the writings of a man who was anything but embarrassed by his successful territorial ambitions are out of fashion. Perhaps it is necessary to adopt a new approach in order to appreciate them fully: to regard them as a privileged insight into the mind and motivations of a man who really did make a difference to history—both through his actions in life, and through his reputation and legend after death.

Whatever form or focus it may take, the fascination of posterity with the Caesar-image is unending. Much more could be said about his depiction in art and music, poetry and drama, and how these have influenced the transmission of the legend from first-century BC Rome to the present day. Perhaps, though, it is best to leave the last word to Caesar himself. Early in March of 49, soon after crossing the Rubicon, he wrote a letter to Cornelius Balbus and Gaius Oppius, two of his close friends and dependants. They were also associates of Cicero, and provided a link between Cicero and Caesar at this difficult time. In it, he reflects on his position as dictator, and the unhappy precedent set by the dictatorship of Sulla (81–80 BC). Ironically, though Sulla became unpopular, and though he enacted much controversial legislation which was later overturned, he did at least survive to resign and retire, unlike Caesar:

I am so pleased that you indicate in your letter how much you approve what I did at Corfinium [see *CW* 1.16–23]. I shall gladly follow your advice, all the more so because I had myself already decided to do this, and to appear as lenient as possible, and make an effort to reconcile Pompey. Let us try in this way to win back everyone's good will and enjoy a lasting victory. For others have not been able, by cruelty, to avoid incurring hatred or to hold on to their success for long, except for Lucius Sulla—and I am not about to follow *his* example. (In Cicero, *Letters to Atticus* 9.7.c1)

SELECT BIBLIOGRAPHY

Texts of The Gallic War

The most accessible Latin texts of *The Gallic War* are the Oxford Classical Text of R. du Pontet (1900), and the Loeb volume (with facing translation) by H. J. Edwards (Harvard University Press, 1919). There is also a Teubner text, edited by O. Seel (Leipzig, 1961) and a Budé (with facing French translation) by L.-A. Constans (Paris, 1972).

The Late Republic

The classic account is that of Th. Mommsen, *Römische Geschichte*, iii: *Von Sullas Tod bis zur Schlacht von Thapsus* (3rd edn., Berlin, 1920). H. H. Scullard, *From the Gracchi to Nero: 133 BC–AD 68* (5th edn., London, 1982), offers a very conservative account of events, but provides strong bibliographical material in the endnotes. Much useful discussion of the workings and ethos of politics is contained in C. Nicolet, *The World of the Citizen in Republican Rome* (trans. Falla, London, 1980) and W. V. Harris, *War and Imperialism in Republican Rome* (Oxford, 1985). A number of studies offer distinctive insights into the period: parts of Sir Ronald Syme's *The Roman Revolution* (Oxford, 1939); Ch. Wirszubski's *Libertas as a Political Ideal at Rome* (Cambridge, 1960); A. W. Lintott, *Violence in Republican Rome* (Oxford, 1968); M. Gelzer, *The Roman Nobility* (trans. Seager, Oxford, 1969); J. Hellegouarc'h, *Le Vocabulaire latin des relations et des partis politiques sous la république* (rev. edn., Paris, 1972); P. A. Brunt, *The Fall of the Roman Republic and Related Essays* (Oxford, 1988); E. Rawson, *Roman Culture and Society: Collected Papers* (Oxford, 1991).

Caesar's Life and Career

A very full bibliography on all aspects of Caesar is provided by H. Gesche, *Caesar*, Erträge der Forschung, Band 51 (Darmstadt, 1976). A bi-millenary number of *Greece and Rome*, NS 4 (1957) includes various articles on Caesar. The standard account of his life, with very full and helpful footnotes, is M. Gelzer's *Caesar: Politician and Statesman* (6th edn. [German] 1960; trans. P. Needham, Oxford, 1968). Napoleon III's *Histoire de Jules César* (Paris, 1865: vol. 2 on the Gallic War) has been translated by T. Wright (London, 1865).

Difficulties with Caesar's versions of events are discussed by H.

Hagendahl, 'The Mutiny of Vesontio', *Classica et Mediaevalia*, 6:
1–2 (1944), 1–40; J. H. Collins, 'Caesar as Political Propagandist',
Aufstieg und Niedergang der römischen Welt, 1: 1 (1972), 922–66;
M. Rambaud, 'De la déformation historique', *Revue des études latines*,
50 (1972), 53–8; C. B. R. Pelling, 'Caesar's Battle Descriptions and
the Defeat of Ariovistus', *Latomus*, 40 (1981), 741–66. H. M. Ottmer,
Die Rubikon-Legende (Boppard am Rhein, 1979) discusses the strategies adopted by Pompey and Caesar in the civil war. See also K.
Raaflaub, *Dignitatis Contentio* (Dissertation Basel, 1970 = *Vestigia*,
20 [1974]); H. Strasburger, *Caesar im Urteil seiner Zeitgenossen*
(Darmstadt, 1968); S. Weinstock, *Divus Julius* (Oxford, 1971).

F. Gundolf, *Caesar. Geschichte seines Ruhms* (Berlin, 1925) is
translated by J. W. Hartmann, *The Mantle of Caesar* (London, 1929).
A collection of articles on Caesar's legacy in literature, art, and
music, *Présence de César. Hommage au doyen M. Rambaud* (Paris,
1985) is edited by R. Chevallier.

Writings

Introductory and theoretical material on the Roman historians can be
found in T. A. Dorey (ed.), *Latin Historians* (London, 1966), 65–84
on Caesar, and A. J. Woodman, *Rhetoric in Classical Historiography:
Four Studies* (London and Sydney, 1988) is particularly interesting
on standards of truth and concepts of veracity. F. E. Adcock provides a brief introduction to Caesar as a writer in *Caesar as Man of
Letters* (Cambridge, 1956). More recent is Raditsa in *Aufstieg und
Niedergang der römischen Welt*, 1: 3 (1973), 417–56 (in English).
On *commentarii*, see Kelsey, 'The Title of Caesar's Work', *Transac-
tions of the American Philological Association*, 36 (1905), 211–38;
F. Bömer, 'Der Commentarius', *Hermes*, 81 (1953), 210–50.

M. Rambaud, *L'art de la déformation historique dans les commentaires de César* (2nd edn., Paris, 1966) is a polemical, wide-ranging,
and acute study of Caesar's narrative aims and methods which states
the case for his systematic distortion of events for political ends:
Rambaud has also written a number of commentaries on individual
books of *The Gallic War* (Paris PUF). His approach stands in contrast to that of T. Rice Holmes in *Caesar's Conquest of Gaul* (2nd
edn., Oxford, 1911).

D. Rasmussen, *Caesars Commentarii* (Göttingen, 1963), and
K. Deichgräber, 'Elegantia Caesaris. Zu Caesars Reden und Commentarii', *Gymnasium*, 57 (1950), 112–23, both analyse aspects of the
speeches in Caesar; H. Gärtner, *Beobachten zu Bauelementen in der
antiken Historiographie, besonders bei Livius und Caesar, Historia
Einzelschriften*, 25 (1975) and J. Schlichter, 'The Development of

Caesar's Narrative Style', *Classical Philology*, 31 (1936), 212–24, consider his narrative technique. *GW* 8 is discussed by A. Bojkowitsch, in 'Hirtius als Offizier und als Stilist', *Wiener Studien*, 14 (1926/7), 71–81, 221–32: and by O. Seel in *Hirtius. Untersuchungen über die pseudocaesarischen Bella und den Balbusbrief* (Klio Beiheft 35, 1935). See also J. H. Collins, *Propaganda, Ethics and Psychological Assumptions in Caesar's Writings* (Frankfurt, 1952).

Gauls, Germans, and Britons: The War

The fragments of Posidonius are collected, with a commentary, in three volumes by L. Edelstein and I. G. Kidd (2nd edn., Cambridge, 1988–9); see also A. D. Nock, 'Posidonius', *Journal of Roman Studies*, 49 (1959), 1–15. Of general interest are J. F. Drinkwater, *Roman Gaul: The Three Provinces 58 BC–AD 260* (London and Sydney, 1983); P. B. Ellis, *Caesar's Invasion of Britain* (London, 1978). Bias in Caesar's account is documented by G. Walser in *Caesar und die Germanen*, Historia Einzelschriften, 1 (1956). Camille Jullian's famous *Vercingétorix* (5th edn., Paris, 1911) studies the available source material in considerable detail; also his *Histoire de la Gaule*, iii (3rd edn., Paris, 1923). See also H. Oppermann, 'Zu den geographischen Exkursen in Caesars Bellum Gallicum', *Hermes*, 68 (1933), 182–95; T. Rice Holmes, *Ancient Britain and the Invasions of Julius Caesar* (2nd edn., Oxford, 1936); G. Stümpel, *Name und Nationalität der Germanen. Eine neue Untersuchung zu Poseidonios, Cäsar und Tacitus* (Klio Beiheft 25, 2nd edn., Leipzig, 1963); R. Schieffer, 'Die Rede des Critognatus und Caesars Urteil über den gallischen Krieg', *Gymnasium*, 79 (1972), 477–94.

Relevant to any studies of ancient accounts of warfare are *The Face of Battle* and *The Mask of Command* (London, 1976 and 1987 respectively) by J. Keegan; E. Abramson, *Roman Legionaries at the Time of Julius Caesar* (London, 1979); G. R. Watson, *The Roman Soldier* (London, 1983); L. Keppie, *The Making of the Roman Army* (London, 1984); J. Rüpke, *Domi Militiae* (Stuttgart, 1990). J. Kromayer and G. Veith, *Schlachtenatlas zur antiken Kriegsgeschichte* v (Leipzig, 1929), covers the Gallic War.

TABLE OF EVENTS

(all dates are BC)

100   Gaius Julius Caesar born.

91–88   Social War (of Rome against her Italian allies [*socii*]).

88   Civil war between Marius and Sulla. Sulla marches on Rome with his army, Marius flees.

87   Marius and Cinna lead massacre of Sulla's supporters at Rome. Caesar supposedly nominated as *flamen Dialis*.

86   Death of Marius (during seventh consulship).

85   Sulla completes settlement of Asia.

84   Caesar marries Cornelia, daughter of Cinna (mother of Caesar's daughter Julia). Death of Cinna, Carbo sole consul.

83   Sulla returns to Italy, with Pompey's support.

82   Civil war, Sulla emerges the victor: proscriptions. Success for Pompey in Sicily. Sertorius escapes to Spain.

81   Sulla dictator. Success for Pompey against Marius's supporters in Africa. Radical changes to Roman constitution, including curbs on power of tribunes and other conservative measures.

80   Caesar does military service in Asia.

79   Sulla retires.

78   Death of Sulla. Marcus Lepidus leads march on Rome.

77   Pompey defeats Lepidus, goes to Spain to face Sertorius. Caesar prosecutes Dolabella.

76   Attempt to restore tribunes' powers. Successes for Sertorius in Spain.

75   Limited tribunician powers restored.

74   Command against pirates for Marcus Antonius. Lucullus against Mithridates in east, Caesar part of army.

73   Revolt of former slave Spartacus in Italy. Success for Lucullus.

72   Defeat of Sertorius and settlement of Spain by Pompey. Pirates defeat Antony. Caesar military tribune.

70   Pompey and Crassus consuls. Tribunician powers restored.

69   Caesar quaestor in Further Spain. Death of Cornelia.

67   Pompey to combat piracy in Mediterranean under *Lex Gabinia*.
      Caesar speaks in favour of *Lex*, marries Pompeia.

66   Pompey sent against Mithridates by *Lex Manilia* with sup-
      port from Cicero and Caesar.

65   Caesar curule aedile.

63   Cicero Consul. Catiline's conspiracy, Caesar speaks against
      execution of the citizen conspirators without trial. Caesar
      pontifex maximus. Pompey still in east.

62   Caesar divorces Pompeia after Bona Dea scandal. Pompey
      returns.

61   Caesar proconsul of Further Spain. Victory against Lusitani.

60   The 'first triumvirate'. Caesar elected with Pompey and
      Crassus' support despite strong opposition.

59   Caesar consul (1). Pompey marries Caesar's daughter Julia,
      Caesar marries Calpurnia. *Lex Vatinia*.

58	Publius Clodius tribune, effects exile of Cicero. Cato to annex Cyprus. Ptolemy exiled from Alexandria.	(*GW* 1) Caesar proconsul. Campaign against Helvetii; against Ariovistus and Germans.
57	Riots at Rome. Return of Cicero.	(*GW* 2) Campaign against Belgae.
56	conflict among 'triumvirs' settled by meeting at Luca.	(*GW* 3) Campaigns against Veneti, NW Gallic peoples, Aquitani.
55	Pompey and Crassus consuls. Spain for Pompey, five more years in Gaul for Caesar.	(*GW* 4) Invasion of Usipetes and Tencteri; Caesar crosses Rhine and Channel.
54	Death of Julia. Unrest at Rome.	(*GW* 5) Second expedition to Britain; deaths of Sabinus and Cotta; campaigns against Ambiorix and Eburones, Treveri.
53	Unrest continues. No consuls elected until July. Death of Crassus at Carrhae in Mesopotamia.	(*GW* 6) Second crossing of Rhine; ethnology of Gauls and Germans; conquest of Eburones; invasion of Sugambri.

52   Unrest continues.   (*GW* 7) Revolt of
      Clodius killed.   Vercingetorix.
      Pompey sole consul
      until August. Law of
      Ten Tribunes enables
      Caesar to stand for
      second consulship *in
      absentia*.

51   Curio switches support   (*GW* 8) Revolt of Carnutes
      to Caesar. Cicero   and Bellovaci; siege and fall
      governor of Cilicia.   of Uxellodunum. Negotiations
                                       of Caesar via Curio and
                                       Antony with Senate. Caesar
                                       forced to surrender two legions.

50   Curio suggests Pompey
      and Caesar disarm—
      vetoed. Consul
      Marcellus asks Pompey
      to save Rome. Curio
      and Antony flee. *GW*
      published (?). Attempts
      to make Caesar return
      for trial.

49   Senate gives Pompey authority against Caesar, who crosses
      Rubicon; Caesar dictator (1); defeats Pompeians in Spain.
      Curio dies in Africa.

48   Caesar consul (2). Pharsalus. Death of Pompey. Caesar
      occupies Alexandria; has liaison with Cleopatra.

47   Caesar dictator (2); makes Cleopatra queen, combats Pom-
      peian remnant.

46   Caesar consul (3); defeats Pompeians at Thapsus. Dictator
      (3) for ten years. Cato dies at Utica. Pompey's sons renew
      war in Spain. Caesar's quadruple triumph.

45   Caesar dictator (4) for life, consul (4), receives divine honours,
      defeats Pompeians at Munda.

44   Caesar consul (5). Refuses diadem of kingship at Lupercalia
      (15 February). Murdered on Ides (15) of March.

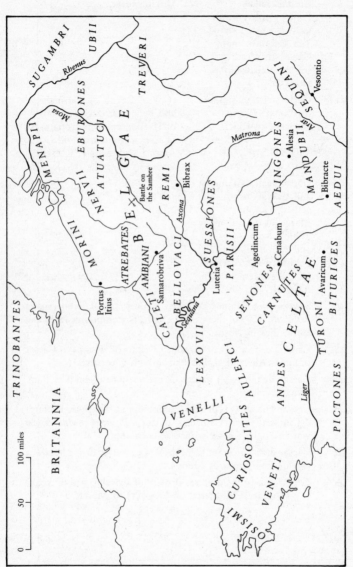

FIG. 2a Map of Northern Gaul

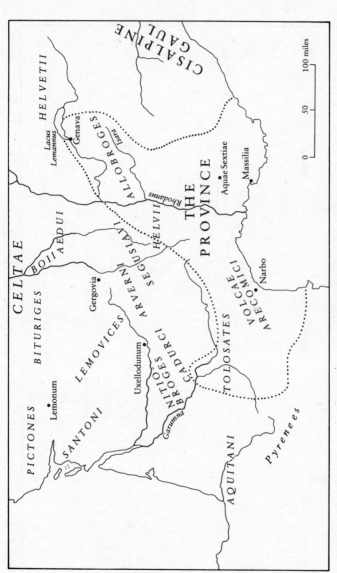

FIG. 2b Map of Southern Gaul

THE GALLIC WAR

The First Book: 58 BC
(AUC 696: Consuls, Lucius Calpurnius Piso Caesoninus, Aulus Gabinius)

War Against the Helvetii: Ariovistus and the Germans

(1) The whole of Gaul is divided into three parts, one of which the Belgae inhabit, the Aquitani another, and the third a people who in their own language are called 'Celts', but in ours, 'Gauls'. They all differ among themselves in respect of language, way of life, and laws. The River Garonne divides the Gauls from the Aquitani, and the Marne and Seine rivers separate them from the Belgae. Of these three, the Belgae are the bravest, for they are furthest away from the civilization and culture of the Province. Merchants very rarely travel to them or import such goods as make men's courage weak and womanish. They live, moreover, in close proximity to the Germans who inhabit the land across the Rhine, and they are continually at war with them. For this reason the Helvetii also exceed the other Gauls in bravery, because they are embroiled in almost daily battles with the Germans, either when they are warding them off from their own frontiers or when they themselves take the fight into enemy territory. The land which the Gauls are said to occupy begins at the River Rhône, and is bounded by the Garonne, the Ocean, and the territory of the Belgae. The part of it inhabited by the Sequani and Helvetii reaches to the Rhine: this land has one frontier to the north. The Belgae come from the most distant regions of Gaul: their lands extend to the lower part of the Rhine, facing north and east. Aquitania reaches from the Garonne to the Pyrenees and that part of the Ocean nearest Spain. It faces north-west.

(2) Among the Helvetii, by far the most aristocratic and the richest man was Orgetorix. During the consulship of Marcus Messalla and Marcus Pupius Piso,* his desire to become king led him to start a conspiracy among the aristocracy, and he persuaded all the citizens to leave their land in

full force. It would be perfectly simple, he said, to win power over the whole of Gaul, so superior were they in courage to all the rest. He persuaded them the more easily because the Helvetii are hemmed in on all sides by the natural terrain: on one side by the Rhine, which is very broad and deep and separates the land of the Helvetii from the Germans, on another by the heights of the Jura mountain range, which stands between them and the Sequani, and thirdly by Lake Lemannus and by the Rhône, which separates them from our Province.* As a consequence their freedom of movement was constrained, and their ability to wage war against their neighbours was also impaired. As they were so fond of waging war, this made the Helvetii very resentful. In comparison with the size of their population, their glorious reputation in war, and their courage, they considered their territory too restricted (it was 220 miles* from north to south, and 165 from east to west).

(3) Mindful of these considerations, and at Orgetorix's instigation, the Helvetii decided to get ready everything they thought was needed for a migration, buy up as many pack animals and waggons as they could, sow as much seed as possible to ensure a supply of corn on the journey, and to establish peaceful relations with neighbouring states. They considered that two years would suffice for these preparations, and passed a law establishing their decision to migrate in the third year.

Orgetorix was put in charge of organizing the migration, and of his own accord he undertook an embassy to the Gallic states. Whilst on his travels he persuaded one of the Sequani called Casticus, the son of Catamantaloedis (who had held the kingship over the Sequani for many years and been named a Friend of the Roman people by the Senate), to seize the kingship in his own state, which his father had previously held. At the same time he persuaded an Aeduan called Dumnorix to do likewise. Dumnorix's brother, Diviciacus, was at that time chief magistrate of the Aedui and a very popular ruler. Orgetorix also gave Dumnorix his daughter in marriage. He assured Dumnorix and Casticus that they would achieve their object with ease, especially since he would

himself be seizing power among the Helvetii, who were beyond
doubt the strongest of all the Gallic peoples; and he promised
them that he would use his strength and his army to help
them win their kingdoms. They were persuaded by his words,
exchanged guarantees, and swore an oath, hoping that, once
they had become kings, through these three very powerful
and determined peoples they could seize control of all Gaul.

(4) News of this plot came to the Helvetii through informers.
In accordance with custom, they made Orgetorix plead his
defence in chains. If found guilty, the law required that he be
burned alive. On the day appointed for the trial Orgetorix
summoned to the court a whole gang of dependants from all
directions, about 10,000 in number; and he assembled likewise
all his many retainers and debtors. By their help he escaped
trial. While the citizens, angry at his escape, were trying to
pursue the case by force of arms, and the magistrates were
mustering a crowd of men from the surrounding countryside,
Orgetorix died—and not without the suspicion, according to
the Helvetii, that it was by his own hand.

(5) After his death, the Helvetii none the less tried to put
their previous decision into action by emigrating from their
own land. As soon as they considered that they were ready
for the enterprise, they set fire to all their own towns (about
twelve in number) and to about 400 villages, as well as all
their private buildings. All the corn, except what they were
to carry with them, they reduced to ashes—so once the hope
of returning home was removed they would be the more
ready to undergo dangers of all kinds. They ordered each
man to bring from his home three months' supply of corn
ready-ground for himself. They persuaded the Raurici, the
Tulingi, and the Latovici (who were their neighbours) to
adopt the same plan: once all their towns and villages were
burned down too they set out together. The Helvetii also
welcomed the Boii (who had lived across the Rhine and had
crossed into the territory of Noricum and beseiged the town
of Noreia) and made alliance with them.

(6) There were only two possible routes for the departure
from their home. One went through the land of the Sequani,
between the Jura mountain range and the Rhône. It was

narrow and difficult, so that the waggons could hardly pass
in single file, and the high mountain which loomed over it
meant that a handful of men could easily block the pass. The
other, which went through our Province, was far quicker and
easier because the Rhône, which flows between the lands of
the Helvetii and those of the Allobroges (who had recently
been pacified),* can be forded at several points. The further-
most town of the Allobroges, on the border with the Helvetii,
is Genava. A bridge connects the town with the Helvetii,
who reckoned they could either persuade the Allobroges to
allow them a passage through their land (for they did not as
yet appear to be reconciled to the Roman people), or force
them to do so. Once everything was ready for the migration
the Helvetii fixed a date by which everyone was to assemble
by the bank of the Rhône. The date was 28 March, in the
consulship of Lucius Piso and Aulus Gabinius.*

(7) When news came to Caesar* that the Helvetii were
trying to journey through our Province he hurried his departure from Rome, and by the longest forced marches possible
he made for Transalpine Gaul and reached Genava. He ordered the whole Province to supply as many men as possible
(for in Transalpine Gaul there was only one legion*), and
gave orders for the bridge at Genava to be destroyed. When
the Helvetii heard of his arrival they sent their most aristocratic citizens to him as envoys, headed by Nammeius and
Verocloetius, to explain their intention of marching, without
doing any harm, through the Province—for they had no other
route. They asked his agreement to their action. Caesar remembered how the consul Lucius Cassius had been killed
and his army beaten by the Helvetii and sent under the yoke,*
and decided to refuse. Nor did he believe that these men,
hostile as they were, would refrain from doing harm and
damage if allowed to march through the Province. Even so,
he told the envoys that he would take a while to consider,
and that they should if they so wished return on 13 April.
Thus a space of time would elapse in which the soldiers he
had ordered could muster.

(8) Meanwhile, he used the legion he had with him and the
soldiers who had assembled from the Province to construct

a sixteen-foot rampart and a ditch, from Lake Lemannus (which flows into the Rhône) to the Jura mountains (which form the border between the Sequani and the Helvetii), a distance of over seventeen miles. When the work was finished he allocated garrisons and fortified outposts: if the Helvetii tried to cross without permission, he could then restrain them more easily. When the day which he had agreed with the envoys came, and they returned to him, he said that in accordance with the practice and precedent of the Roman people he was unable to grant anyone access through the Province, and he made it clear that he would stop them if they tried to use force. Their hopes were crushed: some of the Helvetii lashed boats together and made a number of rafts, others tried to break across the fording-places of the Rhône where the river was at its shallowest, partly in the daytime, but mostly at night. They abandoned these efforts, forced back by the defence-works, the attacks of the soldiers, and by missiles.

(9) Only one way remained, through the land of the Sequani. Because it was so narrow, they could not take this route without the Sequani's consent. When the Helvetii themselves failed to win the Sequani's agreement they sent envoys to Dumnorix the Aeduan, hoping that he could intercede and sway the Sequani.

Because of his popularity and open-handed generosity, Dumnorix was extremely powerful among the Sequani. He was also a friend to the Helvetii, for it was from them that he had taken a wife—Orgetorix's daughter. Spurred on by his eagerness to be king, Dumnorix supported revolution. He also wanted, by services rendered, to put as many states as possible under an obligation to him. So he undertook the negotiations and asked the Sequani to let the Helvetii go through their territory: and he arranged for them to exchange hostages.* The Sequani pledged themselves not to hinder the Helvetii on their journey, while the Helvetii promised not to do any harm or damage as they were passing through.

(10) News came to Caesar that the Helvetii planned to march through the lands of the Sequani and Aedui into the territory of the Santones, which is not far from that of the

Tolosates—a state actually in the Province. If they succeeded, he knew that it would pose a serious threat to the Province to have this warlike nation, which was hostile to the Roman people, so close to such important and completely unprotected corn-producing areas. So he put his legate Titus Labienus in charge of the defence-works which he had constructed, and set out by forced marches for Italy, where he enlisted two legions, and mobilized three more which had been wintering near Aquileia. He then hastened back by the shortest route over the Alps into Transalpine Gaul with these five legions. There the Ceutrones, the Graioceli, and the Caturiges had taken up position on some high ground and tried to hinder the army's march. They were beaten in a series of encounters, after which in seven days he marched from Ocelum (the most distant town of Cisalpine Gaul) into the land of the Vocontii in the Province. From there he led his army into the land of the Allobroges, and from there to that of the Segusiavi. These are the nearest peoples to the Rhône outside the Province.

(11) The Helvetii had already brought their forces through the narrow pass and the land of the Sequani, and had reached the country of the Aedui, which they were pillaging. When the Aedui were unable to protect either themselves or their possessions from the Helvetii they sent envoys to Caesar to ask for help. They had always behaved well, they said, towards the Roman people, so that they hardly deserved to have their land laid waste, their children enslaved, and their towns stormed almost under the gaze of our army. At the same time the Aedui Ambarri, who were relations and kinsmen of the Aedui, informed Caesar that their land too was being laid waste, and that they were having difficulty in protecting their towns from enemy attack. Likewise the Allobroges, who had dwellings and property across the Rhône, fled to Caesar, claiming that everything but their land had been taken from them. For these reasons Caesar decided not to wait until all the property of Rome's allies was destroyed and the Helvetii had reached the territory of the Santones.

(12) There is a river called the Saône, which flows through the lands of the Aedui and Sequani into the Rhône so very

slowly that it is impossible to tell just by looking in which direction it is flowing. The Helvetii crossed it by lashing rafts and boats together. When Caesar learned from his scouts that the Helvetii had brought three-quarters of their forces across, and that about a quarter was left on the near bank of the Saône, during the third watch* he set out from camp with three legions and made for that section of their forces which had not yet crossed. He attacked when they were encumbered with baggage and off guard, and killed a great number: the rest fled and hid in nearby woods. This section consisted of men known as 'Tigurini' after their district; the whole state of the Helvetii is divided into four such districts. In the time of our fathers the Tigurini had migrated on their own; they had killed the consul Lucius Cassius and sent his army under the yoke. So whether by chance or by the gods' design, that section of the Helvetian state which had once inflicted an infamous defeat on the Roman people was also the first to pay the penalty. In doing so, Caesar avenged not only a national but also a private injury: for the grandfather of his father-in-law Lucius Piso was a legate (also called Lucius Piso) killed by the Tigurini in the same battle as Cassius.*

(13) After the battle he had a bridge built over the Saône and led his army across it to pursue the Helvetii. They were thrown into confusion by his unexpected arrival, and when they learned that he had taken only a day to cross the river, a task which had taken them twenty days—and then with extreme difficulty—they sent envoys to him. The embassy was headed by Divico, who had led the Helvetii in the war against Cassius.

He spoke with Caesar to this effect: if the Roman people made peace with the Helvetii they would go to whatever region Caesar decided, and stay wherever he wished them to remain. If, however, he continued to pursue them with war, he should remember both the former misfortunes of the Roman people and the ancient bravery of the Helvetii. He had attacked a single section of their people unexpectedly, at a time when those who had crossed the river could not come to the assistance of their fellows, and so for this reason he

ought not to attribute too much to his own bravery, nor
should he treat them with contempt. The Helvetii had learned
from their fathers and their forefathers to fight with courage
rather than cunning or treachery, and so Caesar should not
allow the place where they were holding talks to win fame
or future renown because of a disaster for the Roman people
and the massacre of an army.

(14) Caesar replied to the envoys as follows: since he remembered those past events which the envoys had mentioned,
he was therefore in no doubt—and indeed he was all the
more indignant because that previous defeat had happened
through no fault of the Roman people. If its army had at that
time been aware of having committed some wrongdoing it
would have been a simple matter to take precautions, but the
Roman army had been taken unawares precisely because it
did not think it had done anything which gave it cause to be
afraid, and so considered it inappropriate to be anxious without good reason. Even if he were willing to forget this old
injury, surely it was impossible to dismiss the remembrance
of recent outrages—that against his will they had tried to
march through the Province by force, and that the Aedui, the
Ambarri, the Allobroges had all been attacked? As for their
haughty boasting about their own victory, and their marvelling
that their outrages had gone so long unpunished, these pointed
the same way. For the immortal gods usually allow those
men they wish to punish for their crimes a time of success
and a period of impunity, so that when a change of fortune
comes they are all the more grieved by it. This being so, he
would none the less still make peace with them if they would
surrender hostages to prove to him their willingness to fulfil
their promises, and if they would make reparation to the
Aedui for the harm done to them and their allies, and likewise
to the Allobroges.

Divico replied that, from the time of their ancestors, the
Helvetii were more accustomed to receive hostages than to
surrender them—and that the Roman people could witness
to the fact. With this reply he departed.

(15) The following day the Helvetii struck camp and moved
out of the area. So did Caesar, who sent all his cavalry ahead

—4,000 in number, recruited from all over the Province, and from the Aedui and their allies—to see where the enemy was marching. But they pursued the rearguard too eagerly, and joined battle with the Helvetii's cavalry on unfavourable ground. A few of our men were killed. The Helvetii were elated by the engagement, because they had routed such a large force of cavalry with only 500 horse. So they began at times to make a bolder stand and, with their rearguard, to provoke our men to fight. Caesar restrained his men from fighting, content for the time being to prevent the enemy from pillaging, foraging, and plundering. In this way they marched for about a fortnight, so that no more than four or five miles lay between the enemy rearguard and our vanguard.

(16) Meanwhile Caesar was daily demanding from the Aedui the corn which had been promised by their government. For because of the cold (Gaul, as has already been said, lies to the north), not only was the corn in the fields not yet ripe, but there was not even a sufficient supply of fodder. He was unable to use the corn which he had transported up the Saône by boat, because the Helvetii had changed the direction of their march away from the river, and he did not want to lose contact with them. The Aedui were fobbing him off from one day to the next: their corn was being collected, they said, it was being transported, it was at hand.

When he realized that he was being put off too long, and that the time had arrived when the corn ought to be distributed to the men, he summoned the leaders of the Aedui. Many of them were present in camp, including Diviciacus and Liscus, who held the highest magistracy of the Aedui, which they call 'Vergobret'.* The Vergobret is annually appointed, and has power of life and death over the citizens. Caesar reproached them severely for failing to offer assistance at such a pressing time, with the enemy so close at hand, when corn could neither be bought nor taken from the fields; and he complained with particular vehemence of having been abandoned, because it was in response to the pleas of a large number of them that he had undertaken this war in the first place.

(17) Then at last Liscus was encouraged by Caesar's speech to reveal what he had previously concealed. There were certain

men, he explained, who had particularly strong influence over the people, and who, in the private sphere, had more power than the magistrates. By their treacherous and wicked statements these men were deterring the people from collecting the corn which they were obliged to provide. It was better, they thought, to submit to Gallic than to Roman rule, if at present they could not win supreme control of Gaul; nor did they doubt that the Romans, if they beat the Helvetii, would then snatch liberty from the Aedui, together with the rest of Gaul. Liscus went on to say that they could not prevent these same men from relaying our plans, and what was going on in the camp here, to the enemy. Worse still, said Liscus, he knew that because he had been forced to report this urgent matter to Caesar he had put himself in great danger, and it was for this reason that he had kept silent as long as possible.

(18) Caesar felt that Liscus' words pointed to Dumnorix, Diviciacus' brother. Because, however, he was unwilling to have the matter discussed in public, he quickly dismissed the meeting, but kept Liscus back. When they were alone he questioned him about what he had said at the meeting. Liscus answered more frankly and confidently.

Caesar questioned other men in secret about the same matter. He found that it was true. Dumnorix was the man: highly audacious, extremely influential with the people—thanks to his open-handed generosity—and ambitious for revolution. For several years he had purchased, at a low price, the collection rights on river tolls and all the Aedui's other taxes—not least because not a single person dared to bid against him.* In this way he had increased his own property and obtained vast resources for the purposes of bribery. He maintained a large cavalry force at his own expense, which he always kept at his side. He had influence even among neighbouring states, as well as among the Aedui. To consolidate this powerful position he had given his mother in marriage to a powerful aristocrat of the Bituriges; he himself had taken a wife from among the Helvetii, and he used his maternal half-sister and other female relations to make marriage alliances with other states. Because of this connection he was a strong supporter of the Helvetii, but he also hated

Caesar and the Romans on his own account because their coming had weakened his own power, while his brother Diviciacus had been restored to his old place of influence and respect. If something were to happen to the Romans, he entertained the highest hopes of winning the Aeduan kingship through the Helvetii; but the power of the Roman people made him despair not only of becoming king, but even of holding on to what influence he already possessed.

As to the unsuccessful cavalry battle which had taken place a few days previously, Caesar learned from these interrogations that the flight had been started by Dumnorix and his cavalry contingent (for Dumnorix was in command of the cavalry force sent by the Aedui to assist Caesar). The rest of the cavalry had been thrown into panic by their flight. (19) All this he knew. But then incontrovertible proof was added to his suspicions: that Dumnorix had led the Helvetii through the land of the Sequani, that he had arranged for the exchange of hostages between the two, that he had done all this not only without the permission of Caesar or the Aedui, but even without the knowledge of either, and that he was being accused by a magistrate of the Aedui. Because of all this, Caesar thought he had good cause either for punishing Dumnorix himself, or for ordering the Aedui to punish him. One consideration, however, acted as a counter to all these. He was familiar with the devotion of Dumnorix's brother Diviciacus to the Roman people, his great goodwill towards Caesar, his outstanding loyalty, his justice, his moderation: Caesar was afraid of upsetting Diviciacus by punishing Dumnorix.

And so, before he attempted to resolve the matter, he gave orders for Diviciacus to be summoned to him. The regular interpreters were sent away, and he spoke with him through Gaius Valerius Procillus, a leader in the Province of Gaul and a close friend of Caesar's, in whom he placed the highest confidence in all matters. At the same time Caesar reminded Diviciacus what had been said about Dumnorix in his presence at the Gallic assembly, and revealed what each man in turn had told him about Dumnorix. Caesar asked Diviciacus, indeed he urged him, not to be offended, but rather, when

the matter was investigated, either to judge Dumnorix himself or to order the state to do so.

(20) Diviciacus embraced Caesar in tears, and began to
plead with him not to judge harshly of his brother. He was
aware that it was all true, and no one was more grieved by
it than he. There was a time when he himself had considerable influence among the Aedui and in the rest of Gaul, while
his brother Dumnorix, being so young, had very little, and
had risen by his help. This same brother was now using his
strength and power not only to lessen Diviciacus' influence
but almost to destroy him. Even so, he felt the influence of
brotherly affection and of public opinion. For if Dumnorix
were punished by Caesar while he, Diviciacus, continued to
hold a position of favour with him, no one would believe
that the punishment was meted out against his wishes—and
as a result, the loyal of all Gaul would turn against him.

As he pleaded with Caesar at length, he wept. But Caesar
took him by the hand, comforted him, and told him to say
no more, making it clear that his influence was valuable, and
that because of his goodwill and his entreaties Caesar would
overlook both the harm done to the Republic and his own
sense of indignation. Then, in Diviciacus' presence, Caesar
summoned Dumnorix and explained the grounds for com-
plaint against him, setting out his own view, and the state's
reasons for protest. He warned Dumnorix to avoid any taint
of suspicion in future, and ended by saying that he was over-
looking the past for Diviciacus' sake. Then, to make sure he
knew what Dumnorix was doing, and with whom he spoke,
Caesar put him under guard.

(21) That same day Caesar's scouts told him that the enemy was encamped in the foothills just over seven miles from
the Roman camp. He sent men to reconnoitre the hill and
find out what sort of ascent there was on the other side of
it. They reported back that it was an easy climb. During the
third watch Caesar ordered Titus Labienus, his second-in-
command,* to take two legions, follow those men who had
spied out the way, and climb to the summit; and he explained his plan. Then, during the last watch of the night
Caesar marched against the enemy along the same route that

they had taken, sending all the cavalry on ahead. Publius Considius, who was considered a man of wide military skill and experience, and who had served in the armies of Lucius Sulla and later Marcus Crassus,* was sent on ahead with the scouts.

(22) By dawn Labienus had taken possession of the summit. Caesar was little more than a mile from the enemy camp; and as he later learned from prisoners, the enemy had not been aware of his own arrival, or that of Labienus either. But Considius galloped up to him and reported that the summit which Caesar had expected Labienus to be occupying was in enemy hands; also that he had recognized them by their Gallic weapons and emblems. So Caesar led his own men instead to a nearby hill and arranged his forces for battle. He had instructed Labienus not to give battle unless his own troops appeared near the enemy camp, so that the attack upon the enemy would come from all sides at once; and so, once he was in control of the summit, Labienus prepared to wait for our men, and avoided engaging. Only late in the day did Caesar at last discover from his scouts that the hill was being held by his own men and that the Helvetii had moved camp— and that Considius had been so terrified that he had reported seeing what he had not in fact seen at all. The rest of that day Caesar followed the enemy at his usual distance, and pitched his camp about three miles from theirs.

(23) Next day, as only two more days remained before it was time to distribute the army's corn rations, and as he was no more than sixteen-and-a-half miles from Bibracte (by far the greatest and wealthiest of the Aeduan towns), he thought it time to make provision for the corn supply. So he shifted his march away from the Helvetii and set out for Bibracte. The enemy learned of this from some runaway slaves belonging to Lucius Aemilius, a squadron-leader in charge of Caesar's Gallic cavalry. Either because they thought the Romans were fleeing in fear from them (which seemed all the more likely, as on the previous day they had not engaged despite seizing a vantage-point), or because they were sure they could cut them off from their corn supply, the Helvetii changed plan, altered their course, and began to pursue and harass our rearguard.

(24) When Caesar saw this he withdrew his forces to the nearest hill, and sent the cavalry to face the enemy assault. Meanwhile he drew up a triple battle line,* consisting of the four veteran legions, half-way up the hill. On top of the height he positioned the two legions he had recently recruited in Nearer Gaul and all the auxiliaries, and filled the whole hill with men. Meanwhile, he gave orders for the soldiers' packs to be piled together in one place, and for those who were positioned in line higher up to stand guard there. The Helvetii followed with all their waggons, and piled up their baggage in a single place. Then, in a compact line they repulsed our cavalry, formed a phalanx,* and moved towards our front line.

(25) Caesar first sent away his own horse out of sight, then did the same with everyone else's, to make the danger equal for everyone and to eliminate any opportunity for flight;* then he encouraged his men and joined battle. The soldiers who were posted higher up threw their javelins and easily shattered the enemy phalanx. Once it was broken, they drew their swords and charged the enemy. The Gauls were severely hindered in the battle by the fact that many of their shields had been pierced and fastened together by the first javelin-cast: the iron became bent, and they could not pull it out—nor could they fight properly with the left hand restricted. So, after persistently shaking their left arm, many of them preferred to throw their shields away and fight unprotected. In the end they were exhausted by their wounds and began to retreat, moving back to a hill which was less than a mile away. They gained it; our men were approaching, as the Boii and Tulingi, who brought up the enemy rear with some 15,000 men, acted as a rearguard. They marched right up to our men, attacked them on their exposed side,* and surrounded them. When the Helvetii, who had retreated to the mountain, saw this, they went back on the offensive and began the battle afresh. The Romans wheeled and advanced in two divisions: the first and second lines facing the enemy forces which had already been defeated and driven off, the third resisting this fresh attack.

(26) The battle continued long and fierce on both fronts. When the Gauls could no longer sustain our assault, the Helvetii retreated once more to the mountain, and the Boii and Tulingi headed for their baggage and waggons. Throughout the whole battle, moreover, despite the fact that it lasted from the seventh hour* until evening, no one could see an enemy soldier turned in flight. Beside the baggage the fight continued far into the night, for they had formed a rampart from the waggons, and from this vantage-point began to throw missiles at our men as they advanced. Down between the waggons and wheels some were throwing pikes and javelins, and wounding our men. After a protracted struggle our men won possession of the baggage and the camp. There the daughter of Orgetorix was taken captive, and one of his sons. About 130,000 of the Helvetii survived this battle, and marched all through that night. They did not break their journey to rest even once, and three days later reached the territory of the Lingones. Because of the legionaries' wounds and the need to bury the dead, our men had been delayed for a period of three days and had not been able to pursue them. Caesar sent messengers with a letter to the Lingones, warning them not to help the Helvetii by providing food or other necessaries: if anyone did offer assistance he would treat them as enemies, just like the Helvetii. After the three-day interval he began the pursuit with all his forces.

(27) The Helvetii were compelled by their total lack of provisions to send envoys to Caesar to discuss surrender. When they met him as he was on the march they threw themselves at his feet, weeping and humbly begging him for peace. He gave orders that the Helvetii should remain where they were and await his arrival, and they obeyed him.

When Caesar arrived he demanded hostages, weapons, and the slaves who had deserted to the Helvetii. While these were being collected and brought together night intervened, and about 6,000 men of the village known as Verbigene set out at dusk from the Helvetii's camp and made for the Rhine and the land of the Germans. Perhaps they were full of fear at being made to hand over their weapons, or perhaps they were encouraged by the hope of safety, thinking that in such a huge crowd of prisoners their flight would be concealed or would even escape notice altogether.

(28) After confirming his suspicion that this escape was taking place, Caesar ordered the peoples through whose territory they were escaping to track them down and bring them back—if they wished to clear themselves of suspicion. When they were returned he treated them as enemies;* as for all the rest, he accepted their surrender after the hostages, weapons, and deserters had been handed over. He ordered the Helvetii, Tulingi, and Latovici to return to the lands from which they had come, and because their crops were all ruined and they had no means of sustenance in their homeland, he commanded the Allobroges to provide them with corn, and told the Helvetii to rebuild the towns and villages which they had burned. His particular reason for this order was that he was reluctant for them to leave the place they had abandoned still unoccupied, in case the Germans who lived across the Rhine crossed out of their own land into that of the Helvetii, because of the fertility of the soil, and settled on the borders of the Province of Gaul and of the Allobroges. At the Aedui's request, he allowed the Boii, who were famous for their great bravery, to settle in Aeduan territory. The Aedui gave farmland to them, and later admitted them to equal rights and freedom.

(29) Tablets were found in the Helvetii's camp, written in Greek characters, and were taken to Caesar. They contained a complete record under several headings—the numbers which had set out from the homeland, those capable of bearing arms, and a separate list of the boys, the old men, and the women. The sum total of all these categories came to 263,000 of the Helvetii: of the Tulingi there were 36,000, of the Latovici 14,000, of the Raurici 23,000, and of the Boii 32,000. About 92,000 of these were capable of bearing arms. The total number was about 368,000. When a census was taken of those who returned home, in accordance with Caesar's orders, the number came to 110,000.

(30) At the end of the war with the Helvetii the leaders of almost all the Gallic states came as envoys to congratulate

Caesar. They were aware, they said, that Caesar's aim had
been to exact punishment in return for outrages long ago
inflicted on the Roman people by the Helvetii. None the less,
the envoys went on, the outcome was as much to Gaul's
advantage as to the Roman people's, for the Helvetii had left
their homes (where they enjoyed great prosperity) with the
express intention of making war upon all Gaul, and snatch-
ing dominion. From an abundance of sites the Helvetii had
intended to select for their home the area which they ad-
judged the most conveniently situated and fertile, and to make
the other states tributary.

The envoys requested Caesar's permission to announce a
meeting of all Gaul for a particular date, for there were
certain requests they wished to make of him, once they had
come to an agreement among themselves. Their request was
granted. They fixed the date of the meeting, and swore an
oath that none but those men designated by common agreement should divulge the proceedings.

(31) When this meeting was ended, the same leaders of the
Gallic states as before returned again to Caesar. They asked
permission to discuss with him in secret both their own welfare
and the good of all. When he agreed, they all wept and threw
themselves at Caesar's feet. They were as anxious, they explained, to ensure that their discussion would not become
public, as they were to obtain what they wanted. For if it
were made public they foresaw for themselves a terrible
punishment. Their spokesman was the Aeduan, Diviciacus,
and he explained that within Gaul as a whole there were two
factions, one led by the Aedui, the other by the Arverni. For
many years the two had been fighting fiercely for supremacy;
then, he said, it came about that the Arverni and Sequani
hired some German mercenaries. Initially about 15,000 of
them crossed the Rhine, but once these wild and savage men
had conceived a passionate desire for the lands of the Gauls,
their way of life, and their wealth, more of them had crossed
the river. There were now about 120,000 of them in Gaul.

Diviciacus went on to say that the Aedui and their dependants had frequently fought with the Germans but had been
defeated, suffering disastrous ruin, and had lost all their

aristocracy, their senate, and their entire cavalry. Broken by these disastrous battles, those men who had previously been pre-eminent in Gaul (by reason of both their own excellence and the hospitality and friendship of the Roman people) were forced to surrender their most aristocratic citizens as hostages to the Sequani, and to bind the state by an oath, never to ask for the hostages' return, nor to beg the help of the Roman people, nor to deny their perpetual subjection to the power and dominion of the Sequani. Alone of all the men of the Aeduan state, he, Diviciacus, could not be constrained to swear the oath or surrender his own children as hostages. For this reason—namely, his lone refusal to be bound by the oath and the giving of hostages—he had fled the state and come to the Senate at Rome to plead for help.

And yet, he continued, a worse fate had befallen the victorious Sequani than the defeated Aedui. For Ariovistus, the king of the Germans, had settled in their territory and seized one-third of their land, which was the best in the whole of Gaul; and he was now ordering the Sequani to vacate another third, because 24,000 men of the Harudes had joined him a few months before, and he was making a place ready for them to settle in. In a few years they would all be driven out of Gaul, and in turn all the Germans would cross the Rhine. After all, there was no comparison between Gallic land and German, nor was there any contest between the two ways of life.

Meanwhile Ariovistus, as soon as he had engaged with the Gallic forces and defeated them (a battle which took place at Admagetobriga), began to issue arrogant and cruel commands—he demanded the children of all the highest-ranking citizens as hostages, and then inflicted all kinds of torture on them as a warning, should anything be done contrary to his will and pleasure. This Ariovistus was a savage, a reckless hothead: they could endure his dictates no longer. Unless Caesar and the Roman people could help, the whole of Gaul would have to do what the Helvetii had once done—leave their homes and seek out another place to dwell in, far away from the Germans, and to risk whatever fortune might befall. If Ariovistus got to hear of this warning, said Diviciacus, he was certain that all the hostages in his keeping would be made to pay the ultimate penalty. But Caesar, either through his own and his army's influence, or because of his recent victory, or through the renown of the Roman people, could discourage him from bringing the Germans over the Rhine in even greater numbers, and could defend all Gaul from Ariovistus' outrages.

(32) At the end of Diviciacus' speech all who were present began, amid much weeping, to petition Caesar for help. But Caesar noticed that of all of them only the Sequani did not act in accord with the rest, but stood looking grave, heads bowed, staring at the ground. Wondering why this was so, he asked them, but they did not reply, and maintained the same grave silence. When he repeatedly questioned them and yet could elicit no response whatever, Diviciacus the Aeduan answered him, and explained that the Sequani had been more unhappy and unfortunate than everyone else, for they alone did not even dare to complain in secret or to beg for help. Even in his absence, they were as afraid of Ariovistus' cruelty as if he were actually present. Everyone else at least had some chance of escape, but the Sequani had received Ariovistus within their own borders—all their towns were in his power, and they must endure whatever torments he inflicted.

(33) On receiving this information Caesar spoke words of encouragement to the Gauls, and promised to take care of the matter. He was confident, he assured them, that Ariovistus would be encouraged to stop his outrageous behaviour by Caesar's special favour and influence. He then dismissed the meeting.

Many considerations persuaded him to think it his duty to consider this matter and to intervene in it. For one thing, the Aedui, who had more than once been named Brothers and Kinsmen* by the Roman Senate, were now enslaved under the dominion of the Germans, and their hostages were in the keeping of Ariovistus and the Sequani. When he considered the great power of the Roman people, this was a strong reproach to himself and to the Roman state. He could see that for the Germans to become accustomed by degrees to crossing the Rhine, and entering Gaul in large numbers, posed a threat to

the Roman people. Nor did he reckon that such fierce barbarians would hesitate—once they had seized the whole of
Gaul—before flooding into the Province as the Cimbri and
Teutoni* had done years before, and then making for Italy,
especially since only the Rhône separated the Sequani from
our Province. These dangers, he believed, must be countered
as swiftly as possible. Indeed, Ariovistus himself had assumed
such arrogance, such an air of haughty pride, as was not to
be borne.

(34) For these reasons Caesar decided to send envoys to
Ariovistus, to ask him to select some location midway between the two sides for a parley. He himself wished to discuss state affairs and business of urgent interest to both parties.
Ariovistus replied to the embassy, saying that had he needed
anything from Caesar he would have approached Caesar—
but if Caesar wanted something from him, Caesar should do
the approaching. Moreover, he went on, he did not dare to
enter those parts of Gaul under Caesar's control without his
army, and he was unable to muster his men in a single place
without going to great trouble and effort over supplies. He
ended by saying that he found it remarkable that either Caesar
or, for that matter, the Roman people was troubled over
Gaul, which he had made his own by right of conquest in
war.*

(35) Ariovistus' words were reported to Caesar, who sent
the envoys back to him with the following message: Ariovistus
had been treated with great kindness by Caesar and the Roman
people when, during Caesar's consulship, he had been pronounced king and Friend by the Roman Senate. Since, however, he had shown his gratitude to Caesar and the Roman
people by being reluctant to attend a parley when invited,
and by seeing no reason to discuss or listen to matters of
concern to both sides, Caesar was making the following
demands of him. First, he should no longer bring large numbers of men over the Rhine into Gaul. Secondly, he must
return the hostages he had taken from the Aedui, and grant
the Sequani full permission to return to the Aedui the hostages they were holding. He was to do no harm to the Aedui,
nor attack them or their allies. If Ariovistus complied with

these instructions he would have the lasting favour and friendship of Caesar and the Roman people; but the Senate had
decided, in the consulship of Marcus Messalla and Marcus
Piso,* that whoever was in command of the Province of Gaul
was empowered to act in the state's interest and defend the
Aedui and the other friends of the Roman people. So if Caesar
did not get what he wanted he would not ignore wrongs
inflicted upon the Aedui.

(36) Ariovistus replied that the laws of warfare said conquerors could rule those they had conquered in whatever way
they chose. Moreover, the Romans were themselves accustomed to ruling the conquered according to their own judgement, rather than another man's orders. If he, Ariovistus,
was not telling the Roman people how to handle their own
jurisdiction, it was not right that they should hinder him in
the exercise of his. After hazarding the fortunes of war, attacking him and being beaten, the Aedui had become his tribute-
payers. Caesar was doing him a great wrong, for his advance
was having a bad effect upon these tax revenues. He was not
going to give the Aedui their hostages back, but neither would
he wrongfully wage war upon them or their allies, if they
stuck to the agreement and paid the annual tribute. If they
did not, the title of Brothers of the Roman people would be
of no use to them at all. As for Caesar's declaration that he
would be mindful of any wrongs done to the Aedui, no one
had ever fought with Ariovistus and not been destroyed.
Caesar could engage when he pleased: then he would understand what the undefeated Germans could achieve by their
courage—men who, with their extraordinary skill in weapons,
had not been beneath a roof in fourteen years.

(37) At the same time as this speech was reported to Caesar,
envoys arrived from the Aedui and Treveri. The Aedui came
to protest about the Harudes, who had only recently been
brought across into Gaul and were ravaging their territory:
not even by surrendering hostages, they said, could they win
peace from Ariovistus. The Treveri complained that a hundred
communities of the Suebi had settled on the banks of the
Rhine, and were trying to cross the river, under the command of two brothers called Nasua and Cimberius. Caesar

was much disturbed by these matters, and realized he must
act swiftly, before this new band of Suebi joined up with
Ariovistus' veteran forces, making the task of defence more
difficult. So he secured the corn supply at great speed, and
then headed towards Ariovistus by forced marches.

(38) After three days' march Caesar was informed that
Ariovistus was making for Vesontio (the main town of the
Sequani) with all his forces to seize control of it, and that he
was already three days out from his own borders. Caesar
knew he must make every effort to prevent this happening,
for the town contained an abundance of the resources necessary for warfare. It was also protected by its natural site in
such a way as to provide a strong position for conducting a
campaign—especially since the River Doubs practically surrounds the entire town, like a circle drawn with compasses.
The remaining perimeter, of not more than 1,600 feet, where
the river does not flow, is filled in by a high mountain, the
roots of which touch the banks of the river on either side. A
wall around its base makes it into a citadel and links it with
the town. Caesar made for this place, marching day and
night; he seized the town and posted a garrison in it.

(39) He remained in Vesontio for a few days to gather
corn and supplies, during which time such a terrible panic
suddenly seized our whole army as severely affected everyone's courage and morale. Our men started asking questions,
and the Gauls and traders replied by describing how tall and
strong the Germans were, how unbelievably brave and skilful
with weapons. Often, they claimed, when they had met the
Germans in battle they had been unable to stand even the
way they looked, the sternness of their gaze. The panic began
among the military tribunes and prefects, and the other men
who, having no great military experience, had followed Caesar
from Rome to court his friendship.* Some of them started
offering various excuses for urgent departure, and asked his
permission to go; others stayed behind out of shame, wanting
to avoid the taint of cowardice. These men could not conceal
their fearful expressions, nor, at times, could they restrain their
tears. They hid themselves away in their tents and bemoaned
their fate, or among their friends lamented the common

danger. Throughout the camp all the men were signing and sealing their wills.

Thanks to their fearful complaining, gradually even men of great military experience began to be affected—the legionary soldiers, centurions, and cavalry officers. Some were eager to appear less cowardly, and declared that it was not the enemy they feared, but the restricted, narrow route of the march, the depths of forest between themselves and Ariovistus, or the arrangement of satisfactory transport for the corn supply. Some even went so far as to tell Caesar that, although he had given the order to strike camp and move out, the soldiers would not obey him and, because of their fear, would refuse to lift the standards.

(40) As soon as Caesar was aware of the situation he called a council, ordered centurions of all ranks to attend, and severely reprimanded them, primarily for thinking that it was their business to inquire or think about either the direction or the strategy of the march. During his consulship, Caesar went on, Ariovistus had eagerly sought friendly relations with the Roman people. Why would anyone now conclude that he was going to abandon his obligations rashly? In fact, he was convinced that once Ariovistus understood the terms he was offering, and considered the fairness of the conditions, he would not spurn the favour either of Caesar or of the Roman people.

And even if Ariovistus did start a war, Caesar continued, spurred on by some mad fury, what was there to fear even then? Why did they despair of their own courage, or of his anxious concern for their well-being? The danger posed by this enemy had already been experienced in the time of our fathers, when the Cimbri and Teutoni were expelled by Gaius Marius. On that occasion it was clear that the army had deserved as much credit as its commander. The same danger had also been experienced more recently during the slave revolt in Italy.* In this instance the slaves were helped to some degree by the experience and training which they had received from us.

From all this, said Caesar, they could see how crucial was firmness of purpose. After all, for a time they had feared the slaves, who were then without weapons: yet later they had defeated those same slaves after they were armed and had won battles. Finally, the Germans were the same people who had often clashed with the Helvetii—and the Helvetii had frequently beaten them, not only within their own borders but also in Germany itself—and yet the Helvetii had proved no match for our army.

Perhaps, he went on, some of those present were disturbed by the defeat and flight of the Gauls. But if they took the trouble to inquire they would discover that the Gauls had been worn down by the long duration of the campaign, before Ariovistus (who had for many months been skulking in his camp in the marshes, giving them no chance to attack him) suddenly launched his assault upon them, when the Gauls had given up hope of battle and had already dispersed. He had won, then, more by tactical planning than by conspicuous bravery. And even if there was a place for these tactics when faced with barbarians of no military skill, not even Ariovistus would pin his hopes on the success of such tactics as a means of beating our army.

As for those who shifted the blame for their own fear on to a pretended anxiety about corn supplies or the narrowness of the route, they were doing so out of presumption. After all, they apparently either doubted their commander's commitment or they were dictating it to Caesar. Yet his attention was taken up with all these things: the Sequani, the Leuci, and the Lingones were supplying corn, and the crop was already ripe in the fields—as for the route of their march, in a short while they would themselves decide it. On the subject of their declared intention not to follow orders and raise the standards, it did not trouble him at all. He was well aware that whenever an army had disobeyed its commander in the past, it was either because fortune had deserted him, as proven by his failure on the field, or because he had been discovered in some crime and found guilty of rapacity. That he, Caesar, was himself guilty of no crime was evident from the whole course of his life: that he was a man who enjoyed good fortune was evident from his campaign against the Helvetii.

And so, Caesar concluded, he would do at once what he

had intended to put off till a later date. The very next night, during the fourth watch, they would strike camp. Then he would know as soon as possible whether their sense of shame and duty was stronger than their fear. Moreover, even if no one at all followed him, then he would still set out, with only the Tenth legion, for he had no doubts about *its* loyalty. Indeed, it would in future serve as his bodyguard.* (Caesar had treated this legion with special favour, and had the fullest confidence in its courage.)

(41) At the end of this speech the change of attitude was quite remarkable, and there arose an immense enthusiasm and eagerness to start the campaign. The Tenth legion was first to express its thanks to Caesar, through the military tribunes, for the excellent opinion he had formed of it, and it declared its readiness to start the campaign. Then the other legions urged their military tribunes and senior centurions to make amends to Caesar. They claimed they had never been in doubt nor afraid, nor did they think the supreme command belonged to them instead of their commander. Their apology was accepted. Through Diviciacus (in whom alone Caesar had particular trust) a route was discovered for the march: by means of a detour of more than forty-six miles it led the army through open country. They set out, as Caesar had said, during the fourth watch. On the seventh day of marching without a break his scouts told Caesar that Ariovistus' army was only twenty-two miles off.

(42) Once Ariovistus learned that Caesar was at hand he sent envoys to him to say that, as far as he was concerned, the parley Caesar had previously demanded could now take place—especially as Caesar had moved nearer, which meant that Ariovistus could now attend without risk. Caesar, who thought that Ariovistus had by now come to his senses (since he was now offering unasked what he had previously refused to do when expressly requested), did not reject this proposal. He was hopeful that in return for the signal services rendered to Ariovistus by both Caesar himself and the Roman people, Ariovistus would abandon his stubbornness once he knew Caesar's terms.

The fifth day following this was appointed for the parley.

In the interim, when envoys went back and forth between the two sides, Ariovistus made it a condition that Caesar should not bring any infantry to the parley, claiming that he feared being surrounded and trapped. Both sides, Ariovistus went on, should come with cavalry—otherwise he would not come at all. Caesar was reluctant to have the parley halted on a pretext, yet did not care to entrust his safety to Gallic cavalry. The most convenient solution, Caesar decided, was to take away the horses of the Gallic cavalry and mount on them instead the soldiers of the Tenth legion, in whom he had the fullest confidence. In this way he would secure a devoted bodyguard, just in case he needed it. There was some wit in doing so, pointed out one soldier of the Tenth: Caesar was doing more for them than he had promised, for he had vowed to keep the Tenth as his bodyguard, but was now enrolling them among the *equites*.*

(43) There was a large level area, and on it a mound of earth of considerable size. The place was almost equidistant from the camps of Ariovistus and Caesar. To this place, as was mentioned above, they came for the parley. Caesar halted the legion which he had mounted on horseback at a distance of 200 paces from the mound. Ariovistus' cavalry stopped at a similar distance, and he stipulated that they should hold the parley on horseback, and bring ten men with them.

When they came to the place, Caesar began by speaking of the benefits conferred by himself and by the Roman Senate, namely, that Ariovistus had been declared king and Friend by the Senate, and that gifts had been showered upon him; Caesar pointed out that the privilege was one granted to few, and usually bestowed in return for signal services. Although Ariovistus had no right of access to the Senate nor any just cause for claim, he had received those rewards through the generosity of Caesar and the Senate. Caesar further pointed out that the reasons for friendship existing between the Romans and the Aedui were appropriate and long-standing, and cited the frequency of decrees of the Senate conferring honour upon the Aedui: they had, Caesar said, always held a position of control over all Gaul, even before they had sought our friendship.

It was the Roman people's custom, Caesar concluded, not only not to deprive their friends and allies of any property, but also to desire the increase of their favour, prestige, and distinction. Who could allow them to be robbed of what they had brought to the friendship of the Roman people? He then set out the same terms that he had given in his instructions to the envoys, namely, to make no war upon the Aedui or their allies, to return the hostages, and if Ariovistus could not send any section of the Germans home, at least to prevent any more from crossing the Rhine.

(44) Ariovistus made a curt reply to Caesar's demands, but then spoke long and loudly of his own excellence. He had not crossed the Rhine of his own accord, but at the express request of the Gauls. He had left his home and family in the sure hope of considerable gains, he held a place in Gaul granted by the Gauls themselves, and hostages which they had willingly surrendered; and he was exacting a tribute by right of war, such as victors usually impose upon the conquered. He had not made war upon the Gauls, but rather they upon him. Every Gallic people had come to attack him and had started operations against him, and their entire force had been routed and overcome by him in a single battle.

If they wished to test the strength of Ariovistus again, he was still prepared to fight it out—but if they wished to enjoy peace, it was not right to refuse payment of the tribute which until now they had willingly paid out. The friendship of the Roman people should be a distinction and protection, not a drawback: that was why he had sought it. If, through the Roman people, the tribute were now paid back and the hostages returned, he would reject their friendship as freely as once he had sought it.

As to the fact that he was bringing hordes of Germans into Gaul, Ariovistus went on, this was for his own protection, not as a means of attacking Gaul. The proof of this was that he would not have come, had he not been asked—and that he had not gone on the offensive, but had defended himself. He had entered Gaul before the Roman people did. Never before had the army of the Roman people moved outside the boundaries of the Province. What did Caesar want with him?

Why was Caesar coming into his territory? This part of Gaul was Ariovistus' province, just as the other part was ours. If he had attacked our lands, it would not be right to give way: likewise, it would be wrong for us to interfere in Ariovistus' jurisdiction.

As for Caesar's statement that the Aedui had been named Brothers, he was not such a barbarian, nor so ignorant of affairs, as to be unaware that neither in the last war against the Allobroges did the Aedui offer the Romans help, nor did they in turn enjoy the assistance of the Roman people in their internal disputes and their contentions with the Sequani. He was bound to suspect that Caesar's friendship was a pretence. After all, he had an army in Gaul—an army to crush him with. Unless Caesar left the area, and took his army with him, he would treat him no longer as a friend but as an enemy. In fact, said Ariovistus, if he killed Caesar he would earn the gratitude of many aristocrats and leaders at Rome. He knew this for a fact from those very men, through their messengers, and by Caesar's death he could win the favour and friendship of them all. If, on the other hand, Caesar departed and handed over full control of Gaul to him, he would give him a great reward; and whatever wars he wanted waged, these would be accomplished without any effort or risk on Caesar's part.

(45) Caesar explained at some length why he could not abandon the business in hand. Neither his own custom, nor the Roman people's, allowed him to desert such loyal allies; nor did he consider that Gaul belonged any more to Ariovistus than to the Roman people. The Arverni and Ruteni had been defeated by Quintus Fabius Maximus,* and then pardoned by the Roman people, but were not turned into a province nor made to pay tribute. If priority of arrival was what counted, then the Roman people's rule over Gaul was fully justified: but if they followed the decision of the Senate, then Gaul—which the Senate had wished to keep its own laws after its defeat—should be free.

(46) During the parley Caesar heard news that Ariovistus' cavalry was coming quite close to the earth mound and riding up to our men, throwing stones and missiles at them. He

finished speaking and returned to his men, ordering them not to throw so much as a single missile in return. For although he realized that a battle between his favourite legion and the enemy cavalry would pose no risk, none the less he considered a fight inadvisable. Thus, once the enemy was beaten they could not say that they had trusted Caesar's assurances and been entrapped by him at a parley. When news of the arrogance with which Ariovistus had behaved at the parley spread to the soldiers—how he had ordered the Romans out of the whole of Gaul, how his cavalry had attacked our men, and how this had led to the breaking-off of talks—they were filled with even greater eagerness and enthusiasm for the fight.

(47) Two days later Ariovistus sent envoys to Caesar. He wished to continue with him discussion of those matters which they had earlier started but not finished. So would Caesar either decide once more the date for a parley, or, if he was reluctant to do so, would he send back an envoy of his own? Caesar saw no reason for talks, the more so since the day before it had proved impossible to prevent the Germans throwing missiles at our men. In his view, to send one of his envoys to Ariovistus would be highly dangerous, as he would be at the mercy of barbarians. The most convenient solution was to send Gaius Valerius Procillus,* the son of Gaius Valerius Caburus who had been granted citizenship by Gaius Valerius Flaccus. Procillus was both a brave and a cultured young man, and because of his loyalty and his fluency in the Gallic language (which Ariovistus, by long custom, habitually used), and also because there was no reason for the Germans to do him any harm, he was sent, along with Marcus Mettius, who enjoyed Ariovistus' friendship. Caesar ordered them to discover what Ariovistus was saying, and report back. When, however, Ariovistus saw them in his camp he cried out before his whole army, asking why they had come—was it to spy? He prevented them from saying anything, and put them in chains.

(48) That same day he struck camp, moved out, and took up a position at the foot of a mountain five-and-a-half miles from Caesar's camp. On the following day he marched his

forces past Caesar's camp, and encamped two miles further on, with the intention of cutting Caesar off from the corn and supplies which were being transported by the Sequani and Aedui. From that day on, for five days without a break, Caesar led out his own forces in front of the camp drawn up in battle formation. Thus, if Ariovistus wanted to engage he would have his opportunity. During these days Ariovistus kept his army in camp, but engaged in a daily cavalry battle. The kind of fighting in which the Germans were practised was this: there were 6,000 cavalry, and the same number of swift and courageous infantry, each of the latter chosen by a cavalryman from the whole force for his protection. In battles they operated together. The cavalry would fall back towards the foot-soldiers, who would quickly mass if trouble loomed. If a cavalryman was badly wounded and fell from his horse, the soldiers would surround him; and if it was necessary to advance some distance or retreat swiftly, they had such speed because of their training that they could keep pace by holding on to the horses' manes.

(49) Caesar realized that Ariovistus was staying in his camp, so to avoid further hindrance to supplies he selected a spot suitable for a second camp, about 600 paces beyond the place where the Germans were positioned. He marched to this spot in a triple-line formation. Then he ordered the first and second lines to stand at the ready, and the third line to construct defences for the camp. This position was, as was just mentioned, about 600 paces from the enemy. Ariovistus sent towards it a force of about 16,000 troops, together with all the cavalry, to terrify our forces and hinder the work of fortification. Nevertheless, Caesar still ordered the two lines to drive away the enemy, as he had earlier decided, and told the third to finish its defence work. Once the camp was fortified, he left two legions there and a section of the auxiliaries. The four remaining legions he led back to the main camp.

(50) Next day he led his forces out of both camps as usual, advanced a short distance from the main camp, and drew up his battle line, thus giving the enemy an opportunity of joining battle. Once he saw that not even then did they emerge, around noon he took his army back to camp. Then

at last Ariovistus sent out a section of his forces to attack the smaller camp. The fight was fierce on both sides until night fell, at which point, after many wounds had been inflicted and also endured, Ariovistus withdrew his forces back to camp.

When Caesar asked some prisoners why Ariovistus did not engage, he discovered that the reason was a custom of the Germans. Using lots and divination, their older women used to declare whether they could join battle with advantage or not—and they said it was not heaven's will that the Germans should win if they joined battle before the new moon.

(51) Next day Caesar left what seemed an adequate garrison for each camp. Then he placed all his auxiliaries before the smaller camp in sight of the enemy, to use them for show (as he was rather weak in numbers of legionary soldiers, in comparison with the numbers of the enemy). He himself drew up a triple battle line and advanced right up to the enemy camp. Then at last, of necessity the Germans led out their own forces from camp and stationed them at equal intervals according to their communities: the Harudes, the Marcomani, the Triboces, the Vangiones, the Nemetes, the Sedusii, and the Suebi. They surrounded their battle line with waggons and carts, so as to leave no hope of flight. There they placed their women, who, with outstretched arms and weeping, begged the men setting out to battle not to hand them over into Roman slavery.

(52) Caesar put five legates and a quaestor* each in charge of a legion, to act as witnesses of each man's valour. He started the battle from the right wing, as he had observed that there the enemy was weakest. At the signal our men attacked the enemy so fiercely, and the enemy rushed forward so suddenly and swiftly, that there was no room for throwing javelins at the foe. These weapons were cast aside as a sword fight ensued. The Germans, as was their custom, quickly formed a phalanx to sustain our attack. Several of our men were found leaping on to the massed enemy, tearing away their shields with their hands, and wounding them from above. Although the enemy line was forced back on the left wing and put to flight, on the right it was pressing on our line by sheer force of numbers. A young man called Publius

Crassus (he was in charge of the cavalry) noticed this, and as he was more at liberty to act than those men who were occupied between the lines, he sent the third line in to help our men in difficulties.

(53) So the battle swung back in our favour, and all the enemy turned tail and did not stop running until they reached the Rhine, nearly five miles away from the field of battle. There a very few trusted in their own strength and aimed to swim across, or found boats and thus ensured their own safety. Ariovistus was of their number. He found a small boat moored to the bank, and escaped in it. Our men pursued all the rest of the enemy with the cavalry and killed them.

Ariovistus had two wives, one a woman of the Suebi (he had brought her with him from Germany) and the other one from Noricum, the sister of King Voccio, who had sent her to be married to him in Gaul. Both wives perished in the flight. One of his daughters also died, but the other was captured. Gaius Valerius Procillus, bound in triple chains, was being dragged by his guards in the flight when he met with Caesar himself, pursuing the enemy with the cavalry. It brought Caesar as much pleasure as the victory itself to see this most worthy provincial, his own companion and close friend, snatched from the hand of the enemy and restored to him: nor had Procillus suffered any terrible fate such as would lessen in any degree Caesar's great pleasure and joy. Procillus recounted how in his presence lots had three times been cast to decide whether he should be burned to death or kept back for a later occasion—but thanks to the lots, he was uninjured. So also Marcus Mettius was found and taken back to Caesar.

(54) News of the battle spread across the Rhine. The Suebi who had come to the banks of the river began to move back home; and when the people who dwell near the Rhine realized their panic, they pursued and killed a large number of them.

Caesar had conducted two major campaigns in a single season, and now, a little later than the time of year required, he led his army to the land of the Sequani to winter quarters. There he put Labienus in charge. He himself set out for Nearer Gaul, to hold assizes.

The Second Book: 57 BC
(AUC 697: Consuls, Publius Cornelius Lentulus Spinther, Quintus Caecilius Metellus Nepos)

Defeats for the Belgic Peoples

(1) As we mentioned above, Caesar was in Nearer Gaul; there he heard a host of rumours, confirmed by a letter from Labienus, that all the Belgae (who make up one-third of Gaul, as we said before) were hatching a plot against the Roman people and exchanging hostages. The reasons for this plot were as follows. First, they were afraid that our army would march against them now all the rest of Gaul had been subdued; secondly, they were being stirred up by a number of the Gauls, some of whom had been unwilling for the Germans to have any further involvement in Gaul, and were equally reluctant for the army of the Roman people to over-winter and become established there. Others were of a volatile and unstable disposition—the sort of men who delight in changes of rule. Yet another group incited the Belgae to conspire because it was common in Gaul for men who possessed some degree of power and the means to hire support to seize regal power—something which would be more difficult to achieve under our rule.

(2) These reports, and Labienus' despatch, prompted Caesar to enlist two new legions* in Nearer Gaul; and once the campaigning season had begun he sent his legate, Quintus Pedius, to lead them to Further Gaul. He himself went to join his army as soon as a supply of fodder became available. To the Senones, and the other Gauls who were neighbours of the Belgae, he gave the task of finding out what the Belgae were doing and of keeping him informed of developments. They all loyally reported that gangs were mustering, and an army assembling in one place. Then he knew it was imperative that he set out for the territory of the Belgae.

Caesar secured a supply of corn, struck camp, and moved out. Within about a fortnight he had reached the borders of

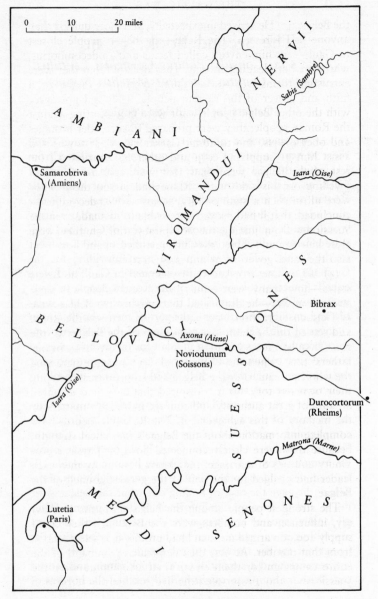

FIG. 3 The Belgian Campaign

the Belgae. (3) He arrived unexpectedly, and more quickly than anyone had foreseen. The Remi—the Belgic people closest to Gaul—sent him envoys called Iccius and Andecomborius, who were both leading citizens. They declared that they were entrusting themselves and all their possessions to the good faith and power of the Roman people. They did not agree with the other Belgic peoples, nor were they plotting against the Roman people: they were prepared to surrender hostages and obey orders, and to admit Caesar into their towns and assist him by supplying corn and other necessaries. All the rest of the Belgae were ready for war, and the Germans dwelling on this side of the Rhine had joined them. They were all in such a state of fury, Iccius and Andecomborius concluded, that it had proved impossible to dissuade even the Suessiones from joining the conspiracy, though they were close kinsmen and shared the same jurisdiction and laws, and also the same government and magistracies.

(4) When Caesar asked the two envoys about the Belgic states—how many were under arms, and what was their strength in war—he discovered that most of the Belgae were of German extraction, and had long ago crossed the Rhine and settled on the western side because of the fertility of the soil. They had forced out the Gauls who dwelt there. In our fathers' time, when the Cimbri and Teutoni were harassing the whole of Gaul, only the Belgae had stopped them entering their own territory. So it transpired that they had acquired an aura of great authority and courage in military matters by the memory of this achievement. The Remi claimed to have complete information about the Belgae's numerical strength, because they were closely connected both by physical proximity and ties of marriage: they knew how many men each leader had pledged for the war at the general council of the Belgae.

The strongest people among the Belgae in terms of bravery, influence, and numbers were the Bellovaci: they could supply 100,000 armed men, and had promised to select 60,000 from that number. At first they demanded command of the entire campaign for themselves. Their neighbours were the Suessiones, who possessed extensive and fertile territories.

Within living memory they had had a king, called Diviciacus,*
who was the most powerful in the whole of Gaul, and controlled a large portion of that region and also of Britain.
Now their king was a man called Galba; because he was a
just and cautious ruler, everyone agreed to give him overall
control of the entire war. He had control of twelve towns,
and was pledging 50,000 soldiers. The Nervii, a people
dwelling far off, and considered particularly fierce by the
Gauls themselves, pledged a similar number. The Atrebates
pledged 15,000, the Ambiani 10,000, the Morini 25,000, the
Menapii 7,000, the Caleti 10,000, the Veliocasses and
Viromandui 10,000 between them, and the Aduatuci 19,000.
The Remi thought that the Condrusi, Eburones, Caeroesi,
and Paemani (who are collectively known as Germans) could
supply about 40,000 men.

(5) Caesar addressed the Remi with words of generous
encouragement. He ordered their whole senate to come before him, and the children of leading citizens to be brought
as hostages. These demands were scrupulously and promptly
carried out. Caesar encouraged Diviciacus the Aeduan warmly,
and explained how important it was, for the Republic and
the common good, to keep the enemy groups apart, so as to
avoid having to engage with such a huge force all at once.
This could be achieved if the Aedui brought their forces into
the Bellovaci's territory and began to plunder their lands.
With these instructions he dismissed Diviciacus.

Once he observed that all the Belgic forces had gathered
together and were marching towards him, and learned from
the scouts he had sent out and from the Remi that they were
getting close, Caesar hastened to take his army across the
River Aisne, which is in the most distant reaches of the Remi's
territory, and pitched camp. Thus one side of the camp was
protected by the river-bank, and the rear was secure from the
enemy; moreover, it ensured that the Remi and other peoples
could ferry supplies to Caesar without danger. There was a
bridge over this river. Caesar garrisoned it, and further along
the river left his legate, Quintus Titurius Sabinus, with six
cohorts; he ordered him to build a camp with a twelve-foot
rampart and an eighteen-foot ditch.

(6) Eight miles away from this camp was a town of the Remi called Bibrax. Whilst actually on the march, the Belgae suddenly turned to attack it with great force. The town barely held out on that day. The siege method of the Gauls and the Belgae is very similar: first, a line of men is placed all around the walls, and they begin to throw stones in the direction of the wall. When the wall has lost all its defenders, they form a 'tortoise',* come in close, and undermine the wall. On this occasion the task was easy: for when such a vast number of men was throwing stones and missiles there was no possibility of anyone remaining standing on the wall.

In command of the town was Iccius, one of the Remi, a man of good birth and reputation among his people. When night fell he sent a man who had been part of the peace embassy to Caesar, to tell him what was happening: unless Caesar sent help, they could not hold out any longer. (7) Around midnight Caesar sent Numidian and Cretan archers and Balearic slingers to help the people of Bibrax, under the leadership of the same men who had come bringing news from Iccius. Their arrival gave the Remi fresh enthusiasm for the fight as well as hope for the defence; and for the same reason it dispelled the enemy's hope of taking the town. So, after lingering in the vicinity, ravaging the lands of the Remi, and setting fire to all the villages and buildings within reach, the whole Belgic army turned and made for Caesar's camp. They pitched camp less than two miles off—a camp which, as the smoke and fires showed, was more than seven miles round.

(8) At first, because the enemy was so numerous, and because of its outstanding reputation for courage, Caesar avoided giving battle. By means of daily cavalry skirmishes, however, he ascertained how brave they really were, and how daring our men could afford to be. Once he realized that our men were not inferior, he chose a place in front of his camp which was naturally convenient, and suitable for forming a battle line. The hill on which the camp was pitched was slightly raised up from the plain, and had enough space in front for a battle line to take up a position at the ready: it sloped steeply on both flanks, but in front rose gently to a ridge and then returned to the level. He constructed a ditch

of about 400 paces at right angles from either side of the hill, and at the ends set up outposts and stationed his artillery: thus, once the battle-line was drawn up, despite their numerical strength the enemy would not be able to fight on the flanks and surround his own men.* He then left the two recently enlisted legions in camp, so they could be mobilized as back-up if necessary. The remaining six he drew up for battle in front of the camp. Likewise, the enemy led their forces out of camp and deployed them for battle.

(9) Between our army and theirs was a small marsh. The enemy waited to see if our men would cross it—but our men were armed and ready to attack them while they were at a disadvantage if they crossed first. Meanwhile a cavalry battle was taking place between the two lines. When neither side took the initiative by crossing first, and when the cavalry battle began to go in our favour, Caesar led his men back to camp. The enemy quickly left and made for the Aisne, which— as was explained—was behind our camp. There they found fording-places, and tried to take a division of their forces across, intending, if possible, to storm the outpost where the legate Quintus Titurius was in command and to destroy the bridge. If this proved impossible, they would devastate the land of the Remi, which was so important to our war-effort, and thus cut off our supplies.

(10) Once Titurius Sabinus had reported this to Caesar he then led all the cavalry, the Numidian light-armed troops, slingers, and archers over the bridge and marched towards the enemy. There a fierce battle was fought. Our men attacked the enemy while they were stuck in the water and killed a large number of them. The rest struggled with great daring to make their escape through the midst of the bodies but were forced back by a shower of missiles. Those who had crossed first were surrounded by our cavalry and cut down.

The enemy realized that their hopes of storming the town and crossing the river were a delusion, and observed that our men did not advance to fight on less favourable ground; moreover, their supplies of corn were starting to run out. So they called a meeting, and decided that the best thing would be for each man to return to his own home: then they could all assemble to defend whichever territory the Roman army invaded first. They could fight better in their own territory than in that belonging to others, and could use their own supplies of corn. They were led to this decision by, among other factors, the consideration that Diviciacus and the Aedui were making for the land of the Bellovaci, whom it was impossible to persuade to linger where they were, rather than going to the help of their own people.

(11) Following this decision, during the second watch they decamped with much noise and uproar and no regular ranks or order of command: for each man was trying to be first on the march and hastening to return home. The result was that the departure looked more like a flight. Caesar learned of it at once through his scouts, and feared a trap. As yet he had no intelligence of the reason for their departure, and so kept the army and cavalry in camp.

At first light, once his spies confirmed what had happened, Caesar sent the cavalry on ahead to slow up their rearguard. He put his legates Quintus Pedius and Lucius Aurunculeius Cotta in charge of them, and ordered his legate Titus Labienus to follow in support with three legions. They reached the rearguard and attacked, then pursued them for many miles and killed a great number as they fled. When our men caught up with those in the rear of the main column they stood their ground, and courageously repelled our attacks. But those who were further ahead seemed far removed from the danger, and were restrained neither by necessity nor by orders: as soon as they heard the battle-cry, they broke ranks and put their hope of safety in flight. The result was that our men, without any risk, killed as many of the enemy as time allowed. At nightfall they stopped and returned to camp as ordered.

(12) Next day, before the enemy could recover from their panic and flight, Caesar led his army into the territory of the Suessiones, which borders that of the Remi, and by a forced march he made for the town of Noviodunum.* On his arrival he tried to attack the town, as he had heard it lacked a garrison. Its ditches, however, were very wide and its walls so high that he was unable to take it by storm, despite the

small numbers defending it. He fortified a camp, and began to construct movable shelters* and prepare other equipment for use in siege operations. In the mean time the Suessiones had returned in full force from the rout and had entered the city the previous night.

The movable shelters were swiftly brought up to the town, earthworks were erected, and towers set up.* Never before had the Gauls seen or heard of such immense siege-works, and they were so disturbed by the Romans' speed of action that they sent envoys to Caesar to negotiate surrender. The Remi interceded for their safety, and their request was granted.

(13) Caesar accepted leading citizens as hostages, including two sons of King Galba himself; all the town's weapons were handed over. He accepted the Suessiones' surrender, and then led his army against the Bellovaci. They retreated into the town of Bratuspantium, taking all their property with them. When Caesar and his army were only about five miles from the town all the elders came out and started holding out their hands to him, and shouting that they entrusted themselves to his power and protection, and were not fighting against the Roman people. It was the same when he reached the town and pitched camp there—on the wall, boys and women with outstretched hands pleaded with the Romans for peace, which it was Caesar's custom to grant.

(14) After the Belgae's retreat Diviciacus had dismissed the Aeduan forces and returned to Caesar. Now he interceded on their behalf. The Bellovaci, he explained, had always been friends and allies of the Aeduan state; by saying that Caesar had enslaved the Aedui, and was inflicting insults and indignities upon them, their leaders had driven them to break off relations with their former allies and make war upon the Roman people. Once they had realized the magnitude of the disaster they had inflicted upon their state, the men who initiated this policy had fled to Britain.* Not only the Bellovaci, but also the Aedui, on their behalf, were begging Caesar to exercise his customary clemency* and mercy towards them. If he did so, he would enhance the authority of the Aedui among all the Belgae; and the Aedui customarily relied upon their help and assistance in any warfare they undertook.

(15) In order to give due respect to Diviciacus and the Aedui, Caesar said that he would spare the Bellovaci and accept them under his protection. As they were an important nation among the Belgae, with a population of significant size, he called for 600 hostages. Once these were handed over and all the town's weapons gathered in, he left Bratuspantium and came to the land of the Ambiani, who straight away surrendered themselves and all their property as well.

On the borders of their territory lived the Nervii. When Caesar inquired about their character and customs he discovered the following: they permitted no merchants within their borders; they did not allow the import of wine and other luxury goods, because they believed such things enfeebled their spirit and weakened their courage. They were fierce men, and very brave, who reproached and condemned all the other Belgae for surrendering to the Roman people and casting aside their ancestral courage: they declared that they would send no envoys, and accept no peace terms.

(16) Caesar had been marching through their territory for three days when he learned from prisoners that the River Sambre was little more than nine miles from his camp. On the other side of this river the Nervii had halted and were awaiting the Romans' arrival, together with two neighbouring peoples whom the Nervii had persuaded to join them in trying their luck in war, namely, the Atrebates and Viromandui. They were all waiting for the forces of the Aduatuci, which were already on their way, and they had sent the women, and those men whose age excluded them from the battle, to a place which was too marshy to be accessible to an army. (17) Once he learned of these events Caesar sent scouts and centurions on ahead to select a suitable place to encamp.

A number of the Belgae and other Gauls who had surrendered were following in Caesar's train and journeying along with our army. Later Caesar discovered from prisoners that during that time some of these men were observing our army's usual order of march. They then went by night to the Nervii and explained to them how a large amount of baggage was placed between the individual legions. Once the first legion had entered the camp, and while the other legions

were still far behind, they said, it would be no trouble to
attack the first legion while it was still encumbered with
heavy packs; and once it was routed and all the baggage
plundered, the other legions would not dare to resist. The
plan of the men who brought this information was helped by
the fact that from ancient times the Nervii had never possessed any cavalry—and even now they show no interest in
cavalry, but place whatever strength they do have in infantry.
As a result, if the cavalry of neighbouring peoples raided
their territory, the Nervii could obstruct it all the more easily. They would do this by cutting into trees and bending
them down—because of the large number of branches sticking out horizontally, all tangled up with brambles and thorns,
they ensured that these hedges provided them with a fortification the size of a wall. Not only was it impossible to penetrate this barrier, it was even impossible to see through it.
As our army's march was being obstructed by these obstacles, the Nervii thought this plan should not be rejected.

(18) The site which our scouts and centurions chose for
the camp was of this kind: a hill sloped down from its summit at an even gradient, along the edge of the Sambre (which
we mentioned above). Another hill sloped up from the river
at a similar gradient, opposite our hill and facing it directly,
clear and open for about 200 paces, but wooded higher up
so that it was difficult to see within. The enemy concealed
themselves in these woods. Down the river on open ground
a few cavalry posts were visible. The river was about three
feet deep.

(19) Caesar sent his cavalry on ahead, and then followed
with all his forces. But he employed a different order and
strategy of march from the one the Belgae had reported to
the Nervii. Because he was approaching an enemy Caesar
was, as usual, leading the six legions carrying only light kit.
He had put the whole army's heavy baggage behind these
legions, while the two legions most recently enlisted brought
up the rear of the whole column and acted as rearguard for
the baggage. Our cavalry, slingers, and archers crossed the
river and engaged with the enemy cavalry, who continually
retreated into the woods and rejoined their comrades before

coming out from the trees and attacking our men again.
When the enemy retreated, our men dared not pursue the
attack beyond the extent of level and open ground. Meanwhile, the six legions had already arrived, measured out the
camp, and begun the work of fortification.

The enemy formed up in battle order within the woods,
and strengthened their resolve; as soon as our army's baggage
came into view of the enemy hidden in the woods (the moment
they had agreed for joining battle) they suddenly rushed out
in full force and launched an attack on our cavalry, which
was easily repulsed and scattered. The enemy then ran at
astonishing speed down to the river, and so seemed—almost
at one and the same moment—to be near the woods, then in
the river, and now already upon us. With similar speed they
made their way up the hill to our camp and attacked the men
who were working on the fortifications.

(20) Caesar had to see to everything at once. The flag
must be unfurled (this was the signal to stand to arms), the
trumpet sounded; the soldiers must be recalled from working
on the defences, and all those who had gone some way off
in search of material for the earthworks had to be ordered
back to camp. He must draw up his battle line, encourage
the men, give the signal. There was too little time, the enemy
pressed on so fast, to complete these arrangements.

Two factors counterbalanced these difficulties. The first
was the knowledge and experience of Caesar's men. Their
training in previous battles had taught them what needed to
be done, so that they could just as easily devise their own
orders as receive them from others. Secondly, Caesar had
forbidden any of his officers to abandon either the defence-
works or their individual legions before the fortification of
the camp was complete. And in fact the enemy was so close
at hand, and moving so swiftly, that these officers no longer
thought of waiting for Caesar's orders but began to make
dispositions of their own accord, as seemed necessary.

(21) Once he had given all the appropriate orders Caesar
ran down where luck would take him to speak his encouragement to the men—and ended up among the Tenth legion.
His speech was long enough only to urge them to remember

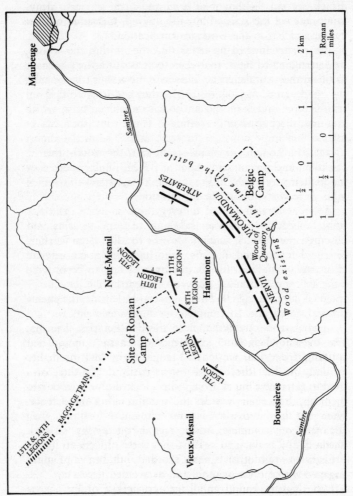

FIG. 4 The Battle on the Sambre

Maubeuge

Sambre

ATREBATES

VIROMANDUI

Belgic Camp

t h e   t i m e   o f   t h e   b a t t l e

Wood of Quesnoy

NERVII

Wood existing

9TH LEGION

Neuf-Mesnil

10TH LEGION

11TH LEGION

8TH LEGION

Hantmont

Site of Roman Camp

12TH LEGION

7TH LEGION

Vieux-Mesnil

Boussières

Sambre

13TH & 14TH LEGIONS

BAGGAGE TRAIN

2 km

1 Roman miles

1   ½   0   ½   1

1   0   1

their long-established record for bravery, and not to lose their nerve but to resist the enemy assault with courage: for the enemy was within missile range of the Roman army. Then he gave the signal for battle. When Caesar moved to the other side to give encouragement he found the men already fighting. Everything happened so quickly, and the enemy were so determined to fight, that there was no time for our men to fit on their emblems* or even to put on helmets and take the covers from their shields. Wherever each man ended up after stopping work on the defences, and whichever signal he saw first, there he took his stand, so as not to waste fighting-time in looking for his comrades.

(22) The Roman army was drawn up so as to take account of the natural terrain, the slope of the hill, and the need of the moment, rather than in accordance with any theoretical military formation. For the legions were resisting the enemy in different directions and different places, while the thick barrier hedges we mentioned before got in their way and obscured the view. It was impossible to allocate assistance, or see what was needed where, or for one man to co-ordinate all commands. The difficult circumstances, therefore, were matched by a number of different outcomes.

(23) The soldiers of the Ninth and Tenth legions had placed themselves on the left flank: they threw their spears and charged upon the Atrebates, whom they happened to be facing. The Atrebates were fatigued and exhausted after running, and suffering from their wounds. Our men, who had the higher ground, quickly forced them into the river. The Atrebates tried to get across but their way was blocked: our men caught them up, drew their swords, and slaughtered many of them. Then our men crossed the river without hesitation. They advanced on to unfavourable ground: the enemy resisted. Battle began again, and again they routed the enemy.

Elsewhere two other legions, the Eleventh and the Eighth, engaged with the Viromandui and overcame them. They then left the higher ground and began to fight actually on the river-bank. Now although the Twelfth were on the right flank, and the Seventh not far off, to the front and on the left flank the camp was almost completely exposed. Under the leadership of their supreme commander, Boduognatus, the Nervii formed up into a dense, compact column and marched upon this part of the camp. Some of them began to encircle the legions on their exposed left flank, the rest made for the higher ground on which the camp stood.

(24) I mentioned earlier* that the enemy's first assault had routed our cavalry and the light infantry which had accompanied it. When these forces of ours returned to camp they ran right up against the enemy advance, and again tried to flee elsewhere. From the main entrance gate* on the crest of the hill the orderlies had seen our men cross the river victorious, and had then gone out in search of plunder; but when they saw the enemy moving about in our camp, they took to their heels and fled. At that moment a roar of confusion went up from the men marching with the baggage-train, and frightened soldiers started to flee in all directions. All this served to terrify the cavalry of the Treveri, who have a reputation for outstanding bravery among the Gauls; they had been sent out by their people as reinforcements and had come to Caesar. When, however, they saw the enemy army swarming all over our camp, our legions hard pressed and on the point of being surrounded, our orderlies, cavalry, slingers, and Numidians spread out, scattered, fleeing in all directions, then they abandoned hope for our cause and made their way home. The Romans were beaten, they announced to their fellow-citizens, the Romans were overcome: the Nervii had taken possession of their camp and their baggage.

(25) After his words of encouragement to the Tenth, Caesar made his way to the right flank. There he saw that his soldiers were hard pressed. Because their standards were crowded together the men of the Twelfth were packed so close that they obstructed one another in the fighting. All the centurions of the fourth cohort were dead, the standard-bearer was slain, the standard lost; all but a few centurions from the rest of the cohorts were wounded or dead. Among the casualties was a senior centurion called Publius Sextius Baculus, a man of immense courage, who was suffering from numerous serious wounds. He could no longer stand upright, and the rest of the men were weakening: some of those at the rear were leaving

the battle and retreating to avoid missiles, while the enemy
did not slacken but pressed on up the hill in front, and
continued to attack on both flanks. Caesar realized that the
outcome rested on a knife-edge—there was no hope of reinforcements—so he snatched a shield from one of the soldiers
at the rear (he had come out without his own shield) and
made his way to the front line. There he called upon the
centurions by name and encouraged the men, ordering them
to advance and open ranks, so they could use their swords
more easily. His coming gave the men fresh hope and heart-
ened them: each one was eager of his own accord to do well
in his commander's sight, even at great personal risk—and
the enemy assault was checked a little.

(26) Caesar now saw that the Seventh legion too, which
had taken up position beside the Twelfth, was being hard
pressed by the enemy. He ordered the military tribunes to
close their legions up gradually, wheel about, and attack the
enemy. By this means, since they could all support one another and need not fear being attacked by the enemy from
behind, they began to resist with greater daring, and to fight
more bravely. Meanwhile the soldiers from the two legions
which had been at the rear of the column to guard the baggage heard of the battle. They sped forward, and came into
enemy view on top of the hill. Titus Labienus, who had
taken over the enemy camp and from his vantage-point saw
what was happening in our camp, sent the Tenth legion to
our men's assistance. When the men of the Tenth discovered
from the fleeing cavalry and orderlies where the fighting was,
and the extent of the danger which now threatened the camp,
the legions, and their commander, they left nothing undone
in terms of speed.

(27) Their arrival transformed our fortunes, so much so
that our men—even those who lay wounded—supported themselves on their shields and began the fight afresh. The orderlies now observed that it was the Nervii who were afraid,
and, weaponless as they were, they charged upon the armed
enemy. So too the cavalry tried to wipe out the shame of its
desertion by fighting everywhere in an attempt to outdo the
legionaries. The enemy, however, even at this critical moment

showed such determination in their bravery that when those in the front rank had fallen the men behind them stood upon the slain and continued the fight from on top of the corpses. When they were overthrown the pile of bodies grew higher, while the survivors used the heap as a vantage-point for throwing missiles at our men, or catching their spears and throwing them back. Not without good reason were they judged to be men of enormous bravery. For they had dared to cross a very wide river, climb its steep banks, and advance on extremely difficult ground: the Nervii's courage had made light of these obstacles.

(28) When the battle was over the name and fighting strength of the Nervii were almost wiped out. We mentioned earlier that the elders were gathered together in inlets and marshes along with the women and children; when news came of the battle, they assumed that nothing stood in the way of the victors, and that for the vanquished nothing was secure. So all the survivors agreed to send envoys to Caesar and surrendered to him. Describing the disaster which had befallen them, the Nervian envoys declared that they had been reduced from 600 senators to three, from 60,000 men capable of active service to a mere 500.

Caesar was eager to preserve their safety and to be seen to exercise clemency towards the wretched people who were pleading with him. He ordered them to confine themselves to their own territories and towns, and commanded their neighbours to refrain from doing the Nervii and their people harm or injury.

(29) We described the Aduatuci above. They were on their way to assist the Nervii in full force when news of this battle made them give up their march and return home. They abandoned all their towns and strongholds and brought all their property to one town which had superb natural defences. All along its circumference it presented sheer cliffs and heights, which at one spot left a gently sloping approach, no more than 200 feet wide. This the Aduatuci had strengthened by a high double wall and were even now putting heavy rocks and sharpened stakes along its length. The Aduatuci were descendants of those Cimbri and Teutoni* who, when marching into

our Province and Italy, had left all the cattle and baggage they could not drive or carry with them on this side of the Rhine: they left a guard—6,000 of their own men—to protect it. Following the destruction of the main force, these men were harassed by neighbouring peoples (sometimes attacking, sometimes defending). Eventually peace was made by common consent and they selected this place to settle in.

(30) As soon as our army arrived the Aduatuci began making frequent sallies from the town and skirmishing with our men. Later, when they were shut in by a rampart four-and-a-half miles in length,* with numerous forts along it, they remained in the town. Moveable shelters were drawn up, an earthwork built; and when the Aduatuci saw a siege-tower constructed in the distance, at first they stood on the wall, mocking and jeering that such a large apparatus was being put together so far off. What hands, what strength were men of such puny stature relying on to move this huge and heavy tower against their wall? (For the main part, Gauls are very tall, and hold our slighter build in contempt.)

(31) But when they saw the tower being moved, and coming close to the walls, the sight of it was so unusual and unexpected that it prompted them to send envoys to Caesar to ask for peace. The envoys spoke to the effect that in their opinion the Romans had divine help in waging war, to enable them to move such tall structures forward so quickly. And so, they declared, they surrendered themselves and all their possessions to the Romans' control. They begged and pleaded for only one favour: if perhaps his clemency and mercy—of which they had heard from others—were to prompt Caesar to spare them, not to be deprived of their weapons. Almost all their neighbours were hostile and looked on their courage with an unfriendly eye. The Aduatuci could not protect themselves against these peoples without weapons. They would rather endure any fate at the hands of the Roman people, if brought to such a pass, than be tortured and killed by peoples among whom they had once reigned supreme.

(32) Caesar answered them that he would spare their state —more because this would accord with habitual practice than because of their merit—if they surrendered before the

battering-ram touched the wall. There could, however, be no formal surrender unless they gave up their weapons. Instead, he would do for them what he had done for the Nervii, and would order the neighbouring peoples not to harm subjects of the Roman people. His offer was reported back to the Aduatuci and they agreed to obey. They threw a large number of weapons down from the wall into the ditch in front of the town: the piles of arms were almost as high as the wall and mound. Even so, it was revealed later that about a third of their weapons had been concealed and kept in the town. They opened their gates and for that day enjoyed peace.

(33) When night fell Caesar gave orders for the gates to be closed and the soldiers to leave the town, to prevent the soldiers doing the inhabitants any harm by night. But the Aduatuci were acting on a predetermined plan, it seemed, in the belief that after the surrender our men would withdraw their guards, or at least keep watch rather less carefully. They equipped themselves with the weapons they had kept concealed, and with shields which, as the pressure of time demanded, were made in haste, of bark or wicker covered with hides. At the third watch they suddenly burst out of the town in full strength, and attacked where the climb up to our defence-works was least steep.

As Caesar had already ordered, a fire-signal was immediately given. Men ran to assemble from the nearest forts. The enemy fought as fiercely as brave men might be expected to when clinging to their last hope of safety, on difficult ground against Romans throwing missiles at them from the rampart and towers, and when their only hope of survival lay in courage alone. About 4,000 men were killed, and the rest forced back into the town. Next day the gates were broken open, for there was no one to defend them. Caesar sent our soldiers inside, and sold everything in the town in one lot. The buyers reported to him a sale numbering 53,000 people.*

(34) At the same time Publius Crassus, whom Caesar had sent with a legion against the Veneti, Venelli, Osismi, Curiosolitae, Esubii, Aulerci, and Redones (the coastal states beside the Ocean), sent him news that all those states had been brought under the power and dominion of the Roman people.

(35) Once this action was over the whole of Gaul was pacified. The fame of this war spread among the barbarians, and was so impressive that the peoples living on the other side of the Rhine sent envoys to Caesar: they promised to give him hostages and to obey his commands. He was, however, in a hurry to reach Italy and Illyricum, and so told the embassies to return to him at the start of the following summer. Then he took the legions to their winter quarters in the lands of the Carnutes, Andes, and Turones, and the other states near to the area where he had been campaigning. He himself set out for Italy.

Because of these achievements reported in a letter from Caesar, a thanksgiving of fifteen days was decreed. This had never been granted to anyone before.*

The Third Book: 56 BC

(AUC 698: Consuls, Gnaeus Cornelius Lentulus
Marcellinus, Lucius Marcius Philippus)

Campaigning Against Maritime Tribes:
Crassus in Aquitania

(1) When Caesar set out for Italy he sent Servius Galba, with
the Twelfth legion and a section of the cavalry, to the lands
of the Nantuates, Veragri, and Seduni. These lands reach
from the territory of the Allobroges, Lake Lemannus, and the
River Rhône, up to the peaks of the Alps. His reason for
sending Galba was that he wanted the pass over the Alps,
which traders habitually used—albeit with great danger, and
on payment of a heavy toll—to remain open. Caesar gave
Galba leave (if he considered it necessary) to post his legion
in the area for the winter.

Galba fought a number of successful engagements and
stormed several of the enemy's forts: they all then sent him
envoys, surrendered hostages, and made peace. Then Galba
decided to station two cohorts among the Nantuates. He
himself wintered among the Veragri with the remaining cohorts of his legion, in a place called Octodurus. This village,
which is set in a valley, has no large area of level ground
around it, but is bordered on every side by lofty heights. As
it was also divided in two by a river, Galba left one half of
the village for the Gauls, and after evacuating its inhabitants
assigned the other half to his cohorts. He fortified the place
with a rampart and ditch.

(2) Several days in winter quarters went by, and Galba
gave orders for corn to be transported to Octodurus. Then
suddenly he learned from scouts that during the night the
Gauls had all left the part of the village he had allotted to
them; also that the heights which loomed over the village
were occupied by a great host of the Seduni and Veragri.

The Gauls' decision to renew hostilities and attack the
legion had emerged for a number of reasons. First, they were

contemptuous of a legion below full strength, which was short of two cohorts, as well as a number of men sent out in small groups to forage for supplies. Moreover, because the ground was uneven they thought that when they ran down from the heights into the valley and threw their missiles our men would not even be able to withstand their first assault. There was also the fact that they were aggrieved because their children had been taken from them as hostages; and they were convinced that the Romans were trying to seize possession of the peaks of the Alps not just to make their route easier, but in fact to take control of them for ever, and to annex the lands bordering the Province.

(3) Work on the winter quarters and the defences was not quite completed, nor had the supply of corn and other necessaries been adequately secured, for Galba had assumed, following the surrender and delivery of hostages, that there was nothing to be feared in terms of an attack. On hearing this news, therefore, he quickly called a council and asked for opinions. The threat had arisen most unexpectedly, and they now saw that almost all the heights were filled with a host of armed men, so that there was no chance of help arriving, or of supplies being brought in, as the access routes were all shut off. Hope was all but abandoned at the council. A number of men declared opinions to the effect that they should abandon the baggage, charge out, and march to a place of safety along the same route by which they had come. The majority, however, resolved to set this aside as a last resort, and in the meantime to await the outcome of events and defend the camp.

(4) In this brief interval they had just enough time to arrange and contrive matters in the way they had decided at the council before a signal was given and the enemy began to charge down on them from all directions, hurling stones and javelins* at the rampart. At first, while they were still fresh, our men fought back bravely, and none of the missiles they cast from the rampart was cast in vain; also, when any section of the camp had lost its defenders and seemed to be hard pressed, they ran to bring help. But they were at a disadvantage because the fighting went on so long, and because

when the enemy grew weary they could leave the battle, and fresh troops took their places. None of this was possible for our men because they were too few in number. In fact, not only were soldiers who were fatigued unable to retire from the fighting, but there was no opportunity even for wounded men to give up the place where they had been posted in order to recover.

(5) The battle went on for more than six hours without a break; our men were running out of weapons as well as strength, while the enemy attacked more fiercely as our men grew weary, and began to break down the rampart and fill in the ditch. Then, as the affair came to a desperate climax, the senior centurion Publius Sextius Baculus (we mentioned his numerous injuries in the battle against the Nervii), together with the military tribune Gaius Volusenus (a man both sensible and brave), ran up to Galba and explained that their one hope of salvation was to try a desperate remedy and attempt a sudden sortie. So Galba summoned the centurions and told the men to leave off the fighting gradually, and just to intercept enemy weapons and rest after their efforts: then after the signal, to sally out from the camp and put all hope of safety in courage.

(6) The men did as they were told. They made a sudden sortie from all the gates of the camp and gave the enemy no chance to realize what was happening, or to close ranks. Now the positions were reversed, and men who had come hoping to take the Roman camp were encircled on all sides and put to death. The total number of Gauls who had come to the camp was reckoned at more than 30,000: more than a third of them were killed, and the rest were terrified and put to flight. They were not even allowed to make a stand on the heights. Once the whole enemy force was routed and the bodies of the slain were stripped of their arms, our men returned to their camp and their own defences.

After this battle Galba was reluctant to take risks too often, and remembered that he had taken up his winter quarters with one set of expectations, but had come face to face with an entirely different set of circumstances. He was particularly worried by the shortage of corn and supplies, and the next

day burned all the buildings in the village and set out to
return to the Province. No enemy barred his way or held up
his march. He led his army to the lands of the Nantuates and
then the Allobroges, where he wintered.

(7) After these events Caesar had every reason to think
that the whole of Gaul had been subdued—the Belgae beaten,
the Germans expelled, in the Alps the Seduni overcome—so
at the start of winter he set out for Illyricum. He wanted to
visit these peoples too and acquaint himself with the area.
Suddenly, however, war broke out in Gaul.

The cause of the war was this. Young Publius Crassus,
together with the Seventh legion, had wintered beside the
Ocean among the people called the Andes. There was very
little corn in those parts, so Crassus sent some prefects and
military tribunes to neighbouring states in search of more
supplies: among them, Titus Terrasidius was sent to the Esubii,
Marcus Trebius Gallus to the Curiosolitae, and Quintus
Velanius and Titus Silius to the Veneti. (8) The influence
of the Veneti is very great indeed along the whole coast in
those parts. Not only do they have a large navy, which they
use for voyaging to Britain, but they also excel in nautical
matters, both theoretical and practical. Since, moreover, they
live beside a particularly fierce and open sea, with only a few
exposed harbours under their own control, practically everyone who regularly sails in their territorial waters must pay
them a tax.

The Veneti took the initiative by detaining Silius and
Velanius, in the expectation of using them to recover the
people they had surrendered to Crassus as hostages. The Gauls
are impulsive and sudden in their decision-making: the neighbouring peoples were influenced by the authority of the Veneti,
and detained Trebius and Terrasidius on the same grounds.
Envoys were quickly despatched between their leaders, and
they swore an oath: they would only act by common consent,
and all would bear the same outcome of fortune. They urged
the other states to choose to maintain the liberty they had
been given by their ancestors, rather than enduring enslave-
ment to the Romans. The coastal peoples were all swiftly won
over to this point of view, and they sent a united embassy to

Publius Crassus. If he wanted Silius, Velanius, Terrasidius, and Trebius back, he must return their hostages to them.

(9) Crassus reported these events to Caesar. As he was some distance away,* Caesar then gave orders for the building of warships on the River Loire (which flows into the Ocean), the appointment of oarsmen from the Province, and a muster of sailors and helmsmen. These matters were soon arranged. Then, as soon as the time of year allowed, Caesar made his way to his army. The Veneti and the other states heard of Caesar's arrival and realized how seriously they had wronged him. They had detained envoys (who had always, in every nation, been entitled to be treated as sacrosanct) and put them in chains. So they began to make ready for war in accordance with the magnitude of the threat, and in particular to prepare what was necessary for their navy. They were especially confident because they put their trust in the nature of their territory. They were aware that on land the roads were intersected by inlets, and that it would be hard for the Romans to travel by water, since they were unfamiliar with the area and harbours were few. They were convinced, moreover, that our armies could not remain much longer in the vicinity, because of their shortage of corn. And even supposing that events did turn out contrary to their expectations, still, they had great seafaring strength, while the Romans had no skill with ships and no knowledge of the waters, harbours, or islands in the areas where the campaign would take place. They also knew that navigating the great unbounded Ocean was quite a different matter from sailing in land-locked waters.*

These plans were adopted. The Veneti fortified their towns and gathered in the corn from the fields. They also assembled as many ships as they could at Venetia (where it was generally agreed that Caesar would begin his campaign). To fight this campaign they made alliance with the Osismi, Lexovii, Namnetes, Ambiliati, Morini, Diablintes, and Menapii. They also summoned assistance from Britain, which lies opposite those regions.*

(10) Despite the difficulties of the campaign, which we have just set out, many factors none the less encouraged Caesar to

undertake the war: the wrong they had done by detaining Roman citizens of equestrian rank, the revival of hostilities following their capitulation, their revolt following the surrender of hostages, and conspiracy among such a large number of states. Most of all, if their behaviour was overlooked the rest of the Gallic peoples might think they could act in a similar fashion. Caesar was aware that almost all Gauls are eager for political change and, because of their fickleness, are soon roused to war; and also that all men naturally long for liberty and despise a state of servitude. Thus he decided to divide up his army and station it at wider intervals.

(11) He sent his legate Titus Labienus with the cavalry against the Treveri, who live close to the Rhine. Labienus' orders were to approach the Remi and the other Belgae and secure their loyalty; and to prevent the Germans—whom the Belgae were rumoured to have summoned to their assistance—from trying to force a crossing over the river by boat. Caesar ordered Publius Crassus to take twelve legionary cohorts and a large force of cavalry and set out for Aquitania, to prevent its peoples sending reinforcements to Gaul and to stop these great nations joining forces.* He sent his legate Quintus Titurius Sabinus with three legions to the Venelli, Curiosolitae, and Lexovii to ensure that their force was prevented from joining in. He put young Decimus Brutus in command of the fleet and of the Gallic ships belonging to the Pictones, Santoni, and the other conquered regions, which he had ordered to assemble; he ordered Brutus to set out as soon as possible against the Veneti. Caesar himself headed in the same direction, taking all the infantry with him.

(12) The sites of their towns were in general of this kind: they were placed on headlands projecting into the sea, and could not be approached on foot when the tide rushed in from the sea, as happened twice every twelve hours.* Nor could they be approached by ship at low tide, because then vessels would run into trouble in the shallows. So making an assault upon such a town, by either means, was an awkward business. For if at any time the Veneti became alarmed by the size of some siege-works, or began to despair because the sea was kept out by the piling up of a massive breakwater as

high as the town walls, then they would bring a large number of ships to land (a task at which they were especially skilled), take all their property out to sea, and sail off to the nearest town. There they would once again put up their defences, with the same advantages of position. The Veneti continued to do this for a large part of the summer, all the more easily because our ships were held back by bad weather—and on the great expanse of the open sea, with its strong currents and few harbours (if any at all), navigation was especially difficult.

(13) The ships of the Veneti were made and armed in the following way: the hulls were rather flatter than on our ships, to make negotiating the shallows and the ebb-tides easier. The prows were very high, and likewise the sterns were fashioned to suit the size of the waves and the weather. The ships were made entirely of oak, to withstand any force or rough treatment. The cross-timbers which supported the decks were made of planks a foot thick, fastened with iron bolts as thick as a man's thumb. The anchors were attached with iron chains, instead of ropes. Instead of sails they had skins and leather stretched very thin—either because they had no linen or did not know how to use it, or (what is more likely) because they thought that linen sails would not be able to withstand satisfactorily the terrible storms and gale-force winds of the Ocean, and the great burden of the ships. The clash between their ships and our fleet revealed that only in speed and oarsmanship did our ships have the advantage, while in all other respects their ships were better adapted and suited to the nature of the locality and the severity of the weather. Our ships were unable to harm theirs by ramming them (they were so strongly built) or, because of their height, to aim missiles at them with any success. For the same reason it was difficult to control them with grappling-irons. Moreover, when the wind began to whip up, they would run before it, and could endure a storm more easily, coming safely to rest in the shallows without fear of rocks or reefs if the tide left them behind. For our ships, on the other hand, every one of these eventualities was a matter of serious concern.

(14) Caesar had taken a number of the Veneti's towns by

storm, but he realized that his great efforts were all in vain, for he could not check the enemy's flight by capturing towns, nor could he do them any damage. He decided to await the fleet. When it arrived it was immediately spotted by the enemy. About 220 of the Veneti's ships—all properly equipped and rigged out with all kinds of weaponry—set out against our fleet.* Between Brutus, who commanded the fleet, and the military tribunes and centurions who captained the individual vessels, there was no complete agreement over how to proceed or what plan of battle to adopt. They already knew that the ram could inflict no damage; and even if turrets were erected, still the sterns of the barbarians' ships were even taller than these, so that our men could not aim missiles satisfactorily from their lower position, while those of the Veneti did all the more harm.

One item, however, which our men had made ready in advance, proved to be of especial importance, namely, sharpened hooks fixed into long poles, not unlike the kind of hooks used for pulling down walls in sieges. Using these hooks, our men seized the ropes binding the enemy yardarms to the masts and drew them tight: then our ship quickly rowed away, and the ropes broke. Now that the ropes were snapped, the yardarms inevitably fell down—the hope of the Gallic ships had depended entirely on their sails and rigging, but when these were taken away, all the advantages of their fleet were removed at a stroke. The rest of the battle depended on courage, in which our soldiers were easily superior—all the more so because the fighting was before the eyes of Caesar and the whole army, so that no action which was at all distinguished for bravery went unnoticed. Our army was positioned on all the hills and heights which offered a good view on to the sea.

(15) Once the yardarms were broken, as we said, and two or three of our ships had surrounded each of the Veneti's, our soldiers battled furiously to climb aboard the enemy vessels. When the barbarians realized what was happening and lost a number of ships, since no reinforcements were available for this action, they tried to seek safety in flight. Now all their ships were turned to sail with the wind when

suddenly a dead calm fell, and they were unable to sail away. This calm was certainly most timely in bringing the engagement to an end, for our men chased each enemy vessel and stormed it, and by nightfall almost none of their number had reached land, though the fighting had lasted from about the fourth hour until sunset.*

(16) With this battle the campaign against the Veneti and the whole of the coastal region came to an end. All the men capable of active service had assembled there, together with all the older men of sense or prestige. Moreover, they had gathered in one place every ship they possessed anywhere, and now the ships were all lost they had no way of retreat left to them, nor any means of defending their towns. They therefore surrendered themselves and all their property to Caesar. Caesar decided that their punishment must be severe, to make these barbarian peoples uphold the law of nations more carefully in future. So he executed all the senate of the Veneti, and sold the rest of the people into slavery.

(17) While the campaign against the Veneti was in progress Quintus Titurius Sabinus arrived in the territory of the Venelli with the forces allocated by Caesar. The leader of the Venelli was called Viridovix; he held the supreme command over all the states which had defected, and had compelled them to provide an army and a large force. Within these few days the Aulerci, Eburovices, and Lexovii had put their senate to death for its reluctance to start a war. They closed their gates and joined forces with Viridovix. Also there assembled from all over Gaul a huge mob of criminals and brigands who were diverted from farming and daily tasks by the hope of plunder and by their enthusiasm for fighting.

Sabinus remained within the camp, which was well sited in all respects. Viridovix encamped facing him, barely two miles off, and each day led out his forces and offered Sabinus an opportunity to fight. Eventually Sabinus not only began to be despised by the enemy, but was even sneered at by our soldiers. He conveyed such an impression of fear that the enemy now dared to approach the rampart of the camp. His reason for acting in this way was the conviction that he ought not, as a subordinate, to engage with a great enemy

host, especially in the absence of his supreme commander—
except on even ground, or if some kind of opportunity arose.

(18) Once their belief in his cowardice was fixed, Sabinus
chose a suitable man of intelligence, a Gaul, from among his
auxiliary forces. With all kinds of promises and substantial
rewards Sabinus persuaded the man to go to the enemy, and
instructed him in what he wanted to happen. Posing as a
deserter, the Gaul went to the Venelli and gave an account
of the Romans' fear: he described how Caesar was in trouble, hard pressed by the Veneti, and how by the following
night at the latest Sabinus would secretly lead his army out
of camp and set out to Caesar's assistance. When they heard
this the enemy all clamoured that such an opportunity for
favourable action should not be lost: they must make their
way to Sabinus' camp. Many factors encouraged the Gauls
to adopt this strategy: Sabinus' previous hesitancy, the deserter's corroboration, their shortage of rations (they had
paid too little attention to this matter), their hopes for the
Venetic war—and the fact that men are generally ready to
believe what they want to believe. Thus encouraged, they did
not dismiss Viridovix and the other leaders from the meeting
before they had their agreement to take up arms and march
on the Roman camp. They rejoiced at this as if victory were
already assured, gathered brushwood and faggots to fill up
the Romans' ditches, and set off for the camp.

(19) The site of Sabinus' camp was on a hill which sloped
up gradually for about a mile. The Gauls made for it at top
speed, so as to give the Romans as little time as possible to
muster and arm themselves. When they arrived, however, they
were out of breath. Sabinus spoke words of encouragement
to his eager men, and gave the signal. While the enemy were
hindered by the baggage they were carrying, Sabinus suddenly
ordered a sortie from two of the gates. Thanks to the advantage of their position, the fatigue and lack of expertise of
the enemy, the courage of our men, and their experience in
previous battles, the result was that the Venelli did not even
withstand our men's first attack, but turned tail. They were
in difficulties: our men, who were still fresh, pursued them as
they fled and killed a large number. The cavalry pursued the

rest: they left only a few who had got away from the rout.

So at one and the same moment Sabinus learned of the naval battle and Caesar learned of Sabinus' victory. All the states at once surrendered to Sabinus. For the Gallic temperament is ready and eager to start wars, but their minds are soft and lacking in determination when it comes to enduring defeats.

(20) At about the same time Publius Crassus had reached Aquitania. This land, as was stated earlier, can be reckoned as one-third of Gaul in terms of both territorial size and population. He knew that he must wage war in places where—only a few years before—the legate Lucius Valerius Praeconinus had been killed following the rout of his army, and where a proconsul, Lucius Mallius, escaped with his life after losing all the army's baggage:* and he knew he needed to exercise no small degree of care. So he saw to it that the corn supply was secure, raised a force of auxiliaries and cavalry, and called up individually a number of brave men besides this from Tolosa and Narbo (these Gallic states are in the Province, very close to Aquitania). Then he led his army into the territory of the Sontiates.

The Sontiates heard of Crassus' arrival, and mustered a large force of men and horses (they were particularly strong in cavalry). Then they attacked the Roman column as it was on the march, and at first began a cavalry battle. But when their cavalry was routed and ours started to press the attack, they suddenly revealed their infantry, which had been posted in ambush in an enclosed valley. Their soldiers attacked and scattered our cavalry, and began the battle again.

(21) The fighting was long and fierce. The Sontiates were confident because of past victories, and thought that the safety of all Aquitania depended on their bravery. Our men, on the other hand, were eager to show what their youthful leader could accomplish in the absence of his commander and the other legions. The enemy suffered heavy casualties and turned tail. Many of them were slain, and Crassus actually turned from his march to begin besieging the town of the Sontiates. They resisted bravely, so he brought up the siege-towers and movable shelters. At one point the Aquitani attempted a sortie,

then at another they took mines up to the earthworks and shelters: they are particularly skilful at mining, since they have mines and quarries at a number of sites. When the Aquitani realized that this was achieving nothing—thanks to the perseverance of our men—they sent envoys to Crassus and asked him to accept their surrender. Their request was granted, and they handed over their weapons as ordered.

(22) Our minds were all concentrated on this action. From another part of town, meanwhile, the commander Adiatunnus attempted a sortie, together with 600 dedicated followers. These followers are called 'soldurii';* they have a rule of life to share all their advantages with those to whom they are joined in friendship. If one of them comes to a violent end, they must either endure the same fate together with him, or must commit suicide. Never within memory has it been found that one of them refused to die following the death of a man bound to him in friendship. With the attempted sortie, a cry went up from that part of the defences. Soldiers ran to arms and a fierce battle began. Adiatunnus was forced back into the town; he then asked of Crassus similar terms of surrender, which Crassus granted.

(23) Crassus received weapons and hostages, and set out for the territory of the Vocates and Tarusates. When the barbarians heard that he had stormed a town with both natural and man-made defences, and within a few days of his arrival, they were alarmed and sent envoys out in every direction. They began to hatch a plot, exchange hostages, and make ready their forces. They even sent envoys to Nearer Spain,* to the peoples closest to Aquitania, summoning reinforcements and leaders. When these arrived they were now possessed of great authority and numbers, and tried to start a war. The leaders they chose were men who had served with Quintus Sertorius* right to the end, and who were considered to have immense expertise in military matters. In accordance with the Roman people's custom, these men began to occupy positions, fortify a camp, and cut our men off from supplies.

Crassus became aware that his own forces were too small to be split up easily, while the enemy, though roaming about and blockading the roads, was still able to leave a sufficient garrison in camp. For this reason the transport of corn and supplies was becoming difficult, and enemy numbers were growing daily. So he decided to fight it out without delay. He referred his decision to a council; and when he realized that everyone supported his view, he decided to give battle the next day.

(24) At dawn Crassus led out his entire force and stationed the men in a double line,* putting the auxiliaries in the centre of the line. Then he waited to see what the enemy's decision would be. The Gauls thought they could engage with impunity because of their great numbers and their long-established glorious reputation in warfare, and because our men were so few. Nevertheless, they decided it was safer to continue blockading the roads and cutting off supplies, and thus to seize victory without suffering harm. Moreover, they thought that if the Romans started to retreat because of their lack of corn, they could attack them while they were encumbered with baggage on the march, and hence in poor heart. The leaders of the Gauls approved this plan, and although the Roman forces were led out, they remained in camp. Crassus took note of the fact, but by delaying and appearing to be frightened the enemy had made our men more eager to fight. They were all heard to shout that there should be no delay in marching to the enemy camp. So Crassus spoke words of encouragement to all his men and set out against the camp of the enemy.

(25) When they reached the camp some of Crassus' men filled in the ditches, while others threw large numbers of missiles and forced the defenders back from the rampart and the defences. He could not trust the auxiliaries sufficiently for battle, but he allotted them the task of supplying stones and missiles, and fetching turves for the Roman earthworks, so that they gave the appearance and impression of being fighting men. At the same time the enemy fought fearlessly and without wavering, and the missiles they cast from their higher position did not fall in vain. Then some of our cavalry went around the enemy camp and reported back to Crassus that the main gate at the back of the camp had not been fortified with equal care, and offered an easy means of entry.

(26) Crassus urged his cavalry officers to rouse their men with promises of great rewards. Then he explained what he wanted to happen. As ordered, they led out the cohorts which had been left to garrison our camp and so were not worn out by exertion. The cavalry commanders took them by a somewhat roundabout route, to avoid being spotted from the enemy camp; but all eyes were turned to the battle, all minds concentrated upon it—and they swiftly reached the defences we mentioned, demolished them, and took up position in the enemy camp before they had even been clearly observed, and before the enemy knew what was happening. Then a shout went up from that quarter, and our men, their strength renewed, began to fight more fiercely—as so often happens when there is hope of victory. The enemy were encircled on all sides, abandoned hope, and struggled to force a way through the defences and seek safety in flight. The cavalry pursued them over the open plains, then returned to camp when the night was far spent. Out of the total of 50,000 men known to have assembled from Aquitania and Calabria, barely a quarter was left.

(27) Once news of the battle spread most of the Aquitani surrendered to Crassus and handed over hostages of their own accord. These included the Tarbelli, Bigerriones, Ptianii, Vocates, Tarusates, Elusates, Gates, Ausci, Garumni, Sibuzates, and Cocosates. A few of the most distant peoples, however, trusted to the onset of winter and failed to surrender like the rest.

(28) The campaigning season was almost over. But although all Gaul was now subdued, the Morini and Menapii still remained ready for war, and had never sent envoys to discuss peace. At almost the same time, therefore, Caesar decided that a war against them could be quickly concluded, and led his army against them. The Morini and Menapii, however, started the war with tactics very different from those employed by other Gauls. They realized that the mighty nations which had engaged in pitched battles had been routed and beaten. They, however, possessed woods and marshlands nearby, into which they shifted with all their property.

Caesar arrived at the borders of the woods and started

building his camp, but during this time there was not an enemy in sight. Then, when our men were spread out at work, the enemy suddenly rushed out of every part of the wood and attacked them. Swiftly our men seized their weapons and forced the enemy back into the woods. A number of them were killed, but our men pursued too far into impenetrable areas, and lost a few of their comrades.

(29) Then, in the time remaining Caesar had all the trees felled to prevent any lateral attack on the soldiers while they were unarmed and unawares. He had all the felled timber placed on the side facing the enemy, and built up as a rampart on either flank. In only a few days a large space was cleared with unbelievable speed. Our men captured the enemy's cattle and the baggage at the rear. The enemy made for the depths of the forest. Then such storms arose that the tree-felling had to be discontinued. The endless rain made it impossible to keep the soldiers any longer in tents. So they devastated the enemy's fields and set fire to their villages and buildings. After this Caesar led his army back and stationed them for the winter among the Aulerci and Lexovii, and the other states which had so recently undertaken hostilities.

The Fourth Book: 55 BC
(AUC 699: Consuls, Pompey, Marcus Licinius Crassus)

Invasion of the Usipetes and Tencteri: Crossing of the Rhine: Caesar in Britain

(1) During the winter which followed, the year of the consulship of Pompey and Marcus Crassus, the Usipetes and Tencteri —two German peoples—crossed the Rhine with a large host of men, not far from the sea into which the river flows. Their reason for making the crossing was this: for a number of years the Suebi had been attacking them and making war upon them, and preventing them from farming their land.*

The Suebi are by far the greatest and most aggressive of all the German peoples. It is said that they possess a hundred villages, from each of which they take a thousand armed men every year for waging war outside their own territory. The men who have remained at home support both themselves and those who are abroad; then the following year they take their turn under arms while the others stay at home. In this way both agriculture and the theory and practice of warfare continue without interruption. There is, however, no private or individual landholding among them, nor is it permissible to remain dwelling in one place for more than a year. They consume little corn, but for the most part live off milk and cattle, and spend much of their time hunting. This activity, together with their diet, daily exercise, and the freedom of their way of life—from childhood they are unaccustomed to duty or discipline, and so do nothing whatsoever against their will—nourishes their strength and produces men of enormous physical stature. They have, moreover, trained themselves by constant practice, so that however cold the region they wear no other clothing than skins, which are so small that most of the body is left uncovered; and they bathe in the rivers.

(2) They do allow traders access, but rather with a view to having buyers for their spoils of war than because they want

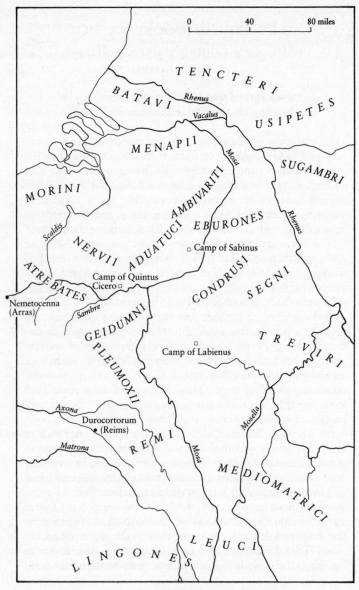

FIG. 5 The Invasion of the Usipetes

anything imported. Furthermore, the Germans do not import for their use the kind of pack-horse which the Gauls so delight in and pay high prices for. They take their own native animals, which are deformed and ugly, and by training them every day make them capable of extreme hard work. During cavalry battles they often jump down from their mounts and fight on foot; for they have trained their horses to remain on the same spot, and then quickly retreat to them in time of need. According to their standards, there is nothing more disgraceful or feeble than using saddles, and so, however few they may be, they will boldly move up to attack any number of cavalry-men on saddled mounts. They forbid the import of wine altogether, believing that it makes men weak and womanish in their capacity for exertion.

(3) As a community they consider it the greatest credit to have as wide a tract of territory as possible next to their borders, as a means of indicating how many states are unable to withstand their strength. Thus, on one side the land bordering the territory of the Suebi is said to be unoccupied for about 600 miles. On the other, the Ubii are close by. By German standards theirs is a large and flourishing nation, and some-what more civilized than the rest of their race:* this is because they live beside the Rhine and traders come to them frequently, and because they are themselves close enough to the Gauls to have become accustomed to their way of life. The Suebi had waged war upon the Ubii many times, but owing to their numbers and importance had failed to expel them from their land. Nevertheless, they made them pay a tribute and reduced them to a state of greater subservience and inferiority.

(4) The Usipetes and Tencteri, whom we mentioned above, were in a similar position. They had endured the aggression of the Suebi for a number of years, but were finally expelled from their land and spent three years wandering in many parts of Germany before coming to the Rhine. The Menapii were living in these regions, and had lands, buildings, and settle-ments on either bank of the river; but they were so terrified by the arrival of this vast host that they evacuated their build-ings over the river, set up garrisons along the nearer bank, and forbade the Germans* to cross. The Germans, meanwhile,

tried everything; but when they could neither fight their way across because they had no boats, nor cross in secret because of the Menapii's guards, they pretended to return to their own territory and their homes. After three days' journey they turned back. Their cavalry completed the entire return journey in a single night, and attacked the Menapii, who had been told by scouts of the Germans' departure and had confidently returned to their settlements across the Rhine, catching them off guard and unawares. They killed them and seized their boats, then crossed the river before those of the Menapii who were on this side of the Rhine found out what was happening. Then they took control of their buildings and spent the rest of the winter living off the Menapii's provisions.

(5) Caesar was informed of this action. He was anxious about the instability of the Gauls, for they are quick to take decisions and ever eager for political change. So he decided not to trust them in anything. For the Gauls make a practice of obliging travellers to stop, even against their will, and of questioning them as to what each one has heard or discovered on every subject. In the towns a crowd surrounds traders and forces them to declare every place they have come from and every matter they learned there. These facts and rumours often prompt them to take decisions on matters of great importance, which they are instantly made to think better of. For they are slaves to vacillating rumours, and most men give them answers made up to suit Gallic wishes. (6) When Caesar learned of this practice he set out to join his army sooner than usual, so as to avoid finding himself confronting a more serious war.

Once he joined the army Caesar realized that what he had feared would happen had in fact occurred. A number of states had sent embassies to the Germans, inviting them to leave the Rhine and promising to procure for them everything they had stipulated. The Germans were encouraged by this hope to roam more widely and penetrate the territory of the Eburones and Condrusi, who are dependants of the Treveri. Caesar summoned the Gallic leaders, but thought it best to conceal what he had discovered: so he soothed and reassured them, and decided to levy a force of cavalry and to wage war against the Germans.

(7) Once the corn supply was secured and the levy of cavalry complete, he began the march into the regions where he heard the Germans were located. When he was only a few days' march away they sent envoys, who made a speech declaring that the Germans had never been the aggressors in waging war upon the Roman people, but they were not refusing to start a fight if they suffered any injury. For the Germans had a custom, handed down from their ancestors, of resisting anyone who made war upon them, and of not suing for peace. They went on to state that they had come against their will after being thrown out of their homes; if the Romans wanted their goodwill they might find them useful friends. So, they concluded, the Romans must either give them land or allow them to hold on to what they had already won by force of arms. They gave way only to the Suebi, for whom not even the immortal gods were a match—certainly there was no one else on earth whom they could not conquer.

(8) Caesar made an appropriate reply to this, but his speech ended by stating that there could be no friendship between them and himself if they remained in Gaul. It was not fair that men who had failed to protect their own territory should be occupying another people's land; nor was there any land in Gaul available to be given out without doing an injustice, especially since they were so very numerous. Even so, if they wished they might settle in the territory of the Ubii, whose envoys were presently with him complaining of outrages done by the Suebi and asking his help. He would issue the Ubii with orders to this effect.

(9) The envoys said that they would report back to their own people and after considering the matter would come back to Caesar in three days. Meanwhile they asked him not to move his camp any closer. Caesar replied that he was unable to grant even that request. For he had learned that several days previously they had sent a large division of cavalry across the Meuse, to loot and forage for corn in the land of the Ambivariti; and he thought that they were awaiting the cavalry's return and that this was the reason they were proposing a delay.

(10) The Meuse flows from the Vosges* mountain range

in the territory of the Lingones, and is joined by a distributary of the Rhine called the Waal, so forming the island of the Batavi. It flows into the Rhine no more than eighty miles from the Ocean.* The Rhine, however, has its source in the land of the Lepontii who live in the Alps. For a long distance it flows swiftly, through the territories of the Nantuates, Helvetii, Sequani, Mediomatrices, Triboci, and Treveri. But when it reaches the Ocean it separates into several channels, thus forming a large number of sizeable islands, before it flows from many mouths into the Ocean. Most of the islands are inhabited by fierce barbarian peoples, some of which are thought to live on fish and birds' eggs.

(11) When Caesar was no more than eleven miles from the enemy the envoys returned to him as had been agreed. They met him on the march and urgently requested him not to proceed further. When they failed to attain this objective they asked him to send ahead to the cavalry, who were in front of the main column, and order them not to engage, and to grant them permission to send an embassy to the Ubii. They made it clear that if this embassy won the sworn support of the senate and leading citizens of the Ubii they would themselves accept the terms Caesar was offering, and asked for an interval of three days in which to accomplish these objectives.

Caesar was of the opinion that all these suggestions were directed to the same end, namely, securing a delay of three days in which their absent cavalry could return. Even so, he declared that he would go no further than four miles that day in search of water, and he ordered them to assemble there in full strength the following day, so that he could learn what it was they were requesting. Meanwhile he sent messengers to the prefects who had gone ahead with all the cavalry, to tell them not to provoke the enemy into fighting, and if they were themselves provoked, to withstand any assault until he had drawn closer with the army.

(12) As soon, however, as the enemy caught sight of our cavalry, which were 5,000 in number, they at once attacked and threw our men into confusion. This was despite the fact that they possessed no more than 800 horse, because those

who had crossed the Meuse in search of corn had not yet returned; they were in no way afraid of our men, since their envoys had just recently departed from Caesar after requesting a truce that day. Our men turned to resist them. Then, as was their usual practice, they dismounted, stabbed our horses, pulled a number of our men down, and routed the rest. They caused such panic among our men that they did not stop running until they came in sight of our column.

Seventy-four of our cavalry were killed in that battle, among them a man of outstanding courage called Piso, an Aquitanian Gaul. He was of a wealthy family—his grandfather had obtained royal power in his own state and been called Friend by our Senate.* He went to the assistance of his brother who was hemmed in by the enemy, and snatched him from danger. But his horse was wounded and he was thrown; he fought bravely, so far as he was able, but was surrounded, sustained many wounds, and fell. His brother had already left the battle, but when he saw this from far away he spurred his horse on, exposed himself to the enemy, and was killed.

(13) After this battle Caesar decided not to give audience to any more envoys, or to accept any terms from men who had first sought peace and then had used snares and treachery to make war unprovoked. Indeed, he judged it the height of folly to wait until the cavalry returned and the enemy's forces were enlarged. He knew how unreliable were his Gallic allies, and he was aware how much prestige the enemy had acquired among them as a result of this one battle. He therefore concluded that the Gauls should be allowed no time to hold discussions. These matters were settled, and he had communicated his plan of not letting a day for battle be missed to his legates and his quaestor,* when a most timely event occurred: the very next day a large crowd of Germans, employing the same treacherous hypocrisy as before, called upon all their leading citizens and elders and came into the camp to see Caesar. They claimed that their intention was to make their excuses for starting a battle in contravention of what had been stated and what they themselves had requested: but at the same time they really intended to use deceit to obtain whatever they could in terms of a truce.

Caesar was delighted that they had put themselves in his power and gave orders for them to be detained. He himself led all his forces out of camp. Because he judged that the cavalry had panicked in the recent battle he ordered it to follow at the rear of the column.

(14) He arranged his forces in a triple column and by completing a seven-mile march swiftly reached the enemy camp before the Germans could be aware what was happening. They were in a sudden panic at the whole state of affairs— our rapid approach, the departure of their leaders, and the lack of time to decide on a strategy or take up arms threw them into confusion as to whether it was best to lead their forces out against the enemy, or defend their camp, or seek safety in flight. Shouting and running to and fro betrayed their fear; then our soldiers, goaded by the previous day's treachery, broke into their camp. There those who were able to grab weapons quickly resisted our men for a little while and gave battle among the waggons and heavy baggage. The Germans had departed from their homes and crossed the Rhine with all their possessions. The crowd of women and children which remained began to flee in all directions. Caesar sent the cavalry to hunt them down.*

(15) The Germans heard the shouting at their back; and when they saw their own people being killed they threw away their weapons, abandoned their military standards,* and burst out of camp. When they reached the confluence of the Meuse and Rhine they abandoned hope of fleeing further and a large number were killed. The rest flung themselves into the river and there they perished, overpowered by fear, fatigue, and the strength of the current.

Every one of our men had survived. A few, however, were wounded. They had returned to camp, and this despite their previous anxiety about such a large-scale campaign, and the fact that the enemy numbered 430,000. Caesar gave the Germans whom he had detained in camp the chance to leave, but they were afraid of punishment and torture at the hands of the Gauls whose lands they had devastated, and declared that they wanted to remain with him. Caesar granted them the freedom to do so.

(16) Once the German campaign was over Caesar decided that for a number of reasons* it was imperative he should cross the Rhine. The most compelling of these reasons was that now he had seen how easily the Germans were induced to invade Gaul, he wanted them to experience fear on their own account—when they realized that the army of the Roman people was both capable of crossing the Rhine and brave enough to venture it. There was also the fact that, after the flight of their comrades, the detachment of the cavalry of the Usipetes and Tencteri (which, as I mentioned above, had crossed the Meuse in search of corn and plunder and had not taken part in the battle) had retreated over the Rhine into the territory of the Sugambri, and made alliance with them. When Caesar sent messengers to them to demand the surrender of those men who had made war upon himself and Gaul, they replied that the Rhine marked the boundary of the rule of the Roman people. If Caesar thought it wrong for Germans to cross into Gaul against his wishes, why was he claiming any rule or power across the Rhine?

The Ubii, however, alone of all the peoples across the Rhine, had sent envoys to Caesar and made a treaty of friendship. They had surrendered hostages, and pleaded forcefully for him to come to their aid, as they were being harassed by the Suebi. If the affairs of the Republic were too pressing to allow him to come, he could just transport his army over the Rhine. That would be enough to help them and bring hope for the future. The fame and reputation of Caesar's army, they went on, was so renowned, because of the expulsion of Ariovistus and the war so recently waged against even the most distant German nations, that the reputation and friendship of the Roman people could protect them. They pledged themselves to provide a large supply of boats to transport the army.

(17) For the reasons which I mentioned, Caesar had determined to cross the Rhine: but as far as crossing by boat was concerned, he judged that it was not sufficiently safe, and he was not convinced that such a method of crossing was in accord with either his own dignity* or that of the Roman people. So despite the extreme difficulty of the task of constructing a bridge which lay before him (because the river

was so broad, swift, and deep), none the less he concluded
that he must attempt a crossing by bridge—or not take his
army across at all.

The plan of the bridge was as follows. Pairs of piles eighteen inches thick and sharpened at the end were measured to
suit the depth of the river and joined together with a two-
foot gap between them. Rafts and cranes were used to lower
the piles into the river-bed and rams to drive them home—
not vertical and straight down like stakes, but lying at an
angle so that they leaned into the current. Opposite these,
and forty feet away on the river-bed, more pairs of piles were
joined in the same way and set at an angled slope, this time
against the force and flow of the current. From above, cross-
beams two feet thick were fitted into the opposing pairs of
piles to fill the gap and join them together to form trestles.
Twin braces at the ends of each pair of piles kept them
apart.* Thus the main piles were arranged in an opposing
manner, both held apart and bound together: as a consequence, the structure was extremely secure, and of such
a nature that the greater the force of the water pressing
upon it, the more firmly its joints were held in position. The
trestles were covered over with planks which joined them
lengthways,* and also with poles and bundles of rods. Even
so, more piles were driven in at an angle further down stream
to serve as props for the bridge: attached to the entire structure they absorbed the force of the current. Finally, more
piles were driven in a little way upstream: if the barbarians
launched logs or ships to demolish the bridge, these would
protect it from being damaged by weakening the impact of
such objects.

(18) Within ten days of the materials being gathered together the entire structure was completed, and the army
transported across. Caesar left a strong garrison at either end
of the bridge and set out for the territory of the Sugambri.
During this time envoys from a number of states approached
him to ask for peace and friendship. He replied in generous
terms, and told them to bring him hostages. The Sugambri,
encouraged by some of the Tencteri and Usipetes who were
with them, had been making ready for flight ever since the

construction of the bridge began; now they departed from
their own land, carried off all their property, and hid themselves in the isolated parts of the forest.

(19) Caesar lingered a few days in their territory, set fire
to all their settlements and buildings, and cut down the corn.
Then he retreated to the land of the Ubii. When he promised
them his help if they were troubled by the Suebi they gave
him the following information: after the Suebi had learned
through scouts that a bridge was being constructed, they had
held an assembly (as was their custom) and then sent messengers in every direction, telling the people to move out of the
towns and to find shelter for their children, wives, and all
their property in the woods. All who were able to bear arms
were to assemble in one place, and the place they chose was
almost in the centre of the territory controlled by the Suebi.
They were waiting here for the arrival of the Romans, where
they had decided to give battle.

By the time Caesar discovered this he had already accomplished all the objectives for which he had decided to take
the army across—namely terrorizing the Germans, wreaking
vengeance on the Sugambri, and liberating the Ubii from a
blockade. So after spending a total of eighteen days on the
other side of the Rhine he judged that he had achieved enough
in terms of both honour and advantage, returned to Gaul,
and tore down the bridge.

(20) The campaign season was almost over, and because
the whole of Gaul looks northwards, winter comes early in
these regions. Despite these facts, Caesar changed his course
to set out for Britain, aware as he was that our enemies in
almost all our wars with the Gauls had received reinforcements from that quarter. He considered, moreover, that even
if the season left no time for a campaign, none the less it
would be a great advantage to him simply to land on the
island and observe the kind of people who lived there, and
the localities, harbours, and approaches. Every one of these
points was unknown to almost all the Gauls. No one, except
for traders, went there as a matter of course, and not even
they knew anything beyond the coastline and the areas facing
Gaul. Thus, when Caesar summoned traders from every region

he was unable to ascertain either the size of the island, the nature and numbers of the peoples living there, their skill in warfare, their established customs, or which harbours were suitable for a fleet of fairly large ships. (21) Before making the landing attempt he needed information on all these matters, and he judged it appropriate to send Gaius Volusenus ahead with a warship. He gave Volusenus instructions to make a thorough reconnoitre and return to him as soon as possible. Then Caesar set out with all his forces for the territory of the Morini, from where the crossing to Britain was shortest. He gave orders for ships from the surrounding areas, together with the fleet which he had had constructed the previous summer for the campaign against the Veneti, to gather there.

Meanwhile his plan became known, and traders relayed it to the Britons. Then envoys approached him from several of the island's communities: they promised to surrender hostages and to obey the rule of the Roman people. Caesar heard them, and made generous pledges, encouraging them to remain loyal to their avowed intentions. Then he sent them home, and with them Commius, a man whom he had made king over the Atrebates after conquering them.* He thought highly of Commius' courage and good sense, and believed him to be loyal to himself; moreover, Commius was thought to possess considerable influence in the area. Caesar ordered Commius to approach what communities he could, urge them to choose loyalty to the Roman people, and declare that Caesar would soon be coming there. Volusenus had spied out the whole area as best he could, considering that he did not dare to disembark and put his safety in barbarian hands. Then he returned to Caesar on the fifth day and reported what he had observed.

(22) While Caesar lingered in this area to make ready his fleet envoys approached him from the majority of the Morini. They made excuses for their strategy of the previous season, on the grounds that it was because they were barbarians and unaccustomed to our ways that they had made war on the Roman people; and they pledged themselves to carry out whatever Caesar ordered. He considered this circumstance most timely, for he was reluctant to leave an enemy at his

back; also, because the season was so advanced, he had no chance of undertaking a campaign against them. He concluded that involvement in such trivial affairs ought not to come before the expedition to Britain. So he demanded from the Morini a large number of hostages, and as soon as these were produced he received them under his protection.

About eighty transport vessels were mustered and collected, a number Caesar considered sufficient to ferry two legions across. Besides this, he divided up the warships in his possession between his quaestor, legates, and prefects. There were also eighteen transport vessels approaching, but a strong wind was holding them back about seven miles off and preventing them from sailing into the same harbour: he assigned these to the cavalry. He handed over the rest of his army to his legates Quintus Titurius Sabinus and Lucius Aurunculeius Cotta: they were to lead it against the Menapii, and against those districts of the Morini which had sent him no envoys. He ordered his legate Publius Sulpicius Rufus to guard the harbour, with a garrison of a size he considered sufficient.

(23) These matters settled, he took advantage of a spell of good weather for sailing and weighed anchor around the third watch. He ordered the cavalry to advance to the farther port, embark there, and follow him. They were rather late in carrying out the order, but he reached Britain with the first ships at around the fourth hour;* there he spied the enemy forces, fully armed and drawn up all along the cliffs. Such was the geography of this place, and so steep the cliffs which bounded the sea, that it was possible for missiles cast from the heights to find their target on the shore. He judged this place wholly unsuitable for disembarkation, so waited at anchor until the rest of the fleet arrived at the ninth hour. Meanwhile he summoned his legates and military tribunes, and set out what he had learned from Volusenus and what he wanted done. He also warned them that military procedure, and especially naval operations (which tend to be subject to instantaneous and irregular changes), required them to carry out all their tasks at a nod and at the right moment. After dismissing them and taking advantage of a favourable wind and tide together, he gave the signal and weighed anchor. He

sailed about six-and-a-half miles further on and landed on a flat and open shore.*

(24) The barbarians, however, had grasped the Romans' strategy and sent their cavalry on ahead, and their chariot-eers (it is their usual custom to use chariots in battle). They followed on with the rest of their forces and prevented our men from disembarking. This led to extreme difficulties, because the ships were too large to be beached except in deep water, while the soldiers, ignorant of the land, their hands full, weighed down by the size and weight of their weapons, at one and the same time had to jump down from the ships, find their feet in the surf, and fight the enemy. The Britons, on the other hand, were either on dry ground or in shallow water, their limbs unencumbered, the ground very familiar. They cast missiles boldly and spurred on their horses, which were well used to such work. This led to panic among our men, who were wholly unaccustomed to this style of fighting, and thus did not display the same eagerness and enthusiasm as they habitually did in infantry engagements. (25) When Caesar observed this he gave orders for the warships, which were of a type less familiar to the barbarians and more man-œuvrable at need, to be moved a short distance from the transport vessels, rowed at speed, and halted on the enemy's exposed flank. From there the enemy could be repelled and driven off with slings, arrows, and artillery machines.

This act was of great assistance to our men. The barbar-ians were thrown into a panic by the appearance of the ships, the movement of the oars, and the unfamiliar machines. They halted and then retreated a short distance. Meanwhile our soldiers were hesitating, chiefly because the sea was so deep; then the man who carried the Eagle of the Tenth legion appealed to the gods to see that his action turned out well for the legion, and said: 'Jump down, soldiers, unless you want to betray our Eagle to the enemy—I at least shall have done my duty to the Republic and to my commander'.* He cried these words in a loud voice, then flung himself away from the ship and began to carry the Eagle towards the enemy. Then our men urged each other to prevent such a disgrace and all together jumped down from the ship. When the men who were on the closest nearby ships saw them do this, they followed them and drew close to the enemy.

(26) Both sides fought fiercely. None the less, our men could not keep ranks or get a firm foothold, neither were they able to follow the standards; rather, different men from different ships grouped round whatever standard they ran up against, and they were in great confusion. The enemy, however, knew all the shallows, so when they caught sight from the shore of some of our men disembarking one by one, they spurred their horses on and attacked while our men were still at a disadvantage, their many surrounding our few. Some began throwing weapons against a whole group of our men on their exposed side. When Caesar noticed this he gave orders for the boats of the warships and likewise the scout ships to be filled with soldiers. Wherever he saw men struggling, there he dispatched assistance. As soon as our men stood on dry ground, closely followed by all their comrades, they charged the enemy and routed them; but they could not pursue them very far, because the cavalry had failed to hold its course and reach the island. This was the one action in which Caesar's previous good fortune was found lacking.

(27) The enemy had been beaten in battle. As soon as they recovered from the rout they at once sent envoys to Caesar to discuss peace terms. They promised to provide hostages and to do whatever he told them. Together with these envoys there came Commius of the Atrebates—I have already described how Caesar sent him on ahead to Britain.* When he disembarked and delivered Caesar's demands to them in the role of envoy they had arrested him and cast him into chains, but when the battle was ended they sent him back. In seeking peace, they blamed the common crowd for what had taken place and begged him to pardon their lack of judgement. Caesar complained that although of their own accord they had sent envoys to the Gallic mainland to seek peace, they had then started a war with no reason; then he declared a pardon for their lack of judgement and demanded hostages. A number of these were surrendered at once, others were summoned from outlying areas and, they claimed, would be handed over in a few days' time. Meanwhile they ordered

their men to return to their lands, and their leaders began to assemble from all directions and commit themselves and their states to Caesar.

(28) These acts established the peace. Four days after the arrival in Britain the eighteen ships which had transported the cavalry (and which were mentioned above) set sail with a gentle breeze and left their more distant port.* When they were drawing near to Britain and were spied from the camp, suddenly a storm arose which was so fierce that not one of the ships could hold her course. Some were carried back to the place from which they had set out. Others, in terrible danger, were swept further down the island's coast, in a westerly direction. They cast anchor but began to fill with seawater, and were thus forced to sail out to sea during a stormy night and make for the Gallic mainland.

(29) As it happened there was a full moon that night. On this day the Ocean tides are usually at their highest—a fact of which our men were unaware. So at one and the same time the tide had flooded the warships by which Caesar had had the army ferried across, and which he had beached, and the storm began to inflict damage on the transport vessels, which were fast at anchor. Nor did our men get any chance to manœuvre them or bring them assistance. Several of the ships were wrecked, the rest had lost their ropes, their anchors, and the rest of their rigging, and were unfit to sail. The inevitable result was panic throughout the army. For there were no other ships to transport them back, and they had no materials of use for naval repairs. Moreover, since it was generally established that they must winter in Gaul, no corn had been provided for wintering in Britain.

(30) Once they learned of this the British leaders who had approached Caesar after the battle held talks among themselves. They realized that the Romans had neither cavalry nor ships nor corn, and understood, from the smallness of the camp, their weakness in manpower—circumstances all the more straitened by reason of the fact that Caesar had brought the legions over without their heavy baggage. Thus they considered it the perfect moment to engineer a renewal of hostilities, to cut our men off from corn and supplies and

prolong the action into the winter. They were confident of overcoming our men or cutting off their escape, and so ensuring that no one would ever again cross to Britain to wage war. So they plotted together once more, and began to leave camp, a few at a time, and to call their men back in secret from the fields.

(31) Even though Caesar had not yet learned of their plans, none the less he suspected it would happen, both because of the fate which had befallen his ships and because the Britons had left off the handover of hostages. So he began to prepare safeguards for every eventuality. Every day he gathered corn from the fields into the camp, and he used timber and bronze from the ships which had been most badly damaged to repair the rest. He gave orders for equipment to be ferried over from mainland Gaul for this purpose. The soldiers carried out these tasks with great enthusiasm, and so by the loss of twelve ships Caesar was able to render the rest sufficiently seaworthy.

(32) While this was going on the legion known as the Seventh had been sent out in a body as usual to find corn. As yet no hint of hostilities had occurred, since some of the Britons were still in the fields, while others were even making frequent visits to the Roman camp. Then the men on guard at the gates of the camp reported to Caesar that a dust-cloud, greater than usual, was visible in the place to which the Seventh had marched. Caesar guessed the truth, that the barbarians had started upon some new stratagem. He gave orders for the cohorts which were then on guard to set out with him to the place, and for two cohorts from the remainder to relieve them on guard-duty: the rest were to arm themselves and follow him without delay.

When they had made their way some distance from the camp he caught sight of his men being hard pressed by the enemy and struggling to hold their position. The legion was crowded together, and missiles were being thrown at it from every quarter. Because all the corn had been cut from the remaining areas, and this place alone was left, the enemy had suspected that our men would come there and had hidden by night in the woods. Then, when our men were scattered and, busy cutting corn, had laid down their weapons, they suddenly attacked, killed a few, cast the remainder into disorder before they could form ranks, and surrounded them at once with cavalry and chariots.

(33) Their method of fighting from chariots is as follows.* First they drive around in all directions, casting missiles and generally throwing army ranks into confusion through the panic caused by the horses and the noise of the wheels. Then, when they have wormed their way in between the cavalry squadrons, they jump down from the chariots and fight on foot. Meanwhile the charioteers gradually make their way out of the fighting, and station their chariots so that, if they are hard pressed by a host of enemies, they have a speedy retreat to their own side. Thus they provide the flexible mobility of cavalry and the stability of infantry in battle. By means of daily practice and exercises they ensure that even on the steepest of inclines they can hold their horses at full gallop, control and turn them swiftly, run along the beam and stand on the yoke—and from there get quickly back to the chariot.

(34) Because this type of fighting was so unusual our men were thrown into confusion by such tactics, but in the nick of time Caesar brought them assistance. For the enemy halted at his coming, while our men recovered from their panic. After this he considered that it was an inopportune moment for going on the offensive and engaging in battle, so he stayed where he was, and after a short while led the legions back to camp. During these events all our men were busy, and the rest of the Britons who were in the fields dispersed. Continual storms followed for a number of days, which kept our men in camp and prevented the enemy from fighting. In the meantime the barbarians sent out messengers in all directions who proclaimed to their own people that our troops were few in number, and declared how great was the opportunity of winning booty and of liberating themselves for ever if they drove the Romans from their camp. In this way a huge force of infantry and cavalry was quickly mustered and approached our camp.

(35) Caesar foresaw that the same thing would happen as

on previous days, namely, that if they were repulsed the enemy would use speed to escape the danger. Nevertheless, he had in his possession about thirty cavalrymen whom Commius the Atrebatian (who was mentioned above) had brought across with him, so he stationed his legions in battle formation in front of the camp. Battle was joined. The enemy was unable to withstand the attack of our soldiers for very long, and fled. Our men pursued for as far as their vigour and strength allowed, killed a number of them, then set fire to all the buildings far and wide and returned to camp.

(36) On the same day the enemy sent envoys to Caesar to sue for peace. Caesar doubled the number of hostages which he had previously demanded from them and ordered that they be taken to the Gallic mainland, because the autumnal equinox* was at hand and he considered that as his ships were damaged the voyage should not be exposed to winter storms. He took advantage of a period of good weather and set sail a little after midnight. All the ships reached the mainland safely, though two of the transport vessels were unable to make the same ports as the rest and were carried a little further south down the coast.

(37) About 300 soldiers had disembarked from these ships and were marching to the camp, when the Morini, whom Caesar had left pacified when he set out for Britain, were led by the hope of booty to surround them with, at first, a small number of men. They ordered our men to lay down their weapons if they did not wish to be killed. Our men, however, formed a circle and began to defend themselves; then about 6,000 of the Morini massed swiftly on hearing the shout. News of this came to Caesar, who sent the entire cavalry to his men's assistance from the camp. Meanwhile our soldiers withstood the attack of the enemy and fought bravely for more than four hours, receiving only a few wounds and killing several of the enemy. After our cavalry came into sight the enemy threw away their weapons and turned tail; many of them were killed. The following day Caesar sent his legate Titus Labienus, with the legions he had brought back from Britain, against the Morini who had renewed hostilities. The marshes which they had used as a refuge in the previous

year* were too dry to offer a place of retreat, so almost all surrendered themselves to Labienus' control.

The legates Quintus Titurius and Lucius Cotta, meanwhile, had led their legions into the territory of the Menapii. There they ravaged the fields, cut down the corn, and burned the buildings, because the Menapii had concealed themselves in the depths of the forests. Then they returned to Caesar, who established winter quarters for all the legions among the Belgae. In all, only two of the British peoples sent him hostages there, while the rest failed to do so. Following receipt of a dispatch from Caesar, a thanksgiving of twenty days was decreed by the Senate for these achievements.*

The Fifth Book: 54 BC
(AUC 700: Consuls, Lucius Domitius Ahenobarbus, Appius Claudius Pulcher)

The Second British Expedition: Deaths of Cotta and Sabinus: Quintus Cicero Against Ambiorix: Labienus Against the Treveri

(1) During the consulship of Lucius Domitius and Appius Claudius, Caesar left his winter quarters for Italy* as he was accustomed to do every year. He ordered the legates whom he had left in charge of the legions to have as many ships as possible built that winter, and the old ones refitted. He specified the form and style of these ships. For speed of loading and beaching he made them a little lower than the vessels we habitually use in the Mediterranean; this was all the more appropriate because he had discovered that the waves there were smaller, because of the frequency of tidal changes.* For cargo, and carrying large numbers of pack animals, he made them slightly broader than the sort we use on other seas. For maximum speed, he ordered them all to be constructed with both oars and sails: their low profile helped this aim considerably. He gave instructions for the tackle for arming the ships to be imported from Spain.

Once the assizes in Nearer Gaul were ended he himself set out for Illyricum, because he was receiving reports that the region nearest to the Province was being ravaged by the raids of the Pirustae. On his arrival he levied troops from the peoples there and told them to muster at a particular place. When news of his action came the Pirustae sent envoys to prove that none of these events had happened as a matter of public policy. They showed themselves ready to make reparation by all possible means for any damage done. Caesar heard their speech, then demanded hostages and ordered them to be produced on a given day. If they failed in this, he made it clear that he would pursue a campaign against their nation. The hostages were brought on the appropriate day as he had demanded, and he appointed arbitrators between the peoples to assess the damages and settle penalties.

(2) These affairs thus settled and his assizes at an end, he returned to Nearer Gaul, and from there set out for his army. When he reached it he made the rounds of all the winter quarters, and discovered that thanks to the soldiers' remarkable zeal—and despite a severe shortage of materials—about 600 ships of the kind we described above had been constructed, together with twenty-eight warships. They were almost ready for launching within a few days. He commended the men and the officers in charge of the business, then set out what he wanted to happen and ordered everyone to assemble at Portus Itius.* He had discovered that the crossing to Britain was easiest from there—a voyage of only about twenty-seven miles from mainland Gaul. Leaving behind what seemed an adequate number of soldiers for the purpose, he took four legions without heavy kit and 800 cavalry, and set out for the territory of the Treveri, who were persistently failing to attend assemblies and obey his commands, and were rumoured to be seeking the support of the Germans living across the Rhine.

(3) In cavalry the Treveri are by far the strongest nation in the whole of Gaul. They also have large infantry forces and, as we mentioned earlier, border the Rhine. Within their nation two men called Indutiomarus and Cingetorix* were competing for supreme power. As soon as the arrival of Caesar and his legions became known, one of the two, Cingetorix, approached Caesar and promised that he and all his people would be loyal and not abandon the friendship of the Roman people; and he revealed what was going on among the Treveri. Indutiomarus, however, began to make ready for war, mustering cavalry and infantry, and hiding those who were not of an age to bear arms in the Ardennes forest. This forest is extremely large and reaches from the Rhine through the middle of the Treveri's land to the borders of the Remi.

Some of the leaders of the Treveri were encouraged by their kinship with Cingetorix, and frightened by the presence of our army, so they approached Caesar. They began to consult him in private about their own affairs, since they could not take measures to protect their nation. Then Indutiomarus was afraid of being abandoned by everyone and sent envoys to Caesar. He claimed that he had been reluctant to leave his own people and approach Caesar, because by staying he would more easily keep the nation loyal, and the ordinary people would not fall into ignorant error with all the aristocracy gone away. In consequence of this the whole nation was under his control, and if Caesar would permit it he would come to his camp and entrust his own fortunes and those of the nation to Caesar's good faith.

(4) Caesar was well aware of the reason for Indutiomarus' words, and of what was deterring him from the policy with which he had begun. Even so, to avoid being forced to waste the campaigning season among the Treveri when everything was ready for the war in Britain, he ordered Indutiomarus to come to him with 200 hostages. Once these were produced, among them his son and all his relations whom Caesar had summoned by name, he comforted Indutiomarus and urged him to remain loyal. All the same, he summoned the leaders of the Treveri and one at a time won them over to Cingetorix. He did this because he realized that Cingetorix, whose good-will towards Caesar himself was evident, deserved this fa-vour; but also because he considered it a matter of importance for Cingetorix's authority among his own people to be as great as possible. Indutiomarus took this restriction of his own influence among his people badly. Previously he had been hostile in his intentions towards us, but now he was even more fiercely ablaze with indignation.

(5) These matters settled, Caesar reached Portus Itius with his legions. There he learned that sixty ships built by the Meldi had been unable to hold their course but were forced back by bad weather. They had returned to the same place from which they had set sail. All the rest he found ready to sail and fully equipped. At the same place cavalry from all over Gaul assembled, about 4,000 in number, and the leaders of all the states. He had decided to leave a few of them—those whose loyalty was evident—in Gaul. The rest he took with him in place of hostages, because he feared that Gaul would revolt during his absence.

(6) Among this majority was Dumnorix the Aeduan, whom we have mentioned before.* Caesar was particularly anxious to keep this man at his side because he knew him to be eager for revolution and eager for power, audacious and influential among the Gauls. There was also the fact that at an assembly of the Aedui Dumnorix had claimed that Caesar was offering him dominion over their nation. It was a claim the Aedui took badly, but they did not dare to send envoys to Caesar to reject or criticize him for it. Caesar had learned of this from his own supporters.

At first Dumnorix pleaded all kinds of reasons why he should be left behind in Gaul. For one thing, he claimed, he knew nothing of sailing and was afraid of the sea; for another —or so he alleged—religious obligations prevented him from going. Once he saw that his request was obdurately refused, and all hope of getting what he wanted was snatched away, he began to stir up the Gallic leaders, to draw them aside individually and urge them to stay behind on the Gallic mainland. He tried to frighten them—not without reason, he asserted, was Gaul being stripped of all her aristocracy: Caesar was afraid to kill them in sight of Gaul, but planned instead to take them all to Britain and there put them to death. He pledged his word to the rest, and demanded an oath that they should carry out whatever they saw was to Gaul's advantage. A number of informers reported this to Caesar.

(7) Caesar had a high opinion of the status and position of the Aedui, so on hearing this he decided that Dumnorix must be checked and deterred by every means possible. He saw Dumnorix's madness spreading abroad, and so it was his duty to watch out that neither he nor the Republic suffered harm. So when he was detained in the area for about twenty-five days (because the north-west wind, which is the prevailing wind in that vicinity, prevented his sailing) he took steps to keep Dumnorix to his allegiance, but just the same he gathered information about all his plans.

At last Caesar had good sailing weather, and ordered his soldiers and cavalry to embark. But while everyone's minds were preoccupied, Dumnorix and the Aeduan cavalry began to leave the camp and go home, without Caesar's knowledge.

When he did learn of it Caesar stopped the expedition and, postponing everything else, sent a large section of the cavalry to pursue Dumnorix and gave orders for him to be dragged back. If he offered armed resistance and would not obey, he told them to kill him: for he judged that a man who had disregarded Caesar's command when Caesar was actually present would certainly not behave like a sensible man in Caesar's absence. As might be expected, when he was summoned to return Dumnorix began his resistance, defending himself by force and appealing to his supporters' loyalty: he continually cried that he was a free man and a citizen of a free state. Caesar's men surrounded and killed him, as ordered. All the Aeduan cavalry, however, returned to Caesar.

(8) After these events Labienus was left on the mainland with three legions and 2,000 cavalry to watch over the harbours, see to the corn supply, find out what was happening in Gaul, and make his plans according to circumstances and events. Caesar set out with five legions and the same number of cavalry as he had left on the mainland. He weighed anchor at sunset. A gentle south-westerly breeze carried him out, but around midnight it dropped and he could no longer maintain his course. He was then carried too far by the flood-tide, and at dawn saw Britain being left behind to port. Then he followed the ebb-tide back and rowed hard to reach that part of the island where he had found the best landing-places the previous summer.* In this the courage of the soldiers was most commendable, for even in the heavily laden transport vessels they managed—by undertaking to row without a break—to keep pace with the course of the warships.

The whole fleet reached Britain at around midday, but there was no enemy visible in the area. Later, however, Caesar learned from prisoners that although a large host of them had arrived, they had panicked at the size of the fleet, which, including last year's ships and the private vessels which certain individuals had had built for their convenience,* was seen to number more than 800 at once. So they had left the shore and hidden themselves away on higher ground.

(9) The army landed and a suitable site for the camp was found. When Caesar learned from prisoners where the enemy

forces were stationed he left ten cohorts and 300 cavalry on the shore to guard the fleet, and during the third watch set out against the enemy. He was the less concerned for the fleet because he was leaving it anchored along a sandy, low-lying coast. He put Quintus Atrius in charge of this garrison. During the night he advanced about eleven miles before catching sight of the enemy forces. They brought their cavalry and chariots forward from higher ground to a river* and began to block the way of our men and to engage in fighting. They were forced back by our cavalry and hid in the forest, where they occupied a place which was strong in both natural and man-made defences. It was apparent that they had previously made this ready to serve in their domestic warfare, for every one of the entrances was blocked off by the felling of a large number of trees. They came out from the forest to fight in small detachments, and prevented our men from coming within the fortifications. But the men of the Seventh legion formed up into a 'tortoise',* piled up a ramp against the fortifications, seized control of the stronghold, and drove the enemy from the forest. They themselves suffered few casualties. Caesar, however, forbade them to pursue the fugitives very far, both because he was not familiar with the terrain and because the day was already far spent, and he wanted there to be enough time left for fortifying the camp.

(10) The following morning he sent the soldiers and cavalry out in three divisions on a foray to pursue fugitives. After they had marched a considerable distance they caught sight of the enemy rearguard. Just then riders came to Caesar from Quintus Atrius and reported that a terrible storm had blown up the night before, and almost all the ships were damaged and cast up on the shore—for the anchors and ropes had failed, and so the sailors and helmsmen could not withstand the force of the storm. As a result, the ships had been dashed one against the other, and serious damage had resulted.

(11) On learning this, Caesar ordered the legions and cavalry to be recalled and to maintain their resistance on the march. He himself returned to the ships. Then he saw everything for himself, almost exactly as he had heard it described by the messengers and dispatch. Yet although about forty ships were

lost, it was apparent that with considerable labour the rest could be rebuilt. So he selected workmen from the legions and ordered more to be summoned from mainland Gaul. He wrote to Labienus to have as many ships as possible built by those legions presently under his command. Then, despite the considerable difficulty and effort involved, Caesar decided the most convenient solution was to beach all the ships and join them with the camp by a single line of fortification. The work lasted for ten days: the soldiers had no break from their efforts even at night. Once the ships were beached and the camp strongly fortified, he left the same forces as before to guard the fleet and returned to the place he had left earlier.

By the time of his arrival even larger British forces had mustered there. By common agreement they had entrusted the supreme command of their campaign to Cassivellaunus, whose lands were separated from the coastal states by a river called the Thames, which is about seventy-three miles from the sea.* Between Cassivellaunus and the other states there had previously been continual warfare, but our arrival frightened the Britons into putting him in charge of the entire war effort.

(12) The inland regions of Britain are inhabited by people whom the Britons themselves claim, according to oral tradition, are indigenous. The coastal areas belong to people who once crossed from Belgium in search of booty and war: almost all of these inhabitants are called by the same national names as those of the states they originally came from. After waging war they remained in Britain and began to farm the land. Population density is high, and their dwellings are extremely numerous and very like those of the Gauls. They have large herds of cattle. They use either bronze or gold coinage or, instead of currency, iron rods of a fixed weight. Tin is found in the midland regions, iron along the coast but only in small quantities. Their bronze is imported. Timber of all kinds is found as in Gaul, except for beech and silver fir. They consider it wrong to eat hare, chicken, or goose, but still they look after them for pleasure and amusement. The climate is more temperate than in Gaul, and the winters milder.*

(13) The island is triangular in shape. One side faces Gaul, and one corner of this side, in Kent, is where almost all ships from Gaul put in to harbour. This corner looks east, the other south: the side stretches for about 460 miles. The second side looks towards Spain and the west: in this direction lies Ireland, which is thought to be half the size of Britain. The crossing from Britain to Ireland is the same as that from Gaul to Britain. Midway lies an island called Mona. There are thought to be several smaller islands besides lying nearby, and several writers have recorded that over the winter solstice there is continual darkness there for thirty days. We were unable to find out the truth of this by inquiries, except that by accurate measurements with a water-clock we observed that the nights were shorter than in mainland Gaul. According to the belief of the Britons, this side is some 640 miles long. The third side looks north, and faces no other land: but it is mainly angled towards Germany. It is thought to be about 730 miles long. Thus the whole island is nearly 2,000 miles in circumference.*

(14) Of all the island's inhabitants, by far the most civilized are those who live in Kent, a region which is entirely coastal. Their way of life is much the same as that of the Gauls. Inland, the people for the most part do not plant corn-crops, but live on milk and meat and clothe themselves in animal skins. All the Britons paint themselves with woad, which produces a dark blue colour: by this means they appear more frightening in battle. They have long hair and shave their bodies, all except for the head and upper lip. Groups of ten or twelve men share their wives in common, particularly between brothers or father and son. Any offspring they have are held to be the children of him to whom the maiden was brought first.*

(15) The enemy cavalry and charioteers clashed fiercely in combat with our cavalry on the march, though the outcome showed that our men were superior in every respect and drove them into the woods and hills. Despite killing a number of the enemy, they pursued too eagerly and lost a number of their own side. After a short time, when our men were off guard and busy fortifying the camp, the Britons suddenly

rushed out of the woods and attacked the guards stationed in front of the camp. A fierce fight ensued. Caesar sent two cohorts to their assistance—the primary cohorts of their respective legions—and they positioned themselves with only a very small gap to separate them. Because our men were frightened by the unfamiliar tactics, the enemy boldly broke through their midst and retreated without casualties. On that day the military tribune Quintus Laberius Durus was killed. The Britons were driven back after more cohorts were sent in support.

(16) Throughout this unusual combat, when the fighting took place in sight of all and in front of the camp, it was evident that because of their heavy weaponry our men were ill equipped for such an enemy. For they could not pursue when the enemy ran, and dared not abandon their close formation. The cavalry fought at great risk too, because the enemy frequently drove away from the fighting on purpose, so when our horsemen had gone some little distance from the legions they could jump down from their chariots and fight on foot with an unfair advantage. In fact, their strategy for cavalry battle brought us into equal danger whether in retreat or pursuit. There was also the fact that they never fought in close formation, but rather in small groups with large spaces between: they had squadrons posted at intervals and each group took over from another in turn, so that fresh troops could take the place of those who were tired out.

(17) The following day the enemy took up a position on high ground far from camp. They began to appear in small detachments and attack our cavalry, though less eagerly than the day before. At midday, though, when Caesar had sent three legions and all the cavalry with his legate Gaius Trebonius to forage for food, the enemy suddenly swept down upon the foragers from all directions with such force that they did not stop before coming up with the standards and the legions. Our legionaries attacked fiercely and drove them back; they did not halt the pursuit until the cavalry saw the legions behind them and had the confidence in their support to drive the enemy headlong. They cut down a large number, and allowed them no opportunity to rally or make a stand

or jump down from their chariots. Directly after this battle the enemy reinforcements which had mustered all dispersed. Thereafter the Britons were never at full strength when they engaged with our forces.

(18) Caesar learned of their plans and led his army to the River Thames in the territory of Cassivellaunus. This river can only be crossed at a single spot,* on foot, and then with difficulty. When he arrived, he observed the large enemy forces drawn up on the opposite bank, the surface of which was protected by a covering of sharpened stakes. Fixed beneath the water, similar stakes were concealed by the river. On learning these facts from prisoners and deserters, Caesar sent the cavalry on ahead and ordered the legions to follow up at once. The soldiers moved with such speed and vigour that—although they had only their heads above water—the enemy could not withstand the assault of the legions and cavalry, abandoned the river-bank, and took to their heels.

(19) As we explained above, Cassivellaunus had given up all hope of a confrontation and dismissed the greater part of his forces, so that about 4,000 charioteers remained.* He kept watch on our marches, withdrawing a short distance from the road and keeping himself hidden in difficult wooded terrain. Wherever he knew we would be marching, he forced men and livestock to leave the fields for the forest. Whenever our cavalry rushed into the fields, ranging too freely in search of plunder and devastation, he sent his charioteers by every path and track out of the woods: the clash between them brought our cavalry into great danger. Thus fear prevented them from ranging more widely. All that remained for Caesar was to forbid anyone straying too far from the column of legions, and to inflict as much harm upon the enemy—by ravaging the fields and starting fires—as the legionary soldiers could manage despite the exertion of the march.

(20) Meanwhile the Trinobantes* (one of the most powerful states in those parts) sent envoys to Caesar and promised to surrender to him and to obey his commands. A young man of that people, called Mandubracius, had approached Caesar on the Gallic mainland looking for his support: for his father, who had won the kingship in that state, had been

killed by Cassivellaunus, while he himself had fled to escape
death. The Trinobantes asked Caesar to defend Mandubracius
from harm at Cassivellaunus' hands, and to send him to their
state to take command and rule over it. Caesar demanded
forty hostages from them, and corn for his army, and sent
Mandubracius to them. They quickly carried out his commands, and sent the required number of hostages and the
corn. (21) Thus the Trinobantes were made secure, and protected from any harm at the soldiers' hands.

Then the Cenimagni, Segontiaci, Ancalites, Bibroci, and
Cassi* sent embassies and put themselves under Caesar's
protection. He learned from them that Cassivellaunus' stronghold, which was protected by woods and marshes, was not
far from his present location: he had gathered quite a large
number of men and cattle there. The Britons, however, apply
the word 'stronghold' to a dense wood which they have
fortified with a rampart and ditch, and where they always
assemble to avoid enemy attack.

Caesar made his way there with the legions, and found it
a place with admirable natural and man-made defences. None
the less, he exerted himself to attack it on two sides. The
enemy lingered a short while, but did not withstand the assault of our soldiers, and burst out from another part of the
stronghold. Large numbers of cattle were found there, and
many of the enemy were caught as they fled and put to
death.

(22) While all this was taking place in that area Cassivellaunus sent messengers to Kent (which, as we explained above,
is by the sea). This was a region ruled over by four kings—
Cingetorix, Carvilius, Taximagulus, and Segovax. He ordered
them to muster all their forces, strike at the Roman fleet's
camp without warning, and launch an assault. When they
reached the camp, however, our men made a sortie. They killed
a large number of the enemy, captured their aristocratic leader
Lugotorix, and returned without casualties. News of this battle
reached Cassivellaunus. He had suffered many defeats and
his lands were ruined: he was particularly disturbed by the
defection of allied states, so finally he sent envoys to Caesar
through Commius the Atrebatian to surrender. Caesar had

decided to winter on the mainland for fear of sudden Gallic uprisings. He realized that not much of the summer remained, and that hostilities could easily drag on, so he demanded hostages and settled the annual tribute which Britain must pay to the Roman people. He ordered Cassivellaunus in strong terms to do no harm to Mandubracius or the Trinobantes.

(23) Once he had received the hostages, Caesar led his army back to the coast, where he found the ships repaired. He had a large number of prisoners, while several of the ships had been destroyed in the storm, so once the ships were launched he decided to transport the army back in two journeys. So it came about that neither this year nor the year before was any ship carrying soldiers lost altogether, despite the large number both of vessels and voyages. Of those ships which were sent back empty from mainland Gaul—both the ones from which the soldiers who crossed first had disembarked and the sixty vessels which Labienus had had built after Caesar sailed—very few reached the rendezvous. Almost all of the rest were forced back. Caesar waited a while for them, but in vain. To avoid being prevented by the season from making the voyage at all (for the autumnal equinox was near), he was forced to pack the soldiers in more tightly than usual; then when a total calm ensued he weighed anchor at the start of the second watch, reached land at dawn, and brought the whole fleet safely to its destination.*

(24) The ships were beached, and an assembly of the Gauls was held at Samarobriva.* Because of a drought the corn had grown only sparsely in Gaul that year, so Caesar was compelled to allocate the army's winter quarters according to a plan different to that of previous years, and to spread the legions across a greater number of states. One legion he allotted to his legate Gaius Fabius, to lead it to the Morini, another to Quintus Cicero, to go to the Nervii, and a third to Lucius Roscius, to Esubian territory. He ordered the fourth under Titus Labienus to winter among the Remi, on the borders of the Treveri. He settled three legions among the Belgae and put his quaestor Marcus Crassus and his legates Lucius Munatius Plancus and Gaius Trebonius in charge of them. One legion, which he had enlisted north of

the Po only recently, he sent with five cohorts to the land of
the Eburones, which lies mainly between the Meuse and the
Rhine. They were ruled by Ambiorix and Catuvolcus. He
ordered his legates Quintus Titurius Sabinus and Lucius
Aurunculeius Cotta to take command of this force.

After allocating the legions in this way he thought that
the shortage of corn would be alleviated. In fact, the winter
quarters of all the legions (except the one he had allotted
to Lucius Roscius to take to a very subdued and peaceful
region) were well within a hundred miles of each other. Meanwhile Caesar decided to wait in Gaul until all the legions
were posted and their quarters fortified.

(25) One of the Carnutes was an aristocrat whose ancestors had held the kingship among their own people; his name
was Tasgetius. In all his campaigns Caesar had enjoyed this
man's exceptional support, and so, in return for his courage
and goodwill, had earlier restored him to the status of his
ancestors. In the third year of Tasgetius' reign, at the open
instigation of many of his own citizens, his enemies killed
him. This event was reported to Caesar. Because the affair
involved a large number of people he was afraid that the
killers would force the state to rebel. So he sent Lucius Plancus
to hasten from Belgium with his legion to the land of the
Carnutes and to winter there; also to arrest and send to him
all those men who had been implicated in the murder of
Tasgetius. In the meantime he was informed by all the legates
and quaestors to whom he had entrusted the legions that
they had reached their winter quarters and fortified them.

(26) About a fortnight after the arrival in winter quarters
revolt and defection suddenly sprang up at the instigation of
Ambiorix and Catuvolcus. Although they had presented themselves to Sabinus and Cotta on the borders of their kingdom,
and had transported corn to the winter camp, messengers
from Indutiomarus of the Treveri spurred them on to rouse
their own people. They suddenly attacked the men who were
sent to fetch wood and then pressed on in large numbers to
the camp to assault it. Our men quickly seized their weapons
and climbed the rampart, while the Spanish cavalry were
dispatched from one direction and emerged the victors after

a cavalry battle. The enemy abandoned hope and withdrew their men from the assault. Then in accordance with their custom they shouted for someone from our side to proceed to a parley: they wanted to say something, they claimed, which was to the advantage of all, and by means of which they hoped that these quarrels could be abated.

(27) A Roman knight* called Gaius Arpineius was sent to parley with them. He was a close friend of Sabinus. With him went Quintus Junius, a certain Spaniard who had previously been used to going to and fro at Caesar's command to Ambiorix. In their presence Ambiorix spoke to the following effect: for all Caesar's marks of favour towards himself he admitted that he was very much obliged; for it was through Caesar's offices that he had been freed from the habitual payment of tribute to his neighbours, the Aduatuci. Also, Caesar had returned his son and his nephew after the Aduatuci had kept them in their midst in chains of slavery among the hostages which were sent to them. His action, he went on, in assaulting the camp was not undertaken of his own free will and decision, but under compulsion from the state. His rule was of such a kind that the masses had as much power over him as he had over them. His state, furthermore, had gone to war because it was unable to withstand a sudden Gallic conspiracy. He could easily prove this by his very insignificance, for he was not so ignorant of affairs as to feel certain of conquering the Roman people with his own forces.

However, Ambiorix went on, the whole of Gaul was in agreement. This was the day appointed for attacking all Caesar's winter camps, so that no one legion could come to the aid of another. One group of Gauls could not easily refuse another, especially when it appeared that a plan for recovering the freedom of all was under way. Since he had now done enough for them in respect of his duty to his country, he had to consider what was due in return for Caesar's favours. Ambiorix warned Sabinus, he pleaded with him for friendship's sake, to look to his own safety and that of his soldiers. A great host of Germans had been hired, and had crossed the Rhine—in two days it would be upon them. It was for Sabinus and Cotta to decide, said Ambiorix, whether they wished to take the men out of winter quarters before the neighbouring peoples were aware, and lead them either to Quintus Cicero or to Labienus, one of whom was about forty-five miles away, the other a little more. Finally Ambiorix made this promise, and confirmed it with an oath—he would give them a safe passage through his land. And by doing this, he claimed, he was acting in the interests of his own state (which would have the burden of wintering them lifted) and doing a favour to Caesar in return for his services. After delivering this speech Ambiorix departed.

(28) Arpineius and Junius reported what they had heard to the legates, who were much disturbed by this sudden turn of events. Even if these were the words of an enemy, they still thought they should not be ignored. They were particularly troubled by the fact that it seemed incredible that an obscure and undistinguished nation like the Eburones dared—on their own initiative—to make war on the Romans. So they brought the matter before a council, where fierce disagreement arose between them. Cotta, together with a number of the military tribunes and leading centurions, thought that nothing should be done on the spur of the moment, and that they should not leave their winter quarters without orders from Caesar. They argued that the German forces, however large, could be held off if their winter camp were fortified. As proof of this there was the fact that they had withstood the enemy's first attack with great bravery, and moreover had inflicted many wounds on them. They were not short of corn supplies—in the meantime help would come both from the winter camps nearby and from Caesar. Lastly, what could be more foolish or shameful than to take advice on a matter of such importance at an enemy's prompting?

(29) Sabinus replied by protesting loudly that by the time the enemy hordes—their numbers swelled by German allies—had arrived, or some disaster had occurred in the winter camps nearby, it would be too late to do anything. They had only a short time to decide. He judged that Caesar had left for Italy: otherwise the Carnutes would never have adopted a plan of killing Tasgetius nor, if Caesar were present, would the Eburones display such scorn for our men in approaching

the camp. He was not, he said, paying regard to an enemy's prompting but to the facts of the case. The Rhine was nearby, the Germans were smarting at the death of Ariovistus and our previous victories, Gaul was incensed by the many slights she had endured after being brought under the rule of the Roman people and by the extinction of her former glory in warfare. Finally, who could be quite sure that Ambiorix had resorted to such a plan except on secure grounds? Either way, his own view was safe—if nothing very untoward occurred, they would reach the nearest legion without risk; if, on the other hand, the whole of Gaul sided with the Germans, their only safety was in flight. What, concluded Sabinus, would be the outcome of the plan proposed by Cotta and others disagreeing with himself? Even if the present threat was no reason to be afraid, the hunger inflicted by a long siege certainly would be.

(30) Following this argument for both views, Cotta and the centurions vigorously opposed Sabinus, but he raised his voice so that a large number of the soldiers could hear him, and said: 'Have it your own way if you must—I am not the man to fear the threat of death most of all among you. These soldiers will understand: if anything untoward happens, they will demand that you justify yourselves. After all, if only you would let them, the day after tomorrow they would join forces with the nearest camp and endure the hazard of war together with all the rest—instead of being isolated and exiled, to perish from hunger or the sword far from reinforcements.'*

(31) They got up from the council, and their friends seized them both by the hand, pleading with them not to let their own stubborn disagreement jeopardize the outcome. There was no difficulty, whether they stayed or left, provided that everyone was in harmony and agreement. If, on the other hand, this dispute continued, they could see no hope of safety. Disagreement over this matter continued until midnight. Finally Cotta was moved to yield. Sabinus' view prevailed.

It was announced that they would set out at dawn. The rest of the night passed in wakefulness, for each soldier looked over his belongings, to see what he could take with him and what items of winter kit he must leave behind. All kinds of reasons were thought up as to why it would be unsafe to remain, and how the men's fatigue and constant watches would intensify the risk. At dawn they set out from the camp, convinced that the advice they had received came not from an enemy but from a true friend, Ambiorix. The column was a very long one, and its baggage extremely heavy.

(32) After the enemy realized, because of all the bustle and watchfulness, that the Romans were on their way, they set up ambushes at two locations in the woods and then began to await the Romans' arrival in a convenient hidden spot about two miles off. When the greater part of the column had descended into a deep ravine they suddenly appeared at both ends of it and began to attack the rearguard and stop the vanguard from climbing up, engaging with our men in a very unequal position.

(33) Because he had anticipated nothing of the kind, it was only then that Sabinus finally showed some anxiety, and ran about arranging his cohorts. Even this he did fearfully, and as if all presence of mind were seen to fail him. This generally tends to happen to men who are obliged to make decisions in the midst of action. Cotta, on the other hand, had considered the possibility that this might happen during their march, and for that reason had not supported the proposal to leave camp. He began to do everything he could to secure the safety of all, and to perform the duties both of a commander (by calling on the men by name and encouraging them) and of an ordinary soldier (by taking part in the fighting). Because the column was so long, it was rather difficult for the commanders to keep a watch on everything and to anticipate what was needed at each point—so they gave orders to pass the word on to abandon the baggage and form a circle. This strategy, though not actually blameworthy in such difficult circumstances, nevertheless had unfortunate consequences. For it weakened the confidence of our soldiers, and made the enemy more eager for the fight. Clearly the Romans would not have done this until they were in a state of total desperation and panic. Another consequence, inevitably, was that soldiers everywhere started to abandon their standards, and all hurried to look for their most treasured possessions

among the baggage and hold on to them. Shouting and weeping filled the air.

(34) The barbarians, on the other hand, did not lack a strategy for reacting to this move. Their leaders gave orders to pass the word all down the line—no one was to leave his post: all the booty was theirs, and whatever the Romans left was set apart for them. In this way they believed everything would be staked on victory. Both in courage and in fighting numbers they were a match for us.

Though abandoned by their commander* and by fortune, our men still knew that in courage lay their only hope of safety. Whenever a cohort made a sally a large number of the enemy facing it fell. Once Ambiorix had noticed this he gave orders to pass the word that his men must throw their weapons from a distance, rather than approaching too close. He also told them to give ground wherever the Romans attacked. His own men's armour was light, and their daily training also ensured that they would be safe from harm. When the Romans retreated to their standards, though, they were to pursue them.

(35) His men carried out his instructions to the letter. Whenever one of the cohorts left the circle and attacked, the enemy retreated at top speed. Inevitably their sally left a gap, exposing our men to missiles on their open flank.* When they began to move back to the post they had left our men were surrounded both by the enemy who had given way and by the closest of those who had remained in position. If they tried to maintain their circle formation instead, their bravery had no scope for action, while at the same time it was impossible in such close formation to avoid missiles thrown from the massive enemy host. Encumbered as they were, our men still put up a resistance, receiving many wounds; the day was more than half over, and they had fought from dawn until the eighth hour* without doing anything to disgrace themselves. Then Titus Balventius, a brave man and strong leader who had been a senior centurion the year before, had both his thighs pierced by a javelin; another senior centurion, Quintus Lucanius, went to the assistance of his son, who was surrounded, and died fighting courageously.

The legate Lucius Cotta, whilst urging on all the cohorts and ranks, was wounded by a stone from a sling which hit him full in the face.

(36) All this threw Sabinus into a panic. He saw Ambiorix from a distance urging on his men, and sent Gnaeus Pompeius* to ask him to spare himself and the Roman soldiers. Ambiorix responded to this appeal by saying that Sabinus was free to parley if he wished: he was hopeful of being able to persuade his force to agree to the Roman soldiers' safety. He promised that no harm should be done to Sabinus himself, and pledged his own word to that effect.

Sabinus reported all this to the wounded Cotta, to get his agreement to the two of them leaving the battle and holding a parley with Ambiorix. He hoped his request to Ambiorix for safety for themselves and their men would be successful. Cotta said that he would not approach an armed enemy, and persisted in this opposition.

(37) Then Sabinus ordered the military tribunes presently at his side and the senior centurions to follow him. When he approached Ambiorix he was told to throw down his weapons: he did as he was told, and ordered his men to do the same. In the meantime, while they negotiated terms, Ambiorix deliberately dragged out their discussion: Sabinus was gradually surrounded and killed. Then indeed they proclaimed the victory in their accustomed way, raised a yell of triumph and made an attack on our ranks, and scattered them. There Lucius Cotta fell fighting, together with most of our soldiers. The rest retreated to the camp they had left behind. Among them was a standard-bearer called Lucius Petrosidius: hard-pressed by a great host of the enemy, he drew his eagle within the rampart and was cut down as he fought bravely before the camp. They barely managed to keep up the fight until nightfall—and when it was dark they abandoned hope of saving themselves and every single one of them committed suicide. A few men who had slipped away from the battle made their way by a haphazard route through the forest to the legate Titus Labienus and his winter quarters. They informed him of all that had occurred.

(38) Ambiorix was ecstatic at this victory. Straight away he

set out with his cavalry for the land of the Aduatuci, which bordered his own kingdom. He marched for a day and a night without resting, and ordered the infantry to follow on. Once he had described what happened the Aduatuci were thoroughly roused. Next day he approached the Nervii and urged them not to let slip a chance to liberate themselves forever and inflict vengeance on the Romans for the wrongs they had suffered at their hands. He explained that two legates had been killed and a large part of the army had perished: it would be no trouble at all to attack the legion wintering under Quintus Cicero and annihilate it. He promised to assist them in the business, and his words easily convinced the Nervii.*

(39) Accordingly messengers were dispatched at once to the Ceutrones, Grudii, Levaci, Pleumoxii, and Geidumni, who were all under Nervian rule. They mustered the greatest forces they could and rushed without warning to the winter camp of Quintus Cicero, who had not yet received news of Sabinus' death. Inevitably it befell Quintus Cicero, as it also had Sabinus, that some of his soldiers who had gone into the woods in search of timber for the defences were cut off by the sudden arrival of enemy cavalry. They were surrounded, and a vast host of Eburones, Nervii, Aduatuci, and their allies and dependants began to attack the legion. Our men swiftly ran to arms and climbed up the rampart. They barely got through the day, for the enemy's hopes were all pinned on a swift result, and they were sure that once this victory was won they would be conquerors for ever.

(40) Quintus Cicero at once sent a dispatch to Caesar, and promised the bearers great reward if they got it through. But all the roads were blockaded, and the messengers were intercepted. That night, with astonishing speed, our men constructed towers—a full 120 of them—out of the timber which they had gathered for the defences. Any defects apparent in the defences were corrected. Next day the enemy attacked the camp in much greater numbers, and filled in the ditch. Our men resisted in the same way as the day before. Day after day the same thing happened. At no time of night was there any break from work: neither the sick nor the wounded

were given a chance to rest. Whatever was needed for the next day's fighting was prepared by night. They made ready large numbers of stakes charred at the point, and many javelins of the type used for fighting on walls. The towers were lined with planks, and battlements and parapets of wickerwork attached.* Cicero himself was in poor health, but did not even allow himself rest at night; eventually he was compelled to spare his exertions by the pressure and insistence of his soldiers.

(41) Now the commanders and leaders of the Nervii who had any means of addressing themselves to Quintus Cicero or any grounds for claiming friendship with him declared that they wanted to parley. Once the opportunity was granted they enumerated the same arguments as Ambiorix had used with Sabinus, namely, that the whole of Gaul was up in arms, the Germans had crossed the Rhine, and the winter camps of Caesar and his legates were under attack. They also reminded him of Sabinus' death, and pointed to Ambiorix to prove their point.* If, said the Nervii, the Romans were hoping to receive support and assistance from comrades already despairing of their own situation, they were much mistaken; where Quintus Cicero and the Roman people were concerned, however, they were not of a mind to refuse anything except the provision of winter quartering, which they did not wish to become a fixed practice. Even so, they would permit the Romans to depart from their camp unharmed and go wherever they wanted without fear. Quintus Cicero made only one reply to this speech—it was not the Roman people's custom, he said, to accept terms from an armed enemy. If they were willing to lay down their weapons he would offer them assistance in sending envoys to Caesar. He was hopeful, in view of Caesar's sense of fairness, that they would obtain what they asked.

(42) The Nervii had hoped to entrap him, but were thus rebuffed. They now encircled the camp with a nine-foot rampart and a ditch fifteen feet wide. They had learned these techniques both from our practice in previous years and from the instruction given by prisoners from our army whom they kept hidden. But as they had no stock of tools suitable for

this purpose they were obliged to cut turves with their swords, and to carry the earth away in their hands and cloaks. From this activity it was possible to reckon the size of their host: for they completed this fortification, which was three miles all round,* in less than three hours. During the days which remained they began to make ready and construct towers (in proportion to the height of the rampart), siege-hooks, and shelters, just as the same prisoners had instructed them.

(43) On the seventh day of the siege a stormy wind blew up. The Nervii started using slings to fire balls of heated clay and burning darts on to the soldiers' cabins, which were thatched in Gallic fashion. They quickly caught fire, and because the wind was so strong the blaze spread into every part of the camp. The enemy gave a great shout as if they were certain of a victory already won, and began to mobilize the towers and shelters, and to use ladders to scale the rampart. Everywhere our soldiers were scorched by the flames and harassed by a cascade of missiles, and they realized that all their baggage and their property was being reduced to ashes. Nevertheless, such was the bravery of our soldiers, and their firm resolution, that not only did none of them abandon the rampart to make his escape but not one of them even so much as looked back. Instead they all fought as fiercely and as bravely as they could. This day was by far the hardest for our men, but it still resulted in a very large number of the enemy being wounded or killed, for they had crowded together under the actual rampart, and so the rearward ranks gave those in front no opportunity to withdraw. Indeed, when there was a short lull in the fire, in one place a tower was brought up to touch the rampart. Then the centurions of the third cohort retreated from where they were stationed and moved back all their men. They began to beckon and call to the enemy to enter if they so wished. Not one of them did dare to make the advance. In fact, stones thrown from all directions brought them tumbling down, and the tower was set on fire.

(44) In this legion there were two centurions, both men of great courage, and close to reaching senior rank. Their names were Titus Pullo and Lucius Vorenus. There was always a

dispute going on between them as to which had precedence over the other, and every year they clashed in fierce rivalry over the most important posts. While the fighting at the defences was at its height Pullo shouted: 'Why are you hesitating, Vorenus? What chance are you waiting for of winning praise for your bravery? This day will decide the contest between us.' With these words he made his way outside the defences and launched an attack where the enemy ranks were densest. Nor indeed did Vorenus remain within the rampart, but followed his rival for fear of what men would think of him. Then Pullo cast his spear against the enemy at close range, and transfixed a Gaul who had run forward from the ranks. He was knocked senseless, so they covered him with their shields and all together threw their weapons at Pullo, giving him no opportunity to withdraw.

Pullo's shield was pierced, and a dart was stuck in his sword-belt—this knocked his sheath and hindered his attempt to draw his sword. While he was in difficulties the enemy surrounded him. To the rescue came Vorenus, his rival, who helped him out of trouble. Straight away the Gauls turned their attention from Pullo to Vorenus, thinking the former had been killed by the dart. With his sword Vorenus fought at close quarters. He killed one man, and drove the rest off a short way. But he pressed forward too eagerly, tripped, and fell into a hollow. Now he was surrounded, and Pullo came to his aid. They killed several Gauls and both returned safely within the defences to great acclaim. Thus fortune played with them both in their rivalry and struggle, so that despite their enmity each helped and saved the other, and it was impossible to decide which should be considered the braver of the two.

(45) The siege became more grim and relentless day by day, especially because so many of our soldiers were wounded and the task devolved on to a handful of defenders. As the situation worsened more and more dispatches and messengers were sent off to Caesar: some of the messengers were caught and tortured in the sight of our men, and then put to death.

Within the camp was a well-born Nervian called Vertico, who had fled to Quintus Cicero for refuge at the start of the siege, and had proved his loyalty to him. He used the hope of freedom and large rewards to persuade one of his slaves to carry a dispatch to Caesar. The slave got the message out attached to a spear, and by mingling freely as a Gaul among Gauls without arousing suspicion he made his way to Caesar. Through him the threat to Quintus Cicero and his legion was discovered.

(46) Caesar received the dispatch at about the eleventh hour of the day,* and at once sent a messenger to the territory of the Bellovaci, to his quaestor Marcus Crassus whose winter camp was about twenty-three miles away. He ordered Crassus' legion to set out at midnight and come quickly to him.* As soon as the messenger arrived Crassus set out. Caesar sent a second messenger to his legate Gaius Fabius, telling him to take his legion to the territory of the Atrebates, through which he knew that he too must march. He wrote to Labienus and told him to bring his legion into Nervian territory if it was possible without endangering the common good. He thought it best not to wait for the rest of the army, which was some distance away. He mustered about 400 cavalry from the winter camps nearby.

(47) At about the third hour* outriders came to tell him that Crassus was arriving. On that day he advanced eighteen miles. He put Crassus in charge of Samarobriva and allocated him a legion, because this was where he was leaving behind the army's baggage, the nations' hostages, state documents, and all the corn which he had transported there to provide food throughout the winter. After a short delay Fabius and his legion (as ordered) met Caesar on the march.

Labienus had received news of the death of Sabinus and the slaughter of his cohorts. Now that all the forces of the Treveri had come upon him, he was afraid that if he set out from his camp it would look as if he was fleeing, and he would be unable to withstand an enemy attack—especially an enemy he knew to be elated because of its recent success. So he wrote to Caesar, explaining how risky it would be to lead his legion out of winter camp. He gave a full account of what had happened in the land of the Eburones, and described how all the infantry and cavalry forces of the Treveri had taken up position three miles from his own camp.

(48) Caesar approved his judgement. Despite the fact that his hope of having three legions was dashed, and he was now reduced to two, he none the less regarded speed as the only means of securing the safety of all. By forced marches he reached Nervian territory. There he learned from prisoners what was happening with Quintus Cicero, and how dangerous the situation was. Then he persuaded one of the Gallic cavalry, by means of a large bribe, to convey a letter to Quintus Cicero. The dispatch he sent was written in Greek* so that if it was intercepted the enemy could not discover our plans. If this Gaul was unable to reach him, Caesar told him to hurl a throwing spear inside the camp defences, with the letter tied to its strap. In it he wrote that he was on his way with the legions and would soon be there; and he urged Quintus Cicero to keep up his former courage.

The Gaul did fear a threat, and so cast his spear as ordered. By chance it stuck in one of our towers. Unnoticed by our men for two days, on the third it was finally spotted by one of the soldiers, removed, and taken to Quintus Cicero. He scanned it through, then read it aloud to an assembly of the troops: this gave rise to great delight among them all. Then, far off, the smoke of burnings was spied, and this put an end to doubt that the legions were at hand.

(49) When the Gauls learned from scouts what was happening they abandoned the siege, and set out against Caesar with all their forces. These totalled about 60,000 men under arms. When the opportunity offered Quintus Cicero asked the same Vertico as we mentioned above for a Gaul to convey a dispatch to Caesar. He warned this man to make his way carefully and with caution. In this letter he described in full how the enemy had departed from him, and had turned their entire force against Caesar. This dispatch reached Caesar at about midnight: he told his men what the situation was, and encouraged them for the fight. At dawn the following day he struck camp and marched for about four miles before the enemy army was spotted across a valley with a stream in it. It would be very risky to engage on unfavourable ground with so small a force; besides, he knew that Quintus Cicero was free of the pressure of the siege, so he could accept with

equanimity the need to slacken the speed of his march. He halted and fortified a camp in the most advantageous position possible. The camp was already small in itself (numbering scarcely 7,000 men, and these without baggage); even so, by making the roadways as narrow as possible he constricted it further, intending to make the enemy treat it with utter derision. Meanwhile he sent scouts out in all directions, and spied out the most convenient route for crossing the valley.

(50) That day there were minor cavalry engagements by the waterside, but both sides held their positions. The Gauls were awaiting larger forces which had not yet arrived, but Caesar hoped to lure the enemy on to his own ground by pretending to be afraid, and so to engage on his side of the valley in front of the camp. If he could not achieve this he hoped that once the routes had been reconnoitred he could cross the valley and the stream with less risk. At dawn the enemy cavalry approached the camp and engaged in battle with our cavalry. Caesar ordered them to give ground on purpose, and retreat to the camp. At the same time he gave orders for the camp to be fortified with a higher rampart on all sides, and the gate to be barricaded—and for these tasks to be carried out with as much rushing about and pretence of panic as possible.

(51) All these factors lured the enemy into bringing their forces over and forming up for battle on disadvantageous ground. Our men had even been withdrawn from the rampart, so they came closer and threw missiles inside the fortifications from all sides. Then they sent heralds all round the camp and told them to announce that any Gaul or Roman who wanted to come over to them before the third hour was free to do so unharmed. But after that time there would be no opportunity. The gates appeared to be barricaded, though in fact it was with only a single layer of turves, and looked impossible to break down, but so deeply did they despise our men that some began to tear down the rampart with their hands, others to fill in the ditches. Then Caesar made a sortie from all the gates, let loose the cavalry, and routed the enemy so swiftly that not a single enemy Gaul halted to resist. He killed a large number of them and stripped them all of their arms.

(52) He was reluctant to pursue them very far, for there were woods and marshes in the way, and he perceived that there was no opportunity for doing the enemy even trivial harm. That same day, all his forces intact, he arrived at Quintus Cicero's camp, and marvelled at the towers, shelters, and fortifications the enemy had built. He called a parade of the legion, and learned that not so much as one soldier in ten was unwounded. All this led him to conclude how great had been their danger, and their courage in dealing with what had happened. He praised both Quintus Cicero and his legion as they deserved; then, one by one, he addressed the centurions and military tribunes, of whose outstanding bravery he had heard from Quintus Cicero.

From prisoners he learned for certain of the disaster which had befallen Sabinus and Cotta. The next day he held an assembly and related what had happened, offering comfort and reassurance to the soldiers. He told them to bear this loss, incurred through the rash fault of his legate, with greater equanimity because amends had been made for the set-back both by the assistance of the immortal gods and by their own courage. The enemy was left with no lasting cause for celebration, nor would their own grief be lasting.

(53) In the meanwhile news of Caesar's victory was carried with incredible speed to Labienus by the Remi. Even though he was some fifty-five miles from Quintus Cicero's winter camp, which Caesar had reached after the ninth hour of the day, before midnight a shout went up at the gates of his camp, which marked the fact of the victory and the congratulations of the Remi to Labienus. The same news reached the Treveri, so Indutiomarus, who had decided to attack Labienus' camp the next day, fled under cover of darkness and took his forces back to the territory of the Treveri.

Caesar sent Fabius and his legion back into winter quarters, and decided that with his three legions he would himself winter around Samarobriva in three camps. Because the disturbances which had arisen in Gaul had been so severe, he decided to remain with his army for the whole winter. For once the set-back of Sabinus' death became known almost all the Gallic states began to discuss war, sending messengers and embassies to all areas to find out what plan of action the rest were adopting, and where the war should begin, and holding assemblies by night in lonely places. Hardly a moment passed all through the winter without Caesar dealing with some cause of anxiety, or receiving some news of the plans and rebellion of the Gauls. Included among this was the information brought by his quaestor Lucius Roscius, who commanded the Thirteenth legion: a large Gallic force from the states known as Aremorican had assembled in order to launch an attack, and were no more than seven miles from his winter camp. On receiving news of Caesar's victory, however, they had departed, and in such haste that their departure looked more like a flight.

(54) Nevertheless Caesar summoned the leaders of each state to him. By frightening some (when he declared that he knew what was going on) and exhorting others he kept a large part of Gaul loyal. Even so the Senones, a people who are particularly strong and influential among the Gauls, by popular decision attempted to put one Cavarinus to death. He was the man Caesar had made king among them. At the time of Caesar's arrival in Gaul his brother Moritasgus was king, and his ancestors before him. Cavarinus realized what was happening and fled, so they pursued him right to the border and expelled him from the kingship and his home. Then they sent envoys to Caesar to offer excuses. Although he had ordered their entire senate to come to him, they did not obey him. The barbarian Gauls attached great importance to the fact that they had found some people to take the lead in starting war, and this effected a striking change of heart among them all. So except for the Aedui and Remi— whom Caesar always held in particular esteem, the former for their long-standing loyalty to the Roman people, the latter for services recently rendered in the Gallic war—there was scarcely a state which did not fall under our suspicion. I do not know that this is such a cause for surprise, for a number of reasons, but especially because the Gauls were once pre-eminent among all nations for their excellence in war, and hence were deeply mortified at having so ruined this reputation as to bow to the dictates of the Roman people.*

(55) Thus Indutiomarus and the Treveri spent the entire winter sending envoys over the Rhine, approaching states for support, pledging money, and claiming that most of our army had been wiped out, and only a much smaller section of it remained. Even so they failed to persuade a single German state to cross the Rhine, for the Germans declared that they had tried crossing twice before—in the war of Ariovistus and the migration of the Tencteri: they were not about to try their luck another time. Disappointed of his hope, Indutiomarus still began to muster forces, train them, obtain horses from neighbouring peoples, and with large bribes to lure outcasts and criminals from all over Gaul to support him. By these means he had acquired such influence in Gaul that embassies flocked to him from all directions, and individuals and governments both sought his favour and friendship. Then he realized that people were approaching him of their own accord. In one direction were the Senones and Carnutes, driven by their sense of guilt, in another the Nervii and Aduatuci, preparing for war with the Romans. He would not, therefore, lack a willing army if he began the march from his own borders. So he called an assembly under arms.

(56) This is the habitual method of initiating hostilities among the Gauls: by a communal law all the men of fighting age are accustomed to muster under arms, and the man who is last to arrive is first tortured as the army looks on and then is put to death. At this assembly Indutiomarus declared Cingetorix an enemy and confiscated his property. Cingetorix was his son-in-law and the leader of the other party; as we showed above, he was a supporter of Caesar who did not waver in his loyalty. This business was now settled. At the meeting Indutiomarus declared that he had been summoned by the Senones and Carnutes and several other Gallic states, and that he would march there through the territory of the Remi, ravaging their lands. Before this, however, he would attack Labienus' camp. He issued instructions as to what he wanted done.

(57) Because Labienus was holding his position in a camp which had strong natural and artificial fortifications he had no fear of any risk to himself or his legion—and he was

considering how to avoid missing any chance of action. So when Cingetorix and his people made known the speech which Indutiomarus had given at the assembly Labienus sent envoys to the neighbouring states and called up cavalry from every region. He set a particular day for their muster. Meanwhile almost every day Indutiomarus and all his cavalry were roaming close to the camp. Some of these occasions were for reconnaissance of the camp's position, others for parleys or to induce fear. The cavalry were throwing missiles inside the rampart at frequent intervals. Labienus kept his men within the fortifications, and reinforced the impression of cowardice by every possible means.

(58) Indutiomarus continued to approach the camp, and his contempt increased day by day. Within the course of a single night, however, Labienus brought inside the walls the cavalry of all neighbouring states which he had had summoned; and so careful was he to keep all his own men within the camp by means of watches that there was no way for the fact of their arrival to be made known or reported to the Treveri. Meanwhile, as was his daily habit, Indutiomarus approached the camp, where he spent most of the day. His cavalry threw missiles and shouted insults to call our men out to fight. Our men gave no reply, and when the enemy felt so inclined, as dusk drew on, they broke up and departed in different directions. Suddenly Labienus sent all his cavalry out from two of the camp gates: he instructed and warned them that once the enemy panicked and fled (he foresaw what would happen, as indeed it did) they should all search only for Indutiomarus. No one was to wound anyone, until he had seen that man killed, for Labienus did not want a respite caused by their pursuit of the others to allow him to escape. He promised substantial rewards to those who killed him, and sent cohorts to the cavalry's assistance.

Fortune approved Labienus' strategy. When they all made for him alone Indutiomarus was caught in the shallows of the river and slain. His head was brought back to camp. As they rode back the cavalry pursued all the Gauls they could and killed them. When this event became known all the forces of the Eburones and Nervii which had mustered dispersed. Soon afterwards Caesar ruled over relative calm in Gaul.

The Sixth Book: 53 BC

(AUC 701: Consuls, Gnaeus Domitius Calvinus, Marcus Valerius Messalla)

Second Crossing of the Rhine: Ethnology of Gaul and Germany: The Search for Ambiorix: Invasion of the Sugambri

(1) For a number of reasons Caesar foresaw disturbances in Gaul on a larger scale, so he decided to hold a levy through his legates Marcus Silanus, Gaius Antistius Reginus, and Titus Sextius. As proconsul Pompey* was staying behind at Rome—despite the fact that he had command of an army—for the sake of the Republic; so at the same time Caesar requested Pompey to order the troops he had levied as consul from Cisalpine Gaul to muster and march to join him in Gaul. Caesar believed that it was vital for the future, in order to match Gaul's opinion of her capabilities, that Italy should appear to possess extensive resources; sufficient, in fact, not only to repair quickly any set-back suffered in the course of a campaign but also to reinforce her army still further. When Pompey had satisfied his obligation both to the Republic and to his friendship with Caesar, the latter's legates swiftly concluded the levy; and before the winter was over three legions had been formed and brought to him in Gaul,* and he had replaced the number of cohorts lost by Sabinus twice over. His speed and strength of numbers proved clearly what the resources and military organization of the Roman people could achieve.

(2) After the death of Indutiomarus which we described, the Treveri transferred supreme rule to his kinsmen, who did not give up seeking support from their German neighbours and promising them money.* After failing to persuade those nearby, they tested the will of those further off, and found a number of states. The swearing of an oath fixed their confederacy, and they exchanged hostages as a guarantee for the money. They joined forces with Ambiorix in a league of alliance.

After Caesar learned of this he saw war being prepared on every side—the Nervii, Aduatuci, and Menapii, together with all the Germans on this side of the Rhine, were in arms. The Senones did not come when he commanded them, and were taking counsel with the Carnutes and neighbouring states, while frequent embassies from the Treveri were urging the Germans to support them; then he decided he must consider war, and quickly.

(3) Thus winter was not yet over when Caesar assembled his four nearest legions and suddenly headed for the land of the Nervii. Before they could either muster or flee he had seized large numbers of men and cattle and turned them over to his soldiers as booty, and then ravaged the fields: he forced them to surrender and give him hostages. This business was quickly concluded, and afterwards he led his legions back to winter quarters. In early spring he called an assembly of Gaul as was his practice; all the Gauls except for the Senones, Carnutes, and Treveri arrived. He therefore judged that this moment marked the beginning of war and of their defection. To give the impression that he regarded everything else as of secondary importance, he shifted the assembly to Lutetia among the Parisii, who were neighbours of the Senones, and in our fathers' time had joined with them in one state; they were not thought to be involved in the conspiracy. Caesar's decision to change venue was announced from his platform, and the same day he set off with his legions against the Senones, and reached their land by forced marches.

(4) On learning of his arrival Acco, who was the ring-leader of the conspiracy, ordered the people to assemble in the towns. They tried to do so, but before they could assemble news came that the Romans were at hand. They were obliged to abandon their purpose and sent envoys to Caesar to beg for mercy, approaching him through the Aedui (for a long time their state had been under the Aedui's protection). At the Aedui's request Caesar freely pardoned them and accepted their excuses, for he judged that summer was a time for active campaigning, not for holding inquiries. He ordered them to surrender a hundred hostages, whom he entrusted to the custody of the Aedui. At the same time the Carnutes sent

envoys and hostages, employing the Remi (whose dependants* they were) to plead their cause. They received a similar
response. Caesar brought the assembly to a close and requisitioned cavalry from the Gallic states.

(5) Now that this region of Gaul was pacified Caesar
concentrated heart and mind entirely on the war with the
Treveri and Ambiorix. He ordered Cavarinus and the cavalry
of the Senones to set out with him, to stem any unrest brew-
ing among that people because of either Cavarinus' quick
temper or the hatred which he had earned. These matters
were now settled; but he was certain that Ambiorix would
not engage in a pitched battle and so began to consider what
strategies were left open to him. Near the borders of the
Eburones were the Menapii, protected by their continuous
stretches of marsh and woodland: of all the Gauls, only this
people had never sent envoys to Caesar to negotiate peace.
He knew that friendship existed between them and Ambiorix;
he was also aware that, through the Treveri, they had formed
an alliance of friendship with the Germans. He judged it
essential to detach these sources of assistance from Ambiorix
before launching a campaign against him. Otherwise Ambiorix
might panic for his own safety and hide among the Menapii,
or be forced to join up with the peoples over the Rhine. This
was the strategy Caesar adopted. He sent the whole army's
baggage to Labienus among the Treveri and ordered two
legions to set out and join him. Caesar himself set out for the
territory of the Menapii, leading five legions now unencumbered by baggage. The Menapii did not muster a force, but
relied on the protection offered by their geographical location: they fled into the woods and marshes and took their
property with them.

(6) Caesar divided his force with his legate Gaius Fabius
and quaestor Marcus Crassus, quickly constructed causeways
over the marshes, and advanced in three divisions, setting fire
to buildings and settlements and seizing a large number of
cattle and people. These actions compelled the Menapii to
send him envoys to sue for peace. He accepted their hostages
and assured them that he would count them among his enemies if they received Ambiorix or his legates within their

borders. These matters settled, Caesar left Commius the Atrebatian and some cavalry as a guard among the Menapii, and then set off against the Treveri.

(7) While Caesar was dealing with this situation the Treveri had mustered a large force of infantry and cavalry and were making ready to attack Labienus and his single legion (which had wintered in their territory). By now they were no more than two days' journey away from him, when they discovered that two legions sent by Caesar had arrived. They pitched camp fourteen miles off, and decided to await German reinforcements. Labienus discovered the enemy's plan, and hoped that their rashness would bring about some opportunity for engagement, so he left a garrison of five cohorts to guard the baggage and set out against the enemy with twenty-five cohorts and a large cavalry force. He constructed a camp at a distance of one mile from the Treveri. Between Labienus and the enemy was a river, difficult to ford and with steep banks. He himself had no intention of crossing it, and did not expect the enemy to do so either, for their hope of seeing the reinforcements was increasing daily.

At a council, Labienus made a public declaration: since the Germans were rumoured to be on their way he would not put his own and the army's fortunes at risk, but at dawn the next day he would strike camp and move out. This news was speedily reported to the enemy, for among so many Gallic cavalrymen native feeling compelled at least some of them to support the Gallic cause. By night Labienus summoned the military tribunes and senior centurions and set out his strategy —to encourage the enemy to suspect a panic, he gave orders that the camp should be struck with more uproar and upheaval than is customary for the Roman people. By this means he created the impression that their departure was a flight. So close were the two camps that before dawn these movements were reported by scouts to the enemy.

(8) When the rear of our column had scarcely marched outside the camp's defences, the Gauls began to spur each other on not to let the booty they hoped for slip from their grasp. Now that the Romans were in a panic, they reasoned, it would take too long to wait for German reinforcements;

and their sense of dignity did not allow them to hesitate about attacking such a small army—especially one fleeing and struggling with baggage—with their substantial force. Without delay they crossed the river and engaged in combat on disadvantageous ground.

Labienus anticipated what would happen, and to lure them all across the river he kept up the same pretence of marching away and calmly continued his progress. Then he sent the baggage on a little way ahead and piled it on a mound. 'Soldiers,' he said, 'you have the chance you have been look-ing for: you have the enemy on difficult and uneven ground. Now show the same courage under my leadership as you have often shown to our commander, Caesar. Imagine that he is present and looking on in person.' He ordered the standards to be turned to face the enemy, and the men to form up for battle; then he sent a few squadrons of cavalry to guard the baggage and posted the rest of the cavalry on the flanks. The war-cry went up and our men quickly threw their javelins at the enemy, who, contrary to their expecta-tion, saw men they thought were running away instead marching towards them on the attack. Not only did they fail to withstand this onslaught, at the first charge they scattered in flight and made for the nearby woods. Labienus pursued them with his cavalry, killed many, and captured a consider-able number. A few days later he received back the allegiance of the Treveri. When the Germans who were on their way with reinforcements heard of the flight of the Treveri they returned home. The kinsmen of Indutiomarus who had started the conspiracy accompanied them as they departed from that people. Leadership and rule was handed over to Cingetorix, who, as we showed, remained loyal from the beginning.

(9) When Caesar arrived among the Treveri from the Menapii he decided for two reasons to cross the Rhine. The first of these was that Germans had sent reinforcements against him to the Treveri; the second was to prevent Ambiorix find-ing refuge among them. Following this decision, he decided to construct a bridge a short way upstream from where he had previously taken the army across. Now that the method of construction was established as well known, the task was

completed, thanks to the strenuous efforts of the soldiers, within a few days. Caesar left a strong garrison at the bridge among the Treveri to stop them causing sudden disturbances, and took the rest of his troops and the cavalry across. The Ubii had previously given him hostages and surrendered to him; to justify themselves they sent Caesar envoys who were to explain that no reinforcements had been sent from their state to the Treveri, nor had they broken their word. They begged and pleaded with him to spare them, and not to let a blanket hatred of Germans result in the innocent paying the penalty for the guilty. If he wanted more hostages, they promised to provide them. Caesar heard their explanation and learned that the reinforcements had been sent by the Suebi. He accepted the Ubii's excuse, and made careful inquiries as to the route of entry to the land of the Suebi.

(10) Meanwhile, after a few days the Ubii informed Caesar that the Suebi were mustering all their forces at a single location, and declaring to the peoples under their rule that they must send infantry and cavalry reinforcements. Once this was made known, Caesar secured the corn supply and selected a suitable place for a camp. He ordered the Ubii to bring their cattle and all their property from the fields into the towns, in the hope that the Suebi, who were ignorant barbarians, would be affected by the lack of food supplies and so could be drawn into fighting on unequal terms. He told them to send scouts to the Suebi at frequent intervals to find out what they were doing. They carried out his orders and after a few days' interval reported back—once reliable news of the Roman army arrived, all the Suebi, with all their own forces and the allied forces which they had mustered, had retreated deep into their most distant territory. There was a forest there of immense size, called the Bacenis: it extended far into their land and formed a natural barrier preventing the Cherusci and Suebi from raiding and inflicting damage on one another. On the edge of this forest the Suebi had decided to await the Romans' arrival.

(11) Since this point has now been reached, it seems not inappropriate to give an account of the customs of Gaul and Germany and the differences between these two nations.

In Gaul there are factions,* not only in every state and every village and district but practically in each individual household as well. The leaders of these factions are the men who in the Gauls' judgement are thought to have the greatest authority; the conclusion of all actions and counsels is referred to their decision and judgement. And so it seems for this reason to be a long-established rule that no ordinary citizen should go without assistance against a man of higher rank and influence. No leader allows his own people to be oppressed and cheated, for if he does he cannot maintain his authority among them.

The same structure holds throughout Gaul as a whole: for all the states are grouped into two parties. (12) When Caesar came to Gaul the Aedui were the leaders of one faction and the Sequani the leaders of the other. From ancient times the Aedui had possessed the highest authority, and their dependants were very numerous, so when the Sequani became less strong in themselves they made an alliance with Ariovistus and the Germans and persuaded them on to their side by means of great expenditure and promises. Then they fought a number of successful battles and, once all the Aeduan aristocracy were dead, they so surpassed the Aedui in power as to win over a large number of their dependants and accept the sons of their leaders as hostages, forcing these men to swear publicly that they would never plot against the Sequani. They also forcibly occupied a section of the neighbouring territory which they had seized, and won supreme control of all Gaul.

This was the necessity which had forced Diviciacus to set off for Rome and the Senate to seek assistance, but he had returned without success. Caesar's arrival brought about a change in this state of affairs. The Aedui got their hostages back, the old relationships of patronage were restored, and new ones effected through Caesar, because those who had allied themselves in friendship with the Aedui saw that they enjoyed better terms and conditions of government, while in other respects their influence and prestige was increased. Thus the Sequani lost supreme control.

Their place was filled by the Remi. Once people realized that they were just as highly favoured by Caesar, those who

because of ancient feuds could not ally themselves with the
Aedui declared themselves instead to be dependants under
the Remi's patronage. The Remi took care to protect these
people, and so held on to their new and suddenly acquired
authority. At that time the state of affairs was such that the
Aedui were considered by far the most important leaders,
while the Remi came second in prestige.

(13) In the whole of Gaul two types of men are counted
as being of worth and distinction. The ordinary people are
considered almost as slaves: they dare do nothing on their
own account and are not called to counsels. When the majority are oppressed by debt or heavy tribute, or harmed by
powerful men, they swear themselves away into slavery to
the aristocracy, who then have the same rights over them as
masters do over their slaves. Of the two types of men of
distinction, however, the first is made up of the druids, and
the other of the knights.

The druids are involved in matters of religion. They manage public and private sacrifices and interpret religious customs
and ceremonies. Young men flock to them in large numbers
to gain instruction, and they hold the druids in great esteem.
For they decide almost all disputes, both public and private:
if some crime has been committed, if there has been murder
done, if there is a dispute over an inheritance or over territory, they decide the issue and settle the rewards and penalties.
If any individual or group of people does not abide by their
decision, the druids ban them from sacrifices. This is their
most severe punishment. Those who are banned in this way
are counted among the wicked and criminal: everyone shuns
them and avoids approaching or talking to them, so as not to
suffer any harm from contact with them. If they seek help at
law, they receive no justice, and they are never given positions of prestige. A chief druid rules over all the rest and has
supreme authority among them. When such a man dies, if
there is an outstanding druid among those remaining he
succeeds to this position, but if there are a number of equal
ability, they decide the leadership by a vote of all the druids,
and sometimes even in armed combat. At a certain time of year
they sit in judgement in a sacred spot in the territory of the

Carnutes, in an area right in the middle of Gaul. Everyone who has a dispute comes to this place from every region, and submits to their decisions and judgements. It is believed that this institution was discovered in Britain and transferred to Gaul; and nowadays those who want to understand these matters in more detail usually travel to Britain to learn about them.

(14) Druids are not accustomed to take part in war, nor do they pay taxes like the rest of the people. They are exempt from military service and from all obligations. Such great rewards encourage many to begin training, either of their own accord or sent by parents and relatives. There they are told to memorize a large number of lines of poetry, and so some spend twenty years in training. Nor do they think it proper to commit this teaching to writing, although for almost all other purposes, including public and private accounts, they use Greek characters. They seem to me to have adopted this practice for two reasons: first, they do not want their teaching spread abroad, and secondly, if those in training rely on written texts they concentrate less on memory. And in fact it does often happen that students who have writing as a safeguard abandon the effort to learn by heart and use their memory. The principal doctrine they attempt to impart is that souls do not die but after death cross from one person to another. Because the fear of death is thereby set aside, they consider this a strong inducement to physical courage. Besides this, they debate many subjects and teach them to their young men—for example, the stars and their movements, the size of the universe and the earth, the nature of things, and the strength and power of the immortal gods.*

(15) The second class is that composed of the knights. When necessity arises and some war flares up—which before Caesar's arrival used to happen almost every year, so that they were either on the offensive themselves or fending off attacks—they are all involved in the campaign. Each man has as many retainers* and dependants about him as is appropriate to his status in terms of his birth and resources. This is the sole form of power and influence they know.

(16) The whole of the Gallic nation is much given to religious practices. For this reason those who are afflicted with

serious illnesses and those who are involved in battles and danger either offer human sacrifice or vow that they will do so, and employ the druids to manage these sacrifices. For they believe that unless one human life is offered for another the power and presence of the immortal gods cannot be propitiated. They also hold state sacrifices of a similar kind. Some of them use huge images of the gods,* and fill their limbs, which are woven from wicker, with living people. When these images are set on fire the people inside are engulfed in flames and killed. They believe that the gods are more pleased by such punishment when it is inflicted upon those who are caught engaged in theft or robbery or other crimes; but if there is a lack of people of this kind, they will even stoop to punishing the guiltless.

(17) The god they worship most of all is Mercury. There are many images of him, and they say that he is the inventor of all the arts and the director of ways and journeys; they believe that he has greatest power over the pursuit of profit and matters of trade. After him they worship Apollo, Mars, Jupiter, and Minerva.* They have practically the same views about these gods as other peoples do—Apollo wards off disease, Minerva imparts the principles of craft skills, Jupiter wields power over the heavens, and Mars controls wars. When they have decided to engage in battle it is to Mars that they will dedicate most of what they may take in the fight. When victorious, they sacrifice the animals they have captured and gather all the rest of the spoils in one place. In many states one may see mounds made out of such objects in holy places, and rarely does it happen that anyone defies the bounds of religion and dares to hide away his spoils at home, or steal them away once they are placed on the mound. The most serious penalty, including torture, is set down for such behaviour.

(18) The Gauls claim that they are all descended from one father, Dis,* and they say that this is the teaching of the druids. For this reason they define the passage of time by nights rather than days: they observe birthdays and the start of months and years in this way, with day coming after night.* As for their mode of life in other respects, they differ from other peoples in that they do not allow their own sons

to approach them in public until they have grown up and can undertake military duties: they consider it a disgrace for a son who is still only a boy to place himself publicly in his father's sight.

(19) After reckoning up the sum, a husband adds to whatever sum of money he has received from his wife as a dowry a similar amount from his own goods. An account is kept of this joint sum of money and the profits are saved. Then whichever partner survives the other receives the joint portion with the accrued profits of previous years. Men have the power of life and death over their wives as over their children. When the head of a noble family dies his kinsmen assemble and, if there is any suspicious circumstance surrounding his death, they interrogate his wives as they would slaves.* If anything is discovered, terrible tortures are inflicted and then they are put to death. By the standards of their civilization Gallic funerals are full of pomp and splendour: they throw on to the pyre everything which they believe was precious to the persons concerned during their lifetime, even living creatures. Indeed, not long before the era recorded in this account slaves and dependants who were thought to be dear to the departed were burned with them at the end of the funeral rites.

(20) The states which are thought to run their public affairs most judiciously have a legal ordinance that if anyone hears rumours or tidings affecting the state from neighbouring peoples, he is to report it to the magistrate and not to discuss it with anyone else.* This is because it is well known that often men who are impetuous and inexperienced are frightened by false rumours and driven into wrongdoing or making decisions about matters of great importance. The magistrates conceal information where it is expedient, and where they judge it appropriate they make it known to the people. It is not permitted to speak about the state except at an assembly.

(21) The customs of the Germans are very different from those of the Gauls. They have no druids to preside over religious matters, nor do they concern themselves with sacrifices. The only things which they count as gods are things

they can see and which clearly benefit them, for example, the Sun, Vulcan,* and the Moon. They have not even heard rumours of any others. They spend their whole life in hunting and military activity, and from childhood they are eager for hard work and endurance. Those who have remained chaste the longest win the highest praise among their own people: some believe that it makes them taller, others that it gives them greater strength and determination. They consider it a matter for shame to have sexual intercourse with a woman before reaching the age of 20—nor does the matter allow for concealment, for both sexes mingle together when they wash themselves in the rivers, and also they wear hides and skins which offer little protection, leaving most of the body naked.

(22) They do not practise agriculture, and the majority of their food consists of milk, cheese, and meat. No one possesses a fixed area of land or estates of his own: rather, every year the magistrates and leading citizens assign each family and clan who have joined forces a tract of land of an appropriate size and location. Then after a year they oblige these men to move on. They cite many reasons for this practice: to prevent people either being ensnared by continuous habit and adopting agriculture in place of their enthusiasm for war; or trying to obtain large estates, the strong driving the weak out of their properties; or building too carefully with the intention of avoiding extreme cold and heat; or to stop the desire for money springing up, for from this arise factions and dissent; or finally, to keep the ordinary people content, since each man can see that his own possessions are equal to those of the men in power.

(23) The highest praise among the German states goes to those who ravage their borders and so maintain the widest unpopulated area around themselves. They think it a true mark of bravery to drive neighbouring peoples from their land and force them to make way, so no one dares to dwell nearby. At the same time they think that this will make them safer by removing the threat of unexpected invasion. In warfare, either when a state wards off attack or when it goes on the offensive, magistrates are chosen to head the campaign and to have the power of life and death. They have no

overall magistrates in peacetime, but the leaders of individual districts and settlements dispense justice among their own people and settle disputes. There is no discredit attached to acts of robbery which take place outside the borders of each state: in fact, they claim that these take place to train their young men and reduce their laziness. And besides, when one of the leaders states at an assembly that he will take command, and that those who wish to support him must declare themselves, then the men who approve him and his cause rise up, pledge their assistance, and win praise from the people. Any who pledge assistance but then do not support him are considered deserters and traitors, and their word is distrusted in every respect from then on. They consider it wrong to violate the obligations of hospitality: they protect their guests from harm, whatever the reason for their presence among them, and treat them as sacrosanct. They open all their houses to such guests and share their food with them.

(24) There was a time when the Gauls were more courageous than the Germans and took offensive military action against them. Because of their high population density and lack of land, they sent colonies across the Rhine. Thus the Volcae Tectosages seized the most fertile areas of Germany, around the Hercynian forest, and settled there. I understand that this forest was known by report to Eratosthenes and certain of the Greeks, but they called it the Orcynian forest.* This people still dwells in the same territory to this day, and has a fine reputation for justice and military glory. These days they endure the same state of poverty, privation, and hardship as the Germans, and have the same kind of food and clothing. The Gauls, on the other hand, live close to the Province and are familiar with imported goods, and this entails an abundant supply of items both luxurious and functional. The Gauls gradually grew accustomed to being defeated, and were beaten in many battles, so now they do not reckon themselves to be even equal in bravery to the Germans.

(25) It takes nine days' march for someone to cross the Hercynian forest (which was mentioned above) travelling light. Its size cannot be described more accurately, for the Germans have no means of measuring units of distance. It begins in

the lands of the Helvetii, Nemetes, and Raurici, runs parallel to the straight course of the River Danube, and reaches to the lands of the Daci and Anartes. At this point it swings to the left in regions away from the river, and because of its great size extends to the borders of many peoples. No one in this part of Germany can claim to have reached its furthest edge—despite journeying for sixty days—or to have heard where it begins. It is agreed that many species of wild animal live there which are not found anywhere else: the most unusual of these, which deserve to be recorded, are described below.*

(26) There is an ox shaped like a stag. In the middle of its forehead a single horn grows between its ears, taller and straighter than the animal horns with which we are familiar. At the top this horn spreads out like the palm of a hand or the branches of a tree. The females are of the same form as the males, and their horns are the same shape and size.*

(27) There are also animals called elks.* Their shape and dappled coat are like those of goats, but they are rather larger, have stunted horns, and legs without joints. They do not lie down to sleep: if they are struck by some unexpected misfortune and fall down, they cannot raise themselves or get up again. They use trees as couches, leaning against them to secure a modicum of repose and so taking their rest. When hunters track their spoor and find their customary resting-place they either weaken the base of the trees there by digging the earth out from under them, or they cut through them—thus the impression is given that the trees are still standing. When the elks lean against the trees as usual, their weight knocks them over: elk and tree fall down together.

(28) A third species of animal is the wild ox.* They are slightly smaller than elephants, and in appearance, colour, and shape they resemble bulls. They are extremely fierce and swift-footed, and attack people and animals on sight. The Germans carefully trap them in pits, and then slaughter them. Such tasks make the young German men tough, and this type of hunting gives them training. Those who kill the most wild oxen display the horns in public as a proof, which wins them considerable acclaim. The oxen cannot grow accustomed to people, or become tame, even if they are caught when young.

The size, appearance, and shape of their horns are very different from the horns of our own cattle. These horns are much prized: the Germans give them a rim of silver and use them as drinking-vessels at magnificent feasts.

(29) Once Caesar learned from the Ubian scouts that the Suebi had retreated to the forest, he became anxious about the corn supply, because (as we explained above) the Germans hardly practise agriculture. So he decided not to proceed further.* None the less, to prevent the barbarians losing all fear of his return, and to hold up their reinforcements, he withdrew his army and broke up a 200-foot length of the bridge at its farthest end, which touched the bank in the territory of the Ubii. At the Gallic end of the bridge he set a four-storey tower and stationed a garrison of twelve cohorts to guard the bridge; he fortified the post with strong defences. He put the young Gaius Volcatius Tullus in charge of the station and garrison. When the corn began to ripen Caesar set off for the campaign against Ambiorix through the Ardennes forest. This forest is the largest in Gaul and stretches from the banks of the Rhine and the land of the Treveri to the Nervii: it is more than 460 miles across.* Caesar sent Lucius Minucius Basilus ahead with all the cavalry, to see if he could gain any advantage by marching swiftly and seizing an opportune moment. He told Basilus to forbid the lighting of fires in camp, so as to prevent any early warning of his approach, and said that he would follow up at once.

(30) Basilus did as he was ordered. Contrary to everyone's expectation the march was quickly completed and he caught many of the people off guard and still in the fields. Acting on their information he made straight for Ambiorix himself at the spot where he was said to be with a few of his cavalry. Fortune* is indeed powerful in all things, and especially in military affairs: for it was by purest chance that he came upon Ambiorix while he was off guard and unprepared. The first people knew of Basilus' arrival was when they saw it— they heard no report or tidings of it. It was equally the operation of fortune that after all his military equipment had been seized, and his horses and carriages captured, Ambiorix himself escaped death. This happened because the building

was surrounded by trees (as are most Gallic dwellings—to avoid the heat they usually look for sites close to woods and rivers), and in such a confined space his friends and comrades held off the assault of our cavalry for a time. During the fight one of his men set him on a horse, and the woods closed over the fugitive. In this way fortune played a part in bringing Ambiorix into danger, and in allowing him to escape.

(31) It is a moot point whether it was deliberate that Ambiorix did not assemble his forces (because he decided not to give battle) or whether he was barred and prevented from doing so by lack of time and the unexpected arrival of our cavalry, and believed that the rest of our army was following behind. It is certain, however, that he sent messengers throughout the land, with orders that each man should look out for himself. Some of his men escaped into the Ardennes forest, others into the long stretches of marshland. Those who were close to the Ocean hid themselves in areas which the tides tend to turn into islands. Many left their own borders and entrusted themselves and their property to total strangers. Catuvolcus, who was king over half the Eburones, and who had joined in this strategy with Ambiorix, was now an old man. He could not endure the effort of either war or exile, and denounced Ambiorix with curses for initiating the plot. Then he killed himself by eating from the yew, a tree which is very widespread in Gaul and Germany.

(32) The Segni and Condrusi, who are to be counted among the German people and who live between the Eburones and the Treveri, sent envoys to Caesar to beg him not to consider them among the number of his enemies, or to judge all the Germans this side of the Rhine to be united in a common purpose. They had never considered war, they had never sent reinforcements to Ambiorix. Caesar investigated the problem by interrogating prisoners, and gave orders that if any of the Eburones had fled to these peoples, and were now gathered there, they must be returned to him. If they did as he ordered, he stated that he would not invade their territory. Then he divided his force in three, and took the heavy baggage of all the legions to Aduatuca. This was the name of a stronghold, practically in the centre of the territory of the

Eburones, where Sabinus and Cotta had settled for the winter. Caesar approved its site for a number of reasons, and in particular because the defence-works constructed in the previous year were still whole, which would spare the efforts of his soldiers. He left the Fourteenth legion, which was one of the three so recently enrolled from Italy, to guard the baggage. He put Quintus Tullius Cicero in charge of this legion and of the camp, and assigned him 200 cavalry.

(33) After dividing up the army Caesar ordered Titus Labienus to take three legions and set out towards the Ocean, to the regions which border the lands of the Menapii. He sent Gaius Trebonius with an equal number of legions to devastate the region bordering the lands of the Aduatuci. He himself decided to take the remaining three legions and march to the River Scheldt,* which flows into the Meuse, and to the farthest reaches of the Ardennes, for he was receiving reports that Ambiorix had headed there with a few cavalry. At his departure Caesar declared that he would return after seven days, on the day when he knew the corn ration was due for the legion which was left behind as a garrison. He urged Labienus and Trebonius to return on that day if they were able to do so without harming the national interest, so that they could discuss their plans, scrutinize the enemy's strategy, and give a fresh impetus to the campaign.

(34) As we explained above, there was no distinct force, no stronghold, no garrison to defend itself in arms. Rather, the whole population was widely scattered. Each one of them had taken up position wherever some secluded valley, wooded location, or impenetrable marsh provided any hope of safety or defence. These places were familiar to the people living nearby. Thus it was a matter requiring considerable care, not to protect the army as a whole (for no danger could befall a united force at the hands of frightened and scattered men), but to keep the individual soldiers safe. This problem, however, did to some extent affect the safety of the whole army. For the desire for booty lured large numbers of them farther afield, while the woods with their strange and hidden tracks prevented them marching in close formation. If Caesar wanted an end of the business, and the execution of a race

of criminals, he must send out more groups of men and disperse the soldiers more widely. If, on the other hand, he wanted his maniples* to remain in formation, as the established and customary tactics of the Roman army required, the actual locality would act as protection for the barbarians—and certain individuals among them were daring enough to set up secret ambushes and encircle scattered Roman soldiers. So far as was possible in such a difficult situation, what could be anticipated—with care—*was* anticipated. Caesar preferred to overlook a chance to inflict injury, even though everyone's heart was burning for revenge, rather than inflict it but do some harm to his soldiers in the process. He sent messengers to the neighbouring states and summoned them all to come in search of booty, and pillage the Eburones. In this way the lives of Gauls, rather than those of legionary soldiers, were put at risk in the woods. At the same time, once this host had surrounded them, the race and name of the Eburones would be wiped out as a punishment for their crime. A large number quickly assembled from every direction.

(35) All this was taking place in every part of the Eburones' territory, and the seventh day was approaching, when Caesar had decided to return to the baggage and the legion. In this the power of Fortune in war, and the great changes of circumstance she brings about, were plain to see. For the enemy, as we explained, was scattered and terrified, and there was no force capable of inflicting even the slightest cause for panic. News had reached the Germans across the Rhine that the Eburones were being pillaged and moreover that everyone was being summoned to join in the hunt for booty. The Sugambri, who live beside the Rhine and who (as we described above) had given refuge to the fleeing Tencteri and Usipetes, mustered 2,000 cavalry. They crossed the Rhine by ship and boat thirty miles downstream of where Caesar had built the bridge and left a garrison behind.

The Sugambri first drew near to the Eburones' borders and captured many of them as they were scattered in flight. They also seized a large number of cattle, which are highly prized by these barbarians. Lured on by the prospect of booty, they advanced further. Neither marsh nor forest stood in the way of these Germans, men born to war and depredation. They asked their prisoners where Caesar was to be found, and learned that he had advanced further and that his whole army had left. Then one of the prisoners said: 'Why are you setting off in pursuit of wretched and scanty loot when you now have the chance of extreme good fortune? Within three hours you can reach Aduatuca, where the Roman army has gathered all its riches. The garrison is so small it cannot even man the wall, and no one dares to venture outside the defences.' Once this expectation opened up the Germans left the plunder they had already taken in a hidden place and made for Aduatuca, following as their guide the very man whose information had led to this discovery.

(36) Throughout all the preceding days Quintus Cicero had been extremely careful to keep the soldiers in camp, as Caesar had instructed. He had not even permitted any of the orderlies to go outside the defences. On the seventh day, however, he gave up hope that Caesar would keep his word about the number of days he would be gone, for he heard that Caesar had advanced further, yet no news reached him of his return. At the same time, Cicero began to be disturbed by the soldiers saying that—inasmuch as no one was permitted to leave camp—his persistence in waiting there virtually amounted to a siege. Moreover, since nine legions and a large cavalry force were on the offensive, while the enemy was scattered and practically wiped out, he did not anticipate that any serious misfortune could occur within three miles of camp. So he sent five cohorts to the nearest fields to fetch corn. There was nothing between the cornfields and the camp but a single hill. Several of the legionaries had been left behind sick; about 300 of them, who by then had regained their health, were sent out together in a separate detachment. Once permission was granted, there went with them a company of orderlies and a large number of pack-horses (which had been left behind in camp).

(37) At this critical moment the German cavalry chanced to arrive, and straight away, keeping the same course by which they had come, tried to invade the camp through the main gate.* Because the trees were in the way on that side they

were not observed until they were actually approaching the camp, with the result that the traders who were encamped under the rampart had no chance to withdraw. Our men, caught unawares by this unexpected event, were thrown into confusion and the cohort on guard barely withstood the first assault. The enemy poured round the other sides of the camp, looking for a way in. Our men just managed to defend the gates—the nature of the site itself, combined with the defence-works, protected the other possible entrance-points. There was panic throughout the camp, some men asking others the reason for the uproar. No one made provision for where the standards must be shifted to, or where the men were to assemble. One man declared that the camp was already taken, another that the barbarians had arrived after the Roman army and its commander had been wiped out. Most of the men conjured up strange superstitious fantasies because of where they were—they visualized the disaster which befell Cotta and Sabinus, who had fallen in the same stronghold. Every one of them was thrown into panic by such fears, and this strengthened the belief of the barbarians that, as the prisoner had told them, there was no garrison within the camp. They tried to break through and urged themselves not to let such a great piece of good fortune slip from their grasp.

(38) Left behind with the garrison, because he was ill, was one Publius Sextius Baculus. He had been one of Caesar's senior centurions (we mentioned* his part in previous battles), and by now had gone five days without food. Baculus was anxious for his own safety and everyone else's, and emerged unarmed from his tent. He saw the enemy looming close and the issue coming to a crisis, so he seized weapons from men standing nearby and took his stand at the gate. The centurions of the cohort which had been on guard-duty followed his lead, and together they held off the attack for a short while. Baculus was badly wounded and lost consciousness: by dragging him back from hand to hand, they just saved him. Thanks to this respite the rest of the men found enough strength to dare to man the defences and offer a show of resistance.

(39) Meanwhile, after the gathering of corn was completed our soldiers heard the shouting. The cavalry hurried ahead and discovered the dangerous situation. The men were thoroughly frightened, but had no defences to retreat behind: they were recent recruits with no experience of military action, and turned expectantly to the military tribunes and centurions, waiting for them to issue orders. No one is so brave that unfamiliar circumstances will not cause him agitation. The barbarians caught sight of the standards in the distance, and left off the siege. At first they assumed that the legions, which according to the prisoners' information had moved some distance away, were returned; but then, feeling only scorn for such a small body of troops, they attacked on all sides.

(40) The orderlies ran ahead to the nearest hill. They were quickly ejected from this position and rushed in among the standards and maniples, which made the soldiers all the more frightened. Some of the men proposed adopting a wedge formation to break through quickly, since the camp was so close and they were sure that even if one section was surrounded and fell, the rest could be saved. Others suggested making a stand on the hill, so that they would all endure the same fate. The veteran soldiers (who, as we mentioned, had been sent out together in a separate detachment) did not agree with this latter proposal. So they encouraged each other, and then, under the leadership of Gaius Trebonius, a Roman knight who had been put in charge of them, they charged through the midst of the enemy and reached camp, every one of them unharmed. The orderlies and cavalry followed on as part of the same charge, and were saved by the bravery of the soldiers. Despite this display, the men who had taken their stand on the hill remained in total ignorance of military tactics: they were unable to stick to the strategy they had adopted (to defend themselves from a higher position), and equally unable to imitate the force and speed which they had seen the others display. So when they tried to make their way back to camp they came down on to unfavourable ground. There were a number of centurions who, because of their bravery, had been transferred from the lower ranks of the

other legions to the higher ranks of this. They were reluctant
to lose their previously good military reputation, and instead
fell, fighting with great courage. Once their courage had forced
the enemy back, some of the soldiers reached camp unharmed
—contrary to expectation; others were surrounded by the
barbarians and killed.

(41) The Germans gave up hope of storming the camp
because they saw that our men were posted at the defences.
They retreated over the Rhine, taking with them the booty
they had hidden in the forest. Even after the enemy's departure there was such panic that during the night, when Gaius
Volusenus (who had been sent with the cavalry) came to the
camp, he could not make the soldiers believe that Caesar was
at hand with his army intact. Panic, indeed, had seized control of their minds so completely that they almost took leave
of their senses, and started declaring that the cavalry had
retreated from battle after all Caesar's forces had been wiped
out, and that if his army had been unharmed the Germans
would not have tried to besiege the camp. Caesar's arrival
put an end to these fears.

(42) Caesar was not inexperienced in the chances of battle,
so on his return he made only one criticism—namely, that
the cohorts had been sent out from their outposts and garrison. He judged that not even the slightest opportunity for
mischance to occur should have been allowed; and that Fortune had shown her strength by the sudden arrival of the
enemy, and still more in turning the barbarians away practically from the rampart itself and the gates of the camp. The
most remarkable thing in all this was the fact that although the
Germans had crossed the Rhine with the intention of ravaging the lands of Ambiorix, by making a detour to the Roman
camp they had done him the greatest service imaginable.

(43) Caesar set out once again to harass the Eburones.
He collected a great host from the neighbouring states and
sent them out in all directions. Every settlement, every building which any of the men caught sight of was set on fire.
Everywhere cattle were driven off. The corn was not only
consumed by huge numbers of pack-animals and people, but
also flattened because of the stormy weather at that time of

year. The result was that any people at present in hiding seemed likely to die for lack of provisions when the army withdrew. This large cavalry force was divided into small groups and sent out in all directions; and it frequently happened that when prisoners were taken they would look around them as if they had just then caught a glimpse of Ambiorix as he fled, and as if he was barely out of sight. The result was that they had great hopes of catching him, and went to enormous trouble, thinking that they would win the highest favour with Caesar. Their efforts were almost superhuman, but always it seemed that something of the highest good fortune was lacking: for Ambiorix repeatedly escaped from hiding-places or woods, making for other regions and areas under cover of darkness. He had only four cavalrymen as his guard; to them alone did he dare to entrust his life.

(44) After ravaging the region in this manner Caesar took his army, minus two cohorts, back to Durocortorum, a town of the Remi. There he called a Gallic assembly and held an inquiry into the plot of the Senones and Carnutes. The ringleader of the plot, Acco, was condemned to death and was punished in accordance with ancestral custom.* Some men were afraid of a trial and fled, and these he outlawed.* He sent two legions to winter on the borders of the Treveri, two to the Lingones, and the other six at Agedincum in the territory among the Senones. When he had ensured the army's supply of corn he set out for Italy as usual to hold assizes.

The Seventh Book: 52 BC

(AUC 702: Sole Consul, Pompey)

Vercingetorix and the Great Revolt

(1) Now Gaul was pacified, Caesar set out for Italy to hold assizes as arranged. There he learned of the murder of Publius Clodius. When he heard news of the senate's decree that all men of an age to do military service must take the oath, he decided to hold a levy throughout his province.*

News of this was quickly brought to Transalpine Gaul. The Gauls exaggerated the reports, and embellished them with rumours, as the occasion seemed to require: Caesar, they said, was being detained because of a revolt at Rome, and was unable to join his army because of the serious unrest. Those who had previously lamented their subjection to the rule of the Roman people now had an opportunity to begin planning a strategy of war more freely and with greater daring.

The Gallic leaders called an assembly in a remote forest location. There they deplored the execution of Acco,* and declared that the same fate could befall them. They bemoaned Gaul's collective lot, and offered all kinds of pledges and prizes in the search for people prepared to start a war and risk their own lives to set Gaul free. First of all, they said, a strategy for cutting Caesar off from his army was essential, before their secret negotiations were revealed. This would be simple, because the legions would not dare to leave winter quarters without their commander, and the commander would not be able to reach his legions without an armed escort. Finally, they agreed, it was preferable to die in battle rather than fail to recover their former military reputation and the freedom which they had inherited from their ancestors.*

(2) Following this debate the Carnutes declared that there was no risk they would not undergo for the good of all, and they promised to take the overall lead in initiating hostilities. For the time being the Gauls could not use hostages to pro-vide guarantees between themselves, for fear their plan should

leak out, so they sought to solemnize it with an oath and pledge, putting their military standards together (a rite of the greatest sanctity). This was to ensure that they would not be deserted by the rest after the war had been started. The Carnutes were warmly congratulated, the oath was taken by all who were present, the timing of their action was decided, and the meeting broke up.

(3) When the day came and the signal was given, the Carnutes charged on Cenabum, led by two reckless characters called Cotuatus and Conconnetodumnus. They slaughtered the Roman citizens who had settled there for business purposes —among them one Gaius Fufius Cita, a respectable Roman knight who presided over the corn supply on Caesar's orders —and plundered their property. News of this spread rapidly to all the Gallic states, for wherever an event of particular note or significance takes place the Gauls shout it abroad in the countryside and the villages; others then take up the cry and pass it on to their neighbours. So it happened on this occasion, for what had taken place at dawn in Cenabum was made known before the end of the first watch in Arvernian territory,* which is about 160 miles away.

(4) There an Arvernian called Vercingetorix* acted in similar fashion. He was the son of Celtillus, and his father had won dominion over the whole of Gaul; for this reason, namely, trying to gain a kingdom, Celtillus had been put to death by the state. Vercingetorix was a young man whose abilities were second to none; he summoned his dependants and easily roused them. Once his plan became known there was a general rush to arms. His uncle Gobannitio, and the other leading men who opposed taking such a risk, tried to restrain him and banished him from the town of Gergovia. Still he persisted, and held a levy of down-and-outs and desperadoes in the open countryside instead. After he had mustered this gang, every Arvernian whom Vercingetorix approached was won over to his own point of view. He urged them to take up arms in order to win liberty for all. Once he had assembled a large force, he exiled the opponents who so recently had themselves expelled him.

Vercingetorix was now proclaimed king by his supporters.

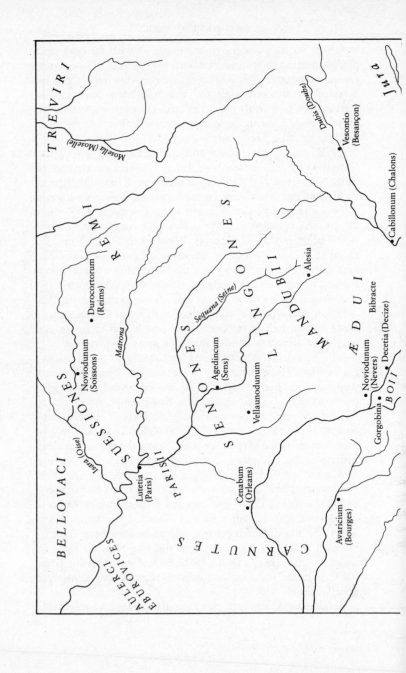

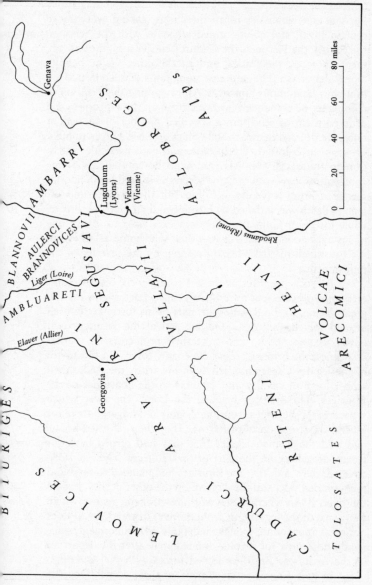

FIG. 6 The Great Revolt of Gaul

He sent out embassies in all directions, asking everyone to remain loyal, and soon formed alliances with the Senones, the Parisii, the Pictones, the Cadurci, the Turoni, the Aulerci, the Lemovices, the Andes, and all the other Gallic peoples along the coast. The supreme command was conferred on him with unanimous approval. After winning this position of command, he demanded hostages from all these peoples, and ordered them to send him a specified number of soldiers at once. He decreed that each state must produce a given number of weapons before a certain date, and paid particular attention to the cavalry. In his command he combined extreme conscientiousness with extreme severity. He used harsh punishments to bring waverers into line. For the more serious offences, death was inflicted by burning and all kinds of torture, while for lesser faults the offender's ears were cut off or one of his eyes gouged out. He was then sent home as an example to others, to strike fear into them by the severity of the punishment.

(5) By such penalties as these Vercingetorix quickly gathered an army. He sent a Cadurcan called Lucterius, a man of great daring, to the Ruteni with part of his force. He himself headed for the Bituriges. On his arrival the Bituriges sent envoys to the Aedui, who were their protectors, to request assistance, the better to resist the enemy force. On the advice of the legates Caesar had left with his army, the Aedui then sent a force of cavalry and infantry to the assistance of the Bituriges. These forces reached the Loire (the river which separates the Bituriges from the Aedui) and lingered there for several days, not daring to cross. They then returned home, and told the Roman legates that they had turned back for fear of treachery on the part of the Bituriges. They had discovered, they said, that the Bituriges had planned to surround them on one side, and the Arverni on the other, if they crossed the river. As to whether they withdrew for this reason which they gave to the legates, or from motives of treachery, it does not seem appropriate to make a definite pronouncement, since we do not know for certain. Immediately after the departure of the Aedui the Bituriges joined forces with the Arverni.*

(6) In Italy Caesar received news of these events. Once he

understood that affairs at Rome were now in a more favourable position—thanks to the resolution of Pompey*—he set
out for Transalpine Gaul. On his arrival he was faced with
a considerable problem—by what strategy was he to reach
his army? For he realized that if he summoned the legions to
the Province they would have to engage in battle while on
the march, and in his absence; but if he made his way to the
army, he perceived that he could not, with any degree of
safety, entrust his life even to the Gauls who at the time
seemed to be peaceable.

(7) Meanwhile Lucterius the Cadurcan, who had been sent
to the Ruteni, won that people over to the side of the Arverni.
He moved on to the Nitiobriges and Gabali and received
hostages from both. Once he had mustered a large force he
made his way into the Province towards Narbo, to launch an
assault. On receiving news of this Caesar decided that setting
out for Narbo must take priority over all his other plans.
When he arrived there he reassured the frightened inhabitants, and stationed troop outposts among the Ruteni who
lived in the Province, and also among the Volcae Arecomici,
the Tolosates, and around Narbo. These were the areas closest
to the enemy. He also ordered a detachment of his forces
from the Province, and the fresh reinforcements which he
had brought from Italy, to assemble in Helvian territory,
which adjoins that of the Arverni.

(8) Lucterius was checked and forced to retire because of
these preparations, as he considered it risky to venture within the outposts. Caesar set out for Helvian territory. The
Cevennes mountains, which separate the Arverni from the
Helvii, made the march difficult because of the very deep
snow there in winter. Even so, with great exertion the soldiers cleared away the snow to a depth of six feet, and opened
up a way. Then Caesar made his way through into the territory of the Arverni. They were caught off guard and unawares—for they thought that the Cevennes protected them
like a wall, and at that time of year the paths had never been
passable before, not even for individual travellers. Caesar
ordered his cavalry to range as widely as possible, striking as
much fear as it could into the enemy.

Rumours and reports of this quickly reached Vercingetorix. The Arverni all surrounded him in a panic, begging him to consider their plight and not to let them be plundered by their foes, especially now the focus of hostilities had clearly shifted on to themselves. He was swayed by their entreaties and transferred his camp from the Bituriges back to Arvernian territory.

(9) Even so, Caesar had remained in this area for two days, as he had anticipated that Vercingetorix's plans would turn out in this way. He then departed from his army, on the pretext of assembling reinforcements and cavalry, and left the young Brutus* in command of the forces, instructing him to let the cavalry range as widely as possible in all directions: he would do his best not to be absent for more than three days. After all this was arranged, to the surprise of his own men he made his way with all possible speed to Vienna.* There he picked up a fresh force of cavalry, which he had sent on there some time before, and without breaking the march by day or night made his way through Aeduan territory into that of the Lingones, where two of his legions were wintering. His purpose in moving with such speed was to forestall the possibility of a plot by the Aedui, perhaps even a plot against his life.

After arriving he sent word to the rest of the legions* and had them all assembled in one place before the news of his presence could reach the Arverni.* On learning of his arrival Vercingetorix brought his army back to the territory of the Bituriges. From there he set out against Gorgobina, a town of the Boii, and began to attack it (Caesar had settled the Boii there after defeating them in the campaign against the Helvetii, and had put them under Aeduan jurisdiction).

(10) This move presented Caesar with a considerable tactical problem. If he detained the legions in a single place for the rest of the winter, then he feared that once a people subject to the Aedui had been defeated the whole of Gaul would desert him, in view of the fact that he had no protection to offer to his friends. On the other hand, he was afraid that if he took his men out of winter quarters too early they would then have difficulties over supplies because of problems

with transportation. Yet it seemed preferable to endure any hardship rather than accept such indignity and lose the good-will of his supporters. So he encouraged the Aedui to transport supplies, and sent messengers on ahead to the Boii to tell them he was on his way, and urge them to remain loyal and resist the enemy's attack with courage. Leaving two of the legions at Agedincum with the heavy baggage of the whole army, he set out for the territory of the Boii.

(11) He reached Vellaunodunum, a town of the Senones, on the following day. To ensure no enemy was left in the rear, and to facilitate the transport of supplies, he laid siege to this town, and within two days had surrounded it with siege-works. On the third day envoys were sent from the town to ask for terms of surrender. He ordered them to collect up their weapons, bring out their horses, and produce 600 hostages. He left his legate Gaius Trebonius to complete these arrangements. He himself set out for Cenabum, a town of the Carnutes, so as to complete his march as quickly as possible.*

News of the siege of Vellaunodunum had only just reached the Carnutes, who were expecting it to be rather a long-drawn-out affair, and were amassing a force to send to the defence of Cenabum. Within two days Caesar arrived; he encamped in front of the town, but the lateness of the hour was against him and he put off the assault until the following day. He commanded his soldiers to prepare what was needed for the attack. As he was afraid that the people would escape from the town by night (for Cenabum was situated beside the bridge over the River Loire) he ordered two legions to keep watch under arms.

Just before midnight the people of Cenabum moved quietly out of the town and began to cross the river. When this was reported to him by the patrols Caesar set fire to the gates, sent in the two legions which he had ordered to stand ready, and took possession of the town. He captured all but a very few of the enemy, because the narrowness of the bridge and the streets cut off the escape of the main body of citizens. He plundered the town and burnt it, gave booty to the soldiers, led his army over the Loire, and made his way to the land of the Bituriges.

(12) When Vercingetorix learned of Caesar's arrival he raised the siege of Gorgobina and set out to meet him. Caesar had begun to besiege Noviodunum, a town of the Bituriges which lay on his route.* Envoys came to him from the town to beg him to pardon them and spare their lives; so in order to bring matters to a conclusion with characteristic speed he ordered them to collect their weapons, bring out their horses, and produce hostages. Some of these hostages had already been surrendered and the remaining tasks were being sorted out, while centurions and a few soldiers had been sent into the town to hunt out the weapons and horses. At that moment the enemy cavalry—which had gone on ahead of Vercingetorix's column—was spied in the distance. The moment the townspeople caught sight of it they began to hope for relief: raising a shout they started to take up weapons, close the gates, and man the wall. The centurions inside the town realized from the way the Gauls were behaving that they were devising some new plan of action, so they drew their swords, seized the gates, and got all their men out safely.

(13) Caesar ordered his cavalry to be led out of camp and engaged the enemy in battle. When his own cavalrymen got into difficulties he sent to their assistance about 400 German horsemen (from the beginning* he had arranged to keep these men with him). The Gauls could not withstand their attack. They were put to flight and withdrew to the main army, with heavy casualties. After their defeat the townspeople were in a panic once more. They seized the men they believed to be responsible for inciting the citizens, led them off to Caesar, and surrendered themselves to him.

Now that these events had been brought to a successful conclusion Caesar set off for Avaricum. This was a very large and well-fortified town in the land of the Bituriges, and in a particularly fertile area of the territory. Once this town was won, he was sure that the nation of the Bituriges would give itself up to his control.

(14) Vercingetorix had suffered one set-back after another— at Vellaunodunum, at Cenabum, at Noviodunum. He summoned his supporters to an assembly, and told them of the need to continue the war according to a totally different

strategy from the one they had adopted until now. They must now concentrate their efforts on cutting the Romans off from food and supplies, by every means possible. This would be easy, Vercingetorix claimed, because they themselves had a large force of cavalry, and also because the time of year was in their favour.* The Romans could not cut forage for themselves, and would inevitably have to separate and go in search of food from buildings—and every day the Gallic cavalry could pick them off. Moreover, he went on, private interests must be sacrificed to the safety of all: they must burn down their buildings and settlements which seemed likely to be within reach of the foraging-parties on either side of their route. They would themselves have sufficient store of the necessary supplies, because they would receive material support from the Gallic peoples in whose territories the war was going on. The Romans, on the other hand, would either be unable to endure such hardship or, at great risk, would advance considerable distances from their camp. It was of small importance whether they killed the Romans or merely seized the baggage without which they could not continue the fight. In addition, he said, they must burn any towns which were not protected from all danger by their fortifications and position: thus there would be no refuge for Gauls to avoid taking part in the campaign, and also no chances for the Romans to carry off plenty of supplies and booty. If these proposals seemed harsh and severe, he concluded, they must remember that it was far worse to have their children and wives dragged off into slavery, and themselves be killed: and this was sure to be their fate if they were defeated.

(15) Vercingetorix's proposal received unanimous support. In a single day more than twenty cities of the Bituriges were set on fire. The same policy was carried out in the other states: fires were visible in every direction. The Gauls were all deeply distressed at this action, but even so they put forward as their consolation the certainty that—now victory was virtually assured—they would quickly recover all that they had previously lost. At a general assembly they debated whether Avaricum should be burned or defended. The Bituriges fell at the feet of all the Gauls, pleading not to be compelled to

burn down, with their own hands, what was nearly the finest city in the whole of Gaul; a city, moreover, which both protected and adorned their nation. They claimed that its site made it easy for them to defend, for it was almost completely surrounded by a river and marsh—there was only one entrance-way, and an extremely narrow one at that. Their plea was granted. Vercingetorix opposed it at first, but later he gave in to the appeals of his own men, out of pity for the people.* Suitable defenders for the town were then selected.

(16) Vercingetorix followed Caesar by short marches, and chose a place for his camp which was protected by marshes and woods, about fifteen miles from Avaricum. There reliable scouts kept him hourly informed of what was going on at Avaricum, and he issued orders for what he wanted done. He kept watch on all our foraging and corn-gathering expeditions. When our men were obliged to scatter and range farther afield he attacked them and inflicted serious harm. Our men countered this as far as they were able by means of forward planning, going out in different directions, and not at fixed times.

(17) Caesar pitched his camp on the side of the town which (as we mentioned above) had a narrow entrance left open by the river and the marshes. There he began to prepare an earthwork, move up siege-shelters, and construct two towers, for the geography of the site made it impossible for him to encircle it with siege-works. He continued to press the Boii and Aedui about the supply of corn. The Aedui were little help, for they carried out his request without enthusiasm; the Boii had few resources, for their state was poor and ineffectual, and they soon consumed whatever they did have. So the army suffered extreme difficulties over the corn supply because of the ineffectiveness of the Boii and the negligence of the Aedui, and because of the burning of buildings, to such an extent that for several days the soldiers went without corn altogether and warded off the worst of their hunger by driving cattle in from far-away villages. Even so, not one of them was heard to utter a word which would disgrace the sovereignty of the Roman people and its previous victories. Indeed, when Caesar spoke to each of the legions while they were busy

with the works, and said that he would put an end to the
siege if they were finding the scarcity of food too hard to
endure, every one of them begged him not to do so. For a
number of years, they said, they had served under his command without incurring any dishonour, or abandoning any
action once they had undertaken it. They would consider it
disgraceful now to leave the siege they had begun; they would
rather endure every hardship than fail to avenge the Roman
citizens who had perished at Cenabum because of Gallic
treachery. This was the decision they entrusted to the centurions and military tribunes, so that they could report it to
Caesar.

(18) The towers were already coming close to the wall
when Caesar learned from prisoners that Vercingetorix had
run out of food supplies and moved his camp nearer to
Avaricum; also that Vercingetorix himself intended to take
his cavalry and the light-armed troops which usually fought
among them, and set a trap—and that he had set out for the
place where he expected our men to go the next day in
search of forage. After receiving this news Caesar silently set
out at midnight, and in the morning reached the enemy camp.
The Gauls had soon learned from scouts of Caesar's coming.
They hid their waggons and heavy baggage in the depths of
the woods, and drew up their entire force in a high, open
place. When news of this came Caesar gave orders for the
men to pile up their packs* and get their weapons ready.

(19) The Gauls were established on this hill, which sloped
gently upward from its base, and was almost entirely surrounded by a marsh, no more than fifty feet wide but virtually
impenetrable. After breaking up their causeways, therefore,
they had complete confidence in the security of their position.
Separated into divisions according to their nationalities, they
had control of all the fords and passes over the marsh. If
the Romans tried to break across the marsh, the Gauls were
determined to attack them from their advantageous position
while they were stuck fast. As a result, an observer looking
at how close the Gauls were would think they were ready to
fight under almost equal battle conditions; but anyone who
perceived that the relative positions of the two armies were

unequal would realize that the Gauls were only making an empty pretence of readiness to engage. The Roman soldiers were furious that the enemy was able to endure the sight of them and stand firm, especially at so short a distance, and they clamoured for the signal to engage; but Caesar explained that victory would inevitably cost them dear in terms of losses and the deaths of many brave men. Moreover, when he saw they were so ready to take any risk to win him honour, he would himself deserve utter condemnation if he did not treat their lives as more valuable than his own safety. That same day, after comforting the soldiers in this manner, he led them back to camp and organized everything else necessary for the siege of Avaricum.*

(20) On returning to his supporters Vercingetorix was accused of treachery—for shifting his camp nearer to the Romans, for setting off with the entire cavalry, leaving a large force without its commander, and because after his departure the Romans had seized their opportunity and arrived so soon. It was impossible, said his accusers, for all this to have taken place by chance and not deliberate design: he preferred to become king of Gaul with Caesar's permission, rather than through their support.

This was the substance of the charges against him. But Vercingetorix replied to the charges by pointing out that as far as moving camp was concerned, he had taken this step because of the shortage of food—and had even done so with their approval. As for coming too close to the Romans, he had been influenced in his decision by the advantage offered by the site in question—for the protection it provided meant that it practically defended itself.* Furthermore, there could have been no need of the cavalry's services in marshland, whereas they had proved useful in the place where they had been sent. It was by deliberate policy that he had not entrusted the supreme command to another man on his departure, to prevent popular pressure forcing anyone into fighting—and he could see that they were all lacking in resolution and wanted to engage only because they could no longer bear this degree of hardship.

If it was by chance that the Romans had arrived on the

scene, he went on, then they had fortune to thank; while if the Romans had been summoned because someone had leaked information to them, they ought themselves to thank the traitor, for enabling them from their advantageous position to find out how few the Romans were, and to despise them as cowards for not daring to engage and instead withdrawing back to camp. He had no desire to win a position of command from Caesar through some act of treachery: such a position was within his grasp in any case, thanks to the victory of which he and all Gaul were already assured. Yes, and he would even give them back his command if they believed they were conferring a distinction upon him greater than the security which they received from him in return. 'So that you understand I am speaking the whole truth concerning these matters,' said Vercingetorix, 'listen to these Roman soldiers here.' He brought forward some slaves captured while foraging a few days previously; they had been tortured, imprisoned, and starved.* They had already been drilled in what to say when they were interrogated, and declared that they were legionary soldiers who had been driven by hunger and lack of provisions to escape the camp in secret and search for whatever corn or cattle they could find in the countryside. The whole army, they claimed, was in similar want, and no one had strength enough to endure any strenuous effort; so their commander had decided that if his army had made no progress with the siege within three days he would withdraw it. 'These are the services I have rendered you,' said Vercingetorix, 'though you accuse me of betraying you. Even though your own blood has not been shed, you see before you a mighty and victorious army reduced to starvation. And I have ensured that no Gallic state will receive the Roman army within its borders when it seeks refuge in ignominious flight.'

(21) The whole host shouted aloud and clashed their weapons together, as is their custom when indicating agreement with someone's proposal.* They declared Vercingetorix the finest of leaders: there could be no doubt of his fidelity, and no better strategy for the campaign. They resolved to send to the town 10,000 picked men from the whole force,

and decided that the safety of all was not to be entrusted to the Bituriges alone. This was because they were aware that the Bituriges would win all the credit* for victory if they held the town.

(22) The Gauls used every kind of ingenuity to counter the extraordinary bravery of our soldiers. They are an extremely resourceful people, and particularly talented at copying and putting into practice anything they are taught. Now, for example, they began using nooses to turn our grappling hooks aside. Once these were made secure, they used ropes to drag them inside the walls. They also started tunnelling beneath our earthwork to undermine it: this was all the more skilfully done because they have many iron-mines, and so are practised experts in every kind of tunnelling. They had covered every section of their wall with towers and overlaid these with hides. Now they made frequent sorties by day and night, trying to set fire to the earthwork or attack our soldiers while they were working on the siege. They tried to match the height of our towers (which increased daily as the earthwork was raised higher and higher) by extending the scaffolding on their own towers. They sabotaged the progress of the mines which we had driven by the use of timbers tempered and sharpened at the end, boiling pitch, and heavy rocks. In this way they prevented us from coming close to the walls of the town.*

(23) All Gallic walls follow virtually the same pattern. At right angles to the wall, along its entire length, beams are placed in the ground at equal intervals, two feet apart. These are secured firmly from the inside, and then covered with large amounts of rubble; the gaps we mentioned between them are filled in with large rocks at the front. Once the beams are laid and joined, another level is added on top; the length of the gaps remains the same, but the second set of beams does not touch the first. Rather, because the spaces in-between the beams are the same, each one is firmly kept separate by single stones. The whole construction is built in this manner until the wall reaches the appropriate height. The finished edifice is not unattractive, with the variations in its appearance and the alternating beams and rocks in straight

lines following the line of their own level. Moreover, it offers an excellent means for practical defence of cities. The stones give protection from fire and the timber from battering rams —for it is impossible to break through continuous beams, usually forty feet long and secured on the inside, or to tear them apart.

(24) All these factors hindered the siege operation. Despite continually being obstructed by the cold and constant rain, by unremitting effort our soldiers still overcame every obstacle. Within twenty-five days they had built an earthwork 330 feet wide and eighty feet high, which almost touched the enemy wall. As was his custom, Caesar stayed by the works, on the alert, and urged the soldiers not to cease their efforts for so much as a moment; shortly before the third watch smoke was observed coming from the earthwork, for the enemy had tunnelled underneath it and set fire to it from below. At that moment a shout went up all along the wall, and the enemy made a sortie from the two gates beside our towers. At long range, some of the enemy began to throw torches and tinder from the wall on to the earthwork. They poured down pitch and other inflammable material, so that it was almost impossible to make a calculated decision about which point the men should head for first or where they should bring help. Even so, it was Caesar's regular practice to keep two legions on watch in front of the camp, and there were more available because they were working on the earthwork in shifts. So it was soon settled that some of our men countered the sorties, while others withdrew the towers and broke up a section of the earthwork. A whole crowd rushed out of camp to put out the fire.

(25) The night was now at an end, yet fighting continued everywhere and the enemy's hopes of victory were continually being renewed, especially since they could see the wooden screens on our towers being burned down and observe how difficult it was for our men to move forward in support while thus exposed. On their side, a constant supply of fresh troops replaced those who were exhausted. They believed that at that very moment the salvation of Gaul hung in the balance; and there then occurred, before our very eyes, something

which seemed to us worth recording, which we believed should
not be passed over. A Gaul stood before the town gate,
opposite our tower, and was throwing lumps of tallow and
pitch—which were passed from hand to hand—into the fire;
he was wounded in the right side by a dart from an artillery
machine,* breathed his last, and fell. One of the Gauls nearby
stepped across the man as he lay there and carried on with
the same task; when he was killed in similar manner by a
dart a third man took over, and likewise a fourth succeeded
him. Nor was that position abandoned by their defenders
before the fire on the earthwork was put out, the enemy
driven off on every side, and the fighting at an end.

(26) The Gauls had tried everything, and everything had
failed. The next day they took the decision to flee from
Avaricum, at Vercingetorix's prompting and instruction. They
hoped that by making the attempt in the silence of the night
they would bring it off without serious casualties on their
own side, especially because Vercingetorix's camp was not
far from the town, while a long stretch of marsh in-between
would hinder the Romans' pursuit. They were making ready
for this nocturnal escape when suddenly the married women
rushed out and threw themselves weeping at the feet of their
men. They begged and pleaded with the men not to abandon
them and the children they had had together to the enemy's
torments, just because their natural physical weakness made
it impossible for them to join the flight. When they realized
that the men were sticking to their plan (for in general, at
times of extreme danger, panic allows no place for pity),
these women began to cry out and alert the Romans to their
flight. The Gauls were so stricken with fear of the Roman
cavalry overtaking them on the road that they abandoned
their plan.

(27) The following day one of the towers was brought
forward and the siege-works which Caesar had set up were
put in order. A fierce rainstorm blew up, and he thought that
this would be a good moment to put his plan into action, for
he could see that the sentries stationed on the wall were
somewhat carelessly posted. So he ordered his men to be
more negligent about carrying out their duties, and explained

what he wanted done. The legions, concealed behind shelters, were outside the camp and ready for action. Caesar urged them all at long last to reap the fruits of victory in return for their great efforts, promised rewards to the first men over the wall, and gave his soldiers the signal. They rushed out from every side and quickly occupied the wall.

(28) This unexpected action panicked the enemy. They were forced down from their wall and towers, and made a stand in close formation in the market-place and open spaces, intending to form a battle line and fight to the death if they met obstruction from any quarter. When they saw that no one was coming down to level ground, but that men were pouring all round the wall, they were afraid of losing their chance to escape altogether. So they threw their weapons away and with a concerted effort made for the furthest reaches of the town. There some of them found themselves crushed in the narrow opening of the gates, and were killed by our soldiers; others got through the gates and were killed by the cavalry.

Not one of our men gave a thought to booty. They were so severely provoked by the massacre at Cenabum and the effort they had put into the siege that they spared neither the elderly, nor the women, nor even the little children.* In the end, of a total number of about 40,000, barely 800 reached Vercingetorix safely; these had run from the town as soon as they heard the shout.

Vercingetorix was afraid that their arrival might evoke the pity of the ordinary Gauls and so lead to a riot in the camp. In silence, therefore, and at dead of night, he intercepted their flight; he posted his close friends and the leaders of the peoples at a distance down the road, and took measures to have the survivors split up and taken to their own peoples in the parts of the camp allotted to each from the start.

(29) The next day he summoned an assembly, spoke words of comfort, and urged them not to be too down-hearted or anxious over this set-back. After all, he said, the Romans had not won because of their bravery or in open battle, but rather by means of trickery and siege-craft in which they themselves were inexperienced. Anyone who expected all outcomes in

time of war to be favourable was mistaken; he himself had never wanted a defence of Avaricum, and they were witnesses to the fact. This set-back they had just received had come about because of the folly of the Bituriges, which everyone else had indulged too far. Even so, he continued, he would swiftly repair the damage with some more significant advances. By strenuous efforts on his part, he would bring in the peoples who were presently at odds with the rest of Gaul and establish a single strategy for the whole of Gaul—such unity of purpose even the entire world could not withstand, and already he had all but achieved it. Meanwhile it was only right that he should ask them, for everyone's safety, to fortify the camp so that they could more easily withstand a sudden enemy attack.

(30) This speech found favour with the Gauls, above all because the set-back he had suffered had not made Vercingetorix down-hearted, or caused him to go into hiding and keep out of everyone's sight. In addition, they thought he showed foresight and perspicacity since he had advised first the burning, then the abandonment of Avaricum even before anything had gone wrong. The result was that, although defeat diminishes the authority of other commanders, the prestige of Vercingetorix, by contrast, grew daily because of the set-back he had suffered. At the same time they began to be hopeful, because of his assurance about making an alliance with the remaining peoples. Then for the first time the Gauls began to fortify their camp. Though unaccustomed to hard work, they were yet so alarmed as to believe they had to put up with whatever he ordered them to do.

(31) Vercingetorix was as good as his word. He spared no pains to try and win the remaining peoples to his side, enticing them with gifts and promises. For this purpose he selected men who were most appropriate, by reason of their skill in speaking or their existing friendships, to be effective in winning them over. He had the men who escaped the storming of Avaricum armed and equipped. At the same time, he made up the strength of his diminished force by demanding from the states a set number of soldiers, stating the required number and the day by which they were to arrive in camp; also he

gave orders for all archers (for Gaul has an enormous number of these) to be mustered and sent to him. By this means he quickly made up the numbers lost at Avaricum. In the meantime there came to him a certain Teutomatus. He was the son of Ollovico, the king of the Nitiobriges (whom our Senate had pronounced a Friend), and had brought a large cavalry force of his own, plus some mercenary horsemen hired in Aquitania.

(32) Caesar lingered several days in Avaricum. There he obtained an abundant supply of corn and other necessities and gave the army a chance to recover from the exertions and shortages it had suffered. Winter was almost over, and the very season demanded that he restart campaigning, so he decided to set out in pursuit of the enemy and see whether he could entice them from the marshes and forest or blockade them. At that moment the leaders of the Aedui came to him as envoys to beg him to help their people in a time of dire necessity. They explained that affairs were in a perilous state: although it was their long-established custom to appoint only one magistrate each year to hold regal power, two men were now holding office, and both of them claimed that they had been legally appointed. One of the two was Convictolitavis, an energetic and distinguished young man; the other was Cotus, a man of aristocratic birth with considerable influence and powerful connections. The brother of the latter, one Valetiacus, had held the supreme magistracy in the previous year. The entire nation was up in arms, the senate was split, and so were the people—and each party had its dependent supporters.* If the wrangling went on any longer the two halves of the state would come to blows. They were relying, concluded the envoys, on Caesar's concern and influence to prevent this happening.

(33) Despite believing that it would be to his disadvantage to move away from the war and the enemy, Caesar was well aware that disputes of this kind often lead to serious setbacks. He was unwilling that a nation of substance—and one closely allied to the Roman people—which he had always fostered and honoured by every possible means should be reduced to armed violence; and wanted to prevent the side

with least confidence in its own strength asking Vercingetorix for reinforcements. He considered it crucial to avert such a turn of affairs.

According to the laws of the Aedui, the supreme magistrate was not permitted to set foot outside Aeduan territory. To avoid appearing to violate their rules and laws in any way, Caesar decided to march to their land in person. He summoned the entire senate and the two men on whom the dispute centred to meet him at Decetia. Almost the entire people gathered there. Caesar was informed that a small number of men had been summoned to meet in secret at a place and time not sanctioned by law. One brother had declared the other elected, although the laws did not permit two men from a single family even to belong to the senate, never mind being appointed as magistrates, during their joint lifetime. So Caesar forced Cotus to give up office; he gave orders that Convictolitavis, who had been appointed by the priests (according to state custom when the succession of office has been broken), should hold power.

(34) This decree settled the dispute. Caesar urged the Aedui to forget their disputes and differences; once all such matters were set aside, they could devote themselves to the campaign and look forward to receiving the rewards which they would earn from him once the conquest of Gaul was complete. He also told them to send all their cavalry and 10,000 infantry to him quickly, so that he could distribute them as protection for the corn supply. Then he divided his army in two, and gave four legions to Labienus to lead against the Senones and the Parisii, while he himself took six legions along the River Allier towards the town of Gergovia, against the Arverni. He shared the cavalry out between them.

On hearing of this move Vercingetorix broke up all the bridges on the Allier and began to march along the opposite bank of the river. (35) The two armies moved away from each other, pitching camp within sight of one another and almost exactly opposite. Vercingetorix posted scouts to stop the Romans building a bridge at any point and moving their force across. Caesar was in a very difficult situation, in danger of having his advance blocked by the river for most of the summer—for the Allier cannot usually be forded before the autumn. To circumvent this potential problem he pitched camp in a wooded location facing one of the bridges which Vercingetorix had torn down. The following day he remained there in hiding with the two legions, and sent the rest of the army on ahead with all the baggage as usual. Some of the cohorts spread out to make it look as if the number of legions remained the same. He ordered this force to advance as far as possible; and when he reckoned that according to the time of day they must all be in camp, he began to rebuild the bridge using the existing piles (for the lower part of these remained intact). The work was soon complete. He took the legions across and chose a suitable place to camp, then called the rest of the army back to him. When Vercingetorix discovered this he moved on ahead by forced marches, so as to avoid being compelled to engage against his will.

(36) It took five days' march for Caesar to reach Gergovia from this position, and on that fifth day a minor cavalry engagement took place. He reconnoitred the city's position. It was located on a high plateau, and every access route presented problems, so that he had no hope of taking it by storm. Nor did he think it advisable to undertake a siege before the corn supply was secured. Meanwhile Vercingetorix, who was camped nearby, had disposed the forces of each individual Gallic state around him at moderate intervals. By seizing control of all the high points on the ridge which gave a view on to the town, they presented an intimidating appearance. Each day at dawn he would order the leaders of the states which he had chosen to assist him in planning the campaign to meet with him, so it would be apparent if there was anything to report or arrange. He let scarcely a day go by without testing his men's courage and morale in an engagement of cavalry and archers mingled together.

Opposite the town there was a hill* at the foot of the plateau, strongly fortified and sheer on every side: if our men could take and hold this, it appeared that they would be able to cut off the enemy's main water supply and prevent them from foraging freely. But the hill was in the control of an enemy garrison, albeit not a particularly strong one. In the dead of night Caesar moved out of camp and expelled the garrison before it could receive reinforcements from the town. After seizing control of the site he posted two legions there; he had a double trench dug, twelve feet wide, from the main camp to the smaller one, so that even individuals could go to and fro in safety from a sudden enemy attack.

(37) While all this was going on at Gergovia the Aeduan Convictolitavis (in whose favour, as we have explained, Caesar awarded a magistracy) was bribed by the Arverni. He then opened negotiations with a number of youths, chief among whom were Litaviccus and his brothers, young men of distinguished family. He shared his bribe-money with them and encouraged them to remember they were born free, born to command. The Aedui, said Convictolitavis, were the only people standing between Gaul and certain victory: the other Gallic peoples were only restrained by the example of loyalty set by the Aedui, and if they abandoned it the Romans would have no position to maintain in Gaul. It was true that Caesar had bestowed some degree of favour on him: but after all, he had done no more than maintain what was an obviously just claim. Why should it be the Aedui who must come to Caesar as arbitrator over their rules and laws, rather than the Romans to the Aedui?

Convictolitavis soon won over the young men, both with his speech and with his bribe. They declared that they would be the very first to support his strategy, and began to look for a way of putting it into practice. For they were not certain that their people could be induced to start a war on impulse. They decided to send Litaviccus at the head of the 10,000 men being sent to Caesar for his campaign, while his brothers went on ahead to Caesar. They also decided a strategy for dealing with all other contingencies.

(38) Litaviccus took over the army. When he was about twenty-seven miles from Gergovia he suddenly called his soldiers together, and in tears said: 'Where are we going, soldiers? All our cavalry, all our aristocracy are dead; two of our leading men, Eporedorix and Viridomarus, have been executed without trial by the Romans on a charge of treachery. Hear about it for yourselves from men who fled from the

actual slaughter. My brothers and all my kinsmen are dead, and grief prevents me from speaking of what has happened.' He had instructed some men in what he wanted them to say. They were now brought forward and explained the same facts as Litaviccus had declared to the assembled company already: namely, that the Aeduan cavalry had been killed because it was alleged that they had negotiated with the Arverni—they had themselves hidden among the throng of troops and fled from the midst of the slaughter.

The Aedui all cried out and begged Litaviccus to decide what they should do. 'As if the matter were open to debate, indeed,' he said, 'and it were not absolutely imperative that we make for Gergovia and form an alliance with the Arverni. Can we doubt that after committing this horrible crime the Romans are already hurrying here to kill us? So, if we have any courage at all, let us avenge the deaths of those who have been so shamefully murdered, and put these brigands to death.' Then Litaviccus pointed out the Roman citizens who were travelling with him, relying on his protection. He stole a large quantity of corn and supplies from them, tortured them cruelly, and had them executed. He sent messengers to all the Aedui, to rouse them with the same lies about a slaughter of cavalry and leading men, and he urged them to avenge their wrongs in the same way as he himself had done.

(39) The Aeduan Eporedorix was a young man of aristo-cratic birth and considerable influence at home; with him was Viridomarus, who was the same age and equally popu-lar, but of lesser birth. For Diviciacus had recommended him to Caesar, and Caesar had raised him from humble status to the highest rank. These two had come along with the cavalry at Caesar's specific request. There was a dispute going on between them about the leadership, and in the earlier conflict over the supreme magistracy both had fought with all their might—one on Convictolitavis' side, the other on that of Cotus. Of the two, Eporedorix reported the matter to Caesar at about midnight as soon as he heard of Litaviccus' plan. He begged Caesar not to let the Aedui defect from their friend-ship with the Roman people because of the young men's misguided scheme, for this would be the outcome if so many

thousands of men joined up with the enemy, since their kins-men could not be indifferent to their safety, while the Aeduan people as a whole could not treat it lightly either.

(40) This news caused Caesar much anxiety, for he had always shown particular favour to the Aeduan people. With-out an instant's hesitation he led four legions, ready for action, and all his cavalry out of camp. At such a moment, when the whole outcome seemed to depend on haste, there was no time to make the camp smaller.* He left his legate Gaius Fabius in command of the camp with two legions. When he gave orders for the arrest of Litaviccus' brothers he discov-ered that they had fled to the enemy shortly before.

Caesar advised his men not to be discouraged at such a critical time by the labour of a march, and such was their eagerness that he advanced twenty-three miles. When he caught sight of the Aeduan column he sent in his cavalry to delay and impede their march, forbidding them to kill any-one. Then he ordered Eporedorix and Viridomarus—who Litaviccus' men thought had been put to death—to mingle with the horsemen and call upon their own side. As soon as they recognized the two men, and saw through Litaviccus' deceit, the Aedui began to hold out their hands and signal surrender, throwing away their weapons and pleading for their lives. Litaviccus fled to Gergovia with his dependants: for according to Gallic custom it is a crime for them to abandon their lord, however desperate the circumstances.

(41) Caesar sent envoys to the Aeduan people to instruct them that as an act of generosity he had preserved the lives of the men whom he was entitled—according to the rules of war—to put to death. He gave over three hours of the night for his army to rest, then struck camp and advanced to Gergovia. In the middle of their march cavalry came from Fabius to report a perilous state of affairs. They explained that the camp had been besieged by a huge force. Fresh troops were constantly replacing the enemy soldiers when they grew weary. By forcing them to struggle without a rest, this enemy was exhausting our men—for the size of the camp necessitated the same troops manning the rampart continually. Many had

been wounded by a hail of arrows and missiles of all kinds; our artillery-machines had proved extremely useful in withstanding these attacks. Now the enemy had withdrawn, Fabius was keeping two gates and blocking up all the others, and setting up barriers on the rampart to make ready for a similar happening the next day. On hearing this news, with the enthusiastic support of the soldiers Caesar reached the camp before sunrise.

(42) While these events were taking place near Gergovia the Aedui received the first messengers from Litaviccus. They gave themselves no time to confirm his story: some acted out of greed, others from motives of rancour or hasty imprudence (which are particularly characteristic of that people), and treated an unsubstantiated report as proven fact. They seized the property of Roman citizens, and started to massacre and enslave them.

Their situation was tottering already, but Convictolitavis sent it tumbling headlong, whipping the ordinary people into a passion so that once their crimes were committed they would be too afraid to come to their senses. By offering him a safe conduct, they persuaded a military tribune travelling to join his legion, one Marcus Aristius, to leave the town of Cabillonum. They also forced the men who had settled there to trade to do likewise. Suddenly attacking them while they journeyed, the Gauls stripped them of all their baggage— when Aristius and the rest fought back, they hounded them for a day and a night. After many were killed on both sides, they called to arms an even larger force.

(43) While this was going on news came that all their soldiers were in Caesar's power. They ran to Aristius and explained that nothing that had taken place was a matter of public policy. They also ordered an inquiry into the stolen property and confiscated the property of Litaviccus and his brothers. Then they sent envoys to Caesar to clear themselves.

All these measures they took to recover their own men. But they were besmirched by their crimes, enticed by the profits to be made from stolen goods, while the number of people involved in what had taken place was large. Alarmed by the thought of being punished, they began to enter secret negotiations for war, and sent embassies to sound out the other Gallic states.

Although Caesar was aware of this, he still addressed the envoys as kindly as he could: he did not think any the worse of their state because of the ignorant folly of the common people, nor was his goodwill towards the Aedui diminished. In fact he expected a fairly serious Gallic uprising. To avoid being surrounded by all the Gallic peoples he decided on a strategy of withdrawal from Gergovia: this was to gather his entire army together, without the departure, which was actually prompted by anxiety about revolt, looking like head-long flight.

(44) As he considered these matters a chance for a success-ful action seemed to present itself. He had gone to the smaller camp to inspect the works, and noticed that a hill under enemy control, and in previous days scarcely visible for the numbers of men on it, was now unoccupied. Puzzled, he asked some deserters, a large number of whom were flocking to him daily, why this was. They all confirmed what Caesar himself had already learned through scouts: that there was a crest along this ridge of high ground which was almost level, but narrow and wooded at the point where it gave access on to the farther part of the town. The Gauls, said the deserters, were much afraid for this place, and were now convinced that once the Romans had one hill under control, if another high point were lost it would be apparent that they were almost encircled and prevented either from escaping or from foraging for food. Vercingetorix had summoned all his men to fortify this crest along the ridge.*

(45) On learning this Caesar sent a number of cavalry squadrons to the place around midnight, and ordered them to cause rather more disruption than usual as they ranged in every direction. At first light he commanded a large number of pack-horses and mules to be led out of camp and had the coverings which stopped their loads chafing removed. The muleteers were told to put on helmets, to look and act like cavalry, and ride around the hill. To maintain this deception

he included a few cavalry, who were to range more widely. He ordered them all to head for the same place by a long route.

All these activities were watched from far off in the town, for there was a good view from Gergovia into the camp; but at such long range it was impossible to find out anything for sure. Caesar sent one of his legions to the same high ground as the cavalry, and when it had advanced a short way he halted it on the lower ground and kept it concealed in the woods. Gallic suspicion grew, and their whole force transferred to the place to secure it. Caesar saw that the enemy camp was unoccupied, so he had his men cover up their emblems* and conceal their standards; then he took the soldiers from the main camp to the smaller one in small groups so as not to attract attention from the town. He explained to his legates (to each of whom he had given command of a legion) what he wanted done. In particular he warned them to keep their soldiers under control and prevent them advancing too far in an eagerness to fight or in hope of booty; he also set out the disadvantage of their less favourable position, which he said only speed could alter—this was a moment for seizing an opportunity, not fighting a full-scale battle. After this briefing he gave the signal and at the same time sent the Aedui by another ascent, on the right.*

(46) In a straight line the wall of the town would be just over a mile from the level where the ascent began, but for the way it curved from side to side along its length. The more the route was made to wind to effect a gentler ascent, the more the distance of the march increased. About half-way up the hill the Gauls had constructed a six-foot wall of large stones, which ran lengthways following the contour-line, to slow down our attack. They had left all the ground below this unoccupied, and filled the upper slopes as far as the town wall with camps packed closely together.

When the signal was given our soldiers quickly reached this line of defence, crossed it, and captured three enemy camps. In fact they acted so quickly in seizing them that Teutomatus, the king of the Nitiobriges, was taken by surprise in his tent whilst enjoying an afternoon nap and just managed to tear himself from the hands of the plundering soldiers and escape half-naked on a wounded horse.

(47) Caesar had achieved what he intended.* He ordered the retreat to be sounded—the Tenth legion (which he was accompanying) halted at once.* The soldiers of the other legions did not hear the trumpet blowing because a rather wide gully was between them. But they were held in check by the military tribunes and legates as Caesar had ordered.

But the men were excited by the hope of a quick victory, and the enemy's flight, and the successful outcome of previous battles—and they believed that there was nothing too difficult for their courage to achieve. So they did not abandon their pursuit until they drew close to the wall and gates of the town. At that moment a shout went up all over Gergovia. Those inside the most distant part of the town were panicked by the sudden uproar, and thought that the Romans were already inside the gates. So they rushed out of the town. The married women began to throw clothing and money from the wall; baring their breasts and leaning forward with outstretched arms they pleaded with the Romans not to kill them, not to act as they had at Avaricum, when they did not even spare the lives of the women and children.

It became apparent that a centurion of the Eighth legion, one Lucius Fabius, had declared among his men that he was stirred by the prospect of rewards such as the ones offered at Avaricum. He refused to let anyone else scale the wall before him. He grabbed three of his fellow-soldiers, got them to hoist him up, and climbed the wall. Then he in turned grasped hold of each of them and hauled them up on to the wall.

(48) In the meantime the Gauls who had assembled in another part of the town to fortify it (as we mentioned above)* first of all heard the shouting, then were roused by a flood of reports that the town was captured by the Romans. They sent cavalry on ahead, and then with a great charge sped off in the same direction. Wherever each man arrived first, there he stood beneath the wall and swelled the fighting strength of his compatriots. A large host gathered; then the married women (who had just now been holding their hands out to

the Romans) started to call upon their men and, in Gallic fashion, to unbind their hair and bring their children forward into view. For the Romans it was an unfair contest, in terms of both ground and numbers. They were tired by their climb and the duration of the fighting, and found it difficult to withstand men who were fresh and unscathed.

(49) When Caesar observed that they were fighting in a disadvantageous position, and that the enemy's numbers were growing, he became anxious for his men and sent to his legate Titus Sextius (whom he had left in charge of the smaller camp). He told him to bring cohorts from camp quickly, and to station them at the foot of the hill on the enemy's right flank. In this way, if he saw that our men were driven from their position he would be able to deter the enemy from pursuing them unchallenged. Then he advanced a short distance with the Tenth from the place where he had halted and awaited the outcome of the battle.

(50) The fighting was now fierce and at close quarters. The enemy relied on their position and numbers, our men on their courage. Suddenly our men caught sight of the Aedui on our exposed flank, although Caesar had sent them off to the right by another ascent, to draw off the enemy. Their weapons resembled those of the enemy so closely that our men panicked. Even though they could see that the Aedui's right shoulders were bared (this was the agreed sign* which regularly distinguished them), the soldiers believed that this was actually a ruse of the enemy's designed to deceive them.

At this moment the centurion Lucius Fabius and the men who had climbed the wall with him were surrounded and killed, then thrown headlong from the wall. Another centurion from the same legion, Marcus Petronius, had tried to break down the gates, but he was overwhelmed by the enemy host and abandoned hope of saving himself. Gravely wounded, he called to his soldiers, who had followed him: 'Since I cannot save myself along with you, I shall at least take care to secure your survival—for it was my desire for glory which made me lead you into danger. When I give you your chance, watch out for your own safety.' At once he plunged into the midst of the enemy, killing two and forcing the rest a little way back from the gate. His men tried to come to his assistance, but he told them: 'Your efforts to preserve my life are futile—already my blood and my strength are draining away. So get away while you can, and make your way back to the legion.' In this manner he soon afterwards fell fighting, and proved the saviour of his men.*

(51) Our men were overwhelmed on every side, and were forced back from their position with the loss of forty-six centurions. But the Tenth legion, which had taken up a support position on rather more even ground, slowed down the Gauls' uncontrolled pursuit. The cohorts of the Thirteenth legion, which had been brought from the smaller camp by the legate Titus Sextius, and had taken up position on higher ground, once more took over from the Tenth. As soon as the legions reached level ground they halted and turned their standards to face the enemy. From the foot of the hill Vercingetorix led his men back inside the fortifications. On that day almost 700 soldiers were lost.

(52) The following day Caesar called an assembly and upbraided the soldiers for their imprudence and over-eagerness in deciding for themselves where to advance and what action to undertake, and for not halting when the signal for retreat was given; also because they could not be restrained by the military tribunes and legates. He explained the significance of disadvantageous ground, and what had motivated him at Avaricum—namely, that even though the enemy were caught without their leader or their cavalry, he had given up the chance of certain victory so as to avoid even small losses in action because of unfair ground. However admirable their courage, which neither the work of fortifying their camp nor the height of the hill nor the wall of the town had been able to check, nevertheless they deserved reproach for their lack of discipline and their presumption in thinking that they knew more about victory and outcomes than their commander did. He was as eager to find level-headedness and restraint in his soldiers as courage and daring.*

(53) Caesar finished his speech by encouraging the soldiers not to be disturbed because of these events, and not to attribute what had resulted from unfair ground to bravery on

the enemy's part. At the end of the assembly, although he was still considering a departure in much the same terms as before, he led the legions out of camp and halted them in battle order on suitable ground. Vercingetorix did come down on to this level ground, but following a successful cavalry skirmish Caesar led his army back to camp.* After doing likewise on the following day Caesar judged that enough had been done to minimize the Gauls' boasting and to improve his own soldiers' morale, so he struck camp and moved out to the Aedui. Not even then did the enemy pursue. On the third day he reached the River Allier, rebuilt the bridges, and took his army across.

(54) On the other side he was greeted by Eporedorix and Viridomarus, and learned that Litaviccus had set out with all his cavalry to rouse the Aedui. It was imperative, therefore, that the two of them should reach the Aeduan people first and reaffirm their loyalty. Caesar already had abundant proofs of Aeduan treachery, and he reckoned that the departure of Eporedorix and Viridomarus was merely speeding up the revolt of that state. Even so, it seemed unwise to detain them, for fear of seeming to insult them or giving the impression that he had something to fear. As they set out he gave a short account of his services to the Aedui. He recalled the subservient position in which he had found them—driven into the towns, deprived of their land, all their supplies stolen, forced to pay tribute, hostages wrested from them in humiliating circumstances—and he recounted too the good fortune and considerable prosperity to which he had brought them, such that they had not only regained their previous distinction, but seemed even to have outdone all previous ages in prestige and influence. With this warning, he dismissed the Aedui from his presence.

(55) Noviodunum was an Aeduan town in a favourable location on the banks of the Loire, to which Caesar had conveyed all his Gallic hostages, his corn, his funds, and most of his own baggage and that of the army. He had also sent there a large number of horses bought for this war in Italy and Spain. When Eporedorix and Viridomarus reached Noviodunum they learned of the situation prevailing in their

state: Litaviccus had been received by the Aedui at Bibracte, which is their most important town, while their magistrate Convictolitavis and a large part of the senate had met with him. An official embassy had been sent to Vercingetorix to obtain peace and a friendly alliance.

The two of them thought this advantageous position too good to throw away, so they killed the soldiers on guard at Noviodunum, and the men who had come there to trade, and shared the money and horses out among themselves. They had the Gallic hostages sent to the magistrate at Bibracte. Judging that they would not be able to hold the town, they set it on fire to prevent the Romans making use of it. All the corn which they could manage at short notice they carried away by boat, and the rest they ruined by drenching or burning it. Then they began to muster a force from the neigh-bouring territories, stationed guards along the Loire, and displayed their cavalry conspicuously everywhere to cause panic: their intention was to cut the Romans off from their corn supply [or to starve them out of the province].* The fact that the Loire was swollen with melt-water greatly strength-ened their hopes, for it seemed altogether impossible to ford the river.

(56) When Caesar learned of all this he decided that if he was going to run the risk of rebuilding the bridges he had to hurry, so that he could fight an engagement before larger forces gathered at the river. As for changing his plan and marching to the Province, he thought that not even fear made it necessary; nor was there only the shame and disgrace of such a course, and the obstacle of the Cevennes, and the problems of the route, to stand in the way—there was also, and most importantly, the fact of his concern for Labienus and the legions he had sent with him, both now cut off. So it was that he completed long forced marches by day and night to surprise everyone by reaching the Loire. The cavalry found a fording-place which was serviceable in an emergency. The men were able to keep their arms and shoulders clear of the water and hold up their weapons; cavalry were posted to break up the force of the current. On first sighting them, the enemy were thrown into such confusion that Caesar got the

army across in safety. In the fields he found a plentiful supply of corn and cattle, and once the army had sufficient stocks of both he began to march to the land of the Senones.

(57) While Caesar was thus occupied, Labienus left the supplementary levy* which had just arrived from Italy to guard the baggage, and set out with four legions for Lutetia. This is a town of the Parisii, sited on an island in the River Seine. When the enemy learned of his coming a large force from the neighbouring states gathered. The supreme command was entrusted to an Aulercan, Camulogenus: despite his relatively advanced age he was singled out for this distinction because of his outstanding knowledge of military matters. When he observed a continuous expanse of marsh which flowed into the Seine and formed a significant obstruction over the whole area, he encamped there and made ready to prevent our men from crossing.

(58) Labienus' first move was to fetch the movable shelters, and to cover the surface of the marsh with wicker hurdles and rubble. Once he saw that this was too difficult, he moved silently out of camp during the third watch, and reached Metiosedum on the same route by which he had come. Metiosedum is a town of the Senones on an island in the Seine, like Lutetia which we mentioned just now. He seized about fifty ships and quickly joined them together into a bridge, then sent his soldiers across on it. Most of the townspeople had been called up for the war: they were so panicstricken by this unprecedented action that Labienus won control of the town without a struggle. He repaired the bridge which the enemy had earlier broken up, then took his army across and began to march downstream towards Lutetia. When refugees from Metiosedum told the enemy what had happened the Gauls gave orders for Lutetia to be burned and its bridges broken up. They advanced from the marsh to the banks of the Seine and took up position opposite Lutetia, facing Labienus' camp.

(59) By now news had come of Caesar's departure from Gergovia, and rumours of the Aedui's treachery and the success of the Gallic uprising were reported. The Gauls began to declare to one another at their meetings that Caesar's

march, and his way over the Loire, had been blocked off, and that he had been forced to make for the Province. But when the news of the Aedui's treachery broke, the Bellovaci—who were already disloyal themselves—began to muster a force and openly make ready for war. Because of this total change of circumstances, Labienus realized that he must adopt a very different strategy from the one he had intended: he must think no longer of ways to make acquisitions, or inflict injury on the enemy in battle, but rather of how to bring his army safely back to Agedincum. On one side threatened the Bellovaci, a nation with a reputation for outstanding bravery in Gaul; Camulogenus held the other, with an army drawn up at the ready. A great river cut the legions off from their baggage and its guards. In the face of these extreme difficulties Labienus saw that they must look to courage to help them.

(60) At dusk he called a council and urged his men to carry out his orders promptly and to the letter. He assigned each of the ships which he had taken from Metiosedum to a Roman knight,* and ordered them to advance four miles downstream in silence, starting at the end of the first watch, and to await him there. To guard the camp he left the five cohorts which he thought were the least determined fighters. The remaining five from the same legion he ordered to set out upstream at midnight with all their baggage, and to make a great uproar about it. He acquired some small boats and sent them to row upstream too, amid much loud splashing. Soon afterwards he himself set out in silence with three legions and made for the location where he had told the ships to put in.

(61) At the time when he arrived a fierce storm had suddenly arisen, so that the enemy scouts who were posted all along the river were caught unawares by our men. Under the control of the Roman knights who had charge of this task, the army and the cavalry were swiftly got across. At almost the same moment, just before dawn, the enemy were told that there was an unusual uproar in the Roman camp—a large column was marching upstream, the sound of oars could be heard coming from the same direction, and a short way

downstream soldiers were being ferried across in boats. On hearing all this the enemy thought that the legions were crossing the river in three places and getting ready to escape because they were so disturbed by the treachery of the Aedui, so they divided their force into three. They left a garrison opposite the camp and sent a small force towards Metiosedum (to advance as far as the ships had done), then led the remainder of their troops against Labienus.

(62) By first light all our men had crossed, and the enemy battle line was in view. Labienus urged the soldiers to be mindful of their former courage and their previous successful engagements, and to imagine that Caesar himself, under whose leadership they had so often overcome their foes, was actually present. Then he gave the signal for battle. At the first clash, on the right wing (where the Seventh legion was positioned) the enemy was driven back and routed. On the left, the position held by the Twelfth legion, the enemy's leading ranks were pierced by weapons and fell; but the survivors still fought fiercely, and no one gave any sign of intending to run away. The enemy leader, Camulogenus, was present among his men, urging them on. Even now the outcome was in doubt, but when the tribunes of the Seventh received a report of what was happening on the left wing they brought the legion round behind the enemy and attacked. Not even then did anyone desert—they were all surrounded and killed. Camulogenus suffered a similar fate.

When the troops who had been left facing Labienus' camp to watch it heard the battle under way they went to the assistance of their comrades and occupied a hill. They were, however, unable to withstand the onslaught of our victorious soldiers. They intermingled with their compatriots in flight, and all who failed to reach the protection of the woods and mountains were put to death by the cavalry.

Labienus had made an end of the business. He now returned to Agedincum, where the whole army's baggage had been left. On the third day he set out from Agedincum with his entire force and made his way to Caesar.

(63) The news of the Aedui's defection extended hostilities. Embassies were sent in every direction, and they did all they

could through favours, influence, and bribery to win the support of the Gallic peoples. They seized the hostages Caesar had left in their charge: by threatening to punish these hostages, they terrified waverers into compliance. The Aedui asked Vercingetorix to come to them and explain his campaign strategies, but when this was agreed they argued that he should hand supreme command to them. Now that the matter was in dispute, an assembly of the whole of Gaul was announced, to be held at Bibracte. The Gauls flocked there in hordes, from every quarter. When the question was put to a popular vote the result was that Vercingetorix was unanimously approved as sole commander.*

Absent from this assembly were the Remi, Lingones, and Treveri. The first two of these nations still held to their friendship with the Romans, but because the Treveri lived too far away, and were presently under German attack, they played no part at all in the campaign and did not support either side. The Aedui took being ousted from supreme control very badly, bewailing their change of fortunes, and began to miss the favour Caesar had shown towards them. Nevertheless, they did not dare to part company with the rest of the Gauls now that the campaign had started. With reluctance the two young men of ambition, Eporedorix and Viridomarus, bowed to Vercingetorix.

(64) Vercingetorix demanded that the other states surrender hostages and named the day for this to be effected.* He ordered all the cavalry, 15,000 in total, to assemble with haste. He also stated that he would be content with the infantry force he had before. After all, he was not going to try his luck, or fight in a pitched battle: since he had cavalry in plenty, it would be easy to cut the Romans off from both regular corn supplies and forage. But the Gauls must agree to destroy their own stocks of corn, and to set their buildings on fire: they must understand that the loss of their property would enable them to achieve perpetual supremacy and liberty. Once these matters were arranged, he demanded 10,000 soldiers from the Aedui and Segusiavi (who live alongside the Province), and in addition 800 cavalry. In charge of them he put Eporedorix's brother, and told him to attack the

Allobroges. In another direction he sent the Gabali and the nearest Arvernian communities against the Helvii, and also sent the Ruteni and Cadurci to ravage the territory of the Volcae Arecomici.

Despite this, in the hope that their minds were still unsettled after the recent war, he sent messengers and embassies in secret to persuade the Allobroges to join him. To their leaders he promised money, and to the state as a whole supreme command over the whole of the Province.

(65) In preparation for all these contingencies, a defence force of twenty-two cohorts, mustered in the Province itself by the legate Lucius Caesar, had been provided. These cohorts were posted throughout the area. Acting on their own initiative, the Helvii joined battle with their neighbours but were routed. After the death of the leader of their state, one Gaius Valerius Donnotaurus, son of Caburus, together with a number of other men, they were forced back behind the walls of their towns. The Allobroges stationed garrisons at frequent intervals along the Rhône, and kept a close and careful watch on their borders.

Caesar was aware that the enemy was the stronger in cavalry, and that because all routes were cut off there was no hope of reinforcements from Italy and the Province. For this reason he sent across the Rhine into Germany, to the peoples which he had subdued in previous years, and demanded from them cavalry and light-armed troops to fight in amongst the horses. When they arrived the horses they were using were hardly suitable, so Caesar took the horses of his military tribunes and the rest of the Roman knights and veterans,* and distributed them among the Germans.

(66) While all this was taking place the enemy force from the Arverni and the cavalry which had been requisitioned from the whole of Gaul were gathering. Caesar was marching to the Sequani over the outer limits of the Lingones' territory, so that he could more easily bring help to the Province. At the same time, once Vercingetorix had mustered a large host of these contingents he marched for three days and then halted about nine miles away from the Romans, arranging his force in three camps. He summoned his cavalry commanders to a

meeting and explained that the moment for victory had arrived. The fact that the Romans were running away to the
Province and leaving Gaul, he went on, was enough to win
them temporary liberty, but it was insufficient to secure peace
and tranquillity permanently. The Romans would surely gather
a larger force and return to prolong the war indefinitely. For
this reason they must attack while the Romans were marching in column and hence encumbered by baggage. If the
soldiers went to help their comrades and were delayed for
that purpose, they could not continue the march. If, on the
other hand, the Roman soldiers abandoned their baggage
and thought only of their own safety—and he was sure this
was the more likely response—they would at a stroke be
stripped of their essential equipment and of their dignity. He
went on to assure his cavalry commanders that they could be
sure not one of the enemy horsemen would dare to advance
even a short distance away from the main column. To encourage them to act bravely he would parade his entire force
in front of the camp and strike fear into the enemy. The
cavalry cried that they must be bound by a solemn oath: no
man was to be received beneath a roof, or have access to his
children, his parents, or his wife, unless he had twice ridden
through the enemy column.

(67) This action was approved and everyone took the oath.
The next day the cavalry was divided into three contingents.
Two adopted battle formation and appeared on either side of
the column, while the third began to impede the march from
the front. On hearing the news of this Caesar ordered his
own cavalry to divide into three likewise, and to attack the
enemy. There was fighting everywhere at once. The column
halted, and the legions withdrew the baggage into their midst.*
If it appeared that our men were in difficulties or hard pressed
in any area, Caesar gave orders for the standards to advance
and the line of battle to form up. This action slowed the
enemy pursuit as well as encouraging our men with the hope
of assistance.

After some time the Germans on the right flank seized a ridge
of high ground. Forcing the enemy down, they routed them,
pursued them right down to the river—where Vercingetorix

and his infantry had taken up position—and killed a number
of them. After observing this, the rest were afraid of being
surrounded and so fled. There was slaughter everywhere.

Three aristocratic Aeduans were captured and taken to
Caesar—the cavalry commander Cotus, who had been locked
in rivalry with Convictolitavis at the previous elections;
Cavarillus, who had been put in charge of the infantry after
the desertion of Litaviccus; and Eporedorix, under whose
leadership the Aedui had campaigned against the Sequani
before the coming of Caesar.

(68) Now all his cavalry had fled, Vercingetorix withdrew
his infantry force, which he had stationed in front of the
three camps, and immediately began the march to Alesia,
which is a town of the Mandubii. He issued orders for the
baggage to be fetched quickly from the camps and to follow
on behind. Caesar had his army's baggage taken to the nearest high ground and left two legions behind to guard it. He
pursued Vercingetorix as long as the light lasted and killed
about 3,000 of the enemy rearguard. The following day he
pitched camp near Alesia. He reconnoitred the city's position
and provoked panic in the enemy; then, after encouraging
the soldiers for the task they faced, he set about the work of
circumvallation.*

(69) The actual stronghold of Alesia* was in an extremely
lofty position on top of a hill, apparently impregnable except
by means of a siege. On two sides the foot of this hill was
washed by rivers, and for about three miles there stretched a
plain in front of the town. Close by in every other direction
more hills of equal height girded the town. Beneath the wall,
where the hill faced east, the Gallic forces filled the entire
space: they had constructed a ditch and a six-foot wall. The
length of the siege-works which the Romans had started
reached ten miles. Camps had been pitched at suitable locations and twenty-three forts built along the line. These forts
were garrisoned in the daytime, to guard against unexpected
sorties; at night sentries and reinforced patrols kept watch
there.

(70) After work on the siege had begun, a cavalry battle took
place in the three-mile stretch of plain which we mentioned

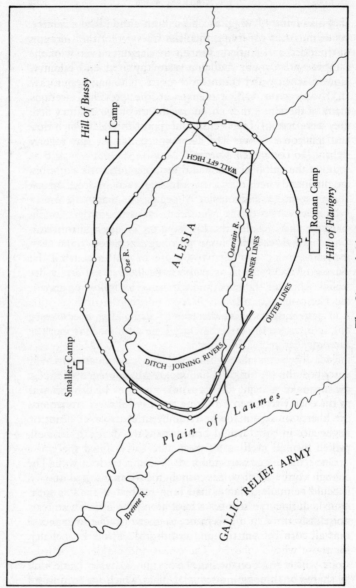

FIG. 7 The Siege of Alesia

above as lying between the hills. Both sides fought fiercely. When our men got into difficulties Caesar sent the Germans to their assistance and stationed the legions in front of the camps to prevent any sudden invasion by the enemy infantry. Now that they had the protection of the legions, our cavalry's courage rose. The enemy were routed. There were so many of them that they got in one another's way as they fled; they were crushed together in a heap at the gates, which they had left too narrow. The Germans pursued them eagerly right up to their ditch and wall. Massive slaughter ensued as some of the Gauls abandoned their horses and tried to cross the ditch and climb over the wall. Caesar ordered the legions he had stationed just outside the camp ramparts to advance a short way. The Gauls inside the fortifications were equally terrified, and sounded the call to arms in the belief that an assault was imminent. Some were in such a panic that they forced their way into the town. Vercingetorix ordered the closing of the gates to stop the camp being completely deserted. After killing many and capturing a number of horses, the Germans withdrew.

(71) Vercingetorix now decided to send all his cavalry away by night before the Romans completed their siege-works. As they left, he told each of them to go to his own people and muster for battle all the men of an age to bear arms. He described the services he had done them and called upon them to take thought for his safety, and not to abandon him to the enemy's torments after he had done so much to secure the liberty of all. Finally he reminded them that any hint of negligence in them would bring about the deaths of 80,000 picked men, as well as his own.

Once the plan was adopted, Vercingetorix had barely enough corn for thirty days, though by practising economy it could be made to last a little longer. Once his orders were issued, during the second watch he sent the cavalry away noiselessly through a gap in our siege-works. He demanded that all corn be sent to him, and decreed the death penalty for those who disobeyed. There was an abundance of livestock which had been wrested from the Mandubii, and this he shared out among individuals. He arranged for corn to be shared out gradually and sparingly, and withdrew all the forces which he had posted in front of the town back inside. Now these arrangements were in place, he began to await reinforcements from Gaul and prepared to conduct his campaign.

(72) All these arrangements were relayed to Caesar by deserters and prisoners. He then decided to set up the following types of fortification. He had a twenty-foot-wide ditch dug, with vertical sides, so that the bottom of the ditch was as wide as its edges at the top. He fixed the position of all the other fortifications 400 paces back from the ditch, with the intention of preventing an unexpected or night-time onslaught on them by the enemy army, and of stopping the enemy aiming missiles at our men while they were busy on the siege-works; for the area he had enclosed was necessarily of considerable size, and it would be difficult to encircle the entire site with a cordon of soldiers. At this distance away, then, he extended two more ditches, of the same depth but fifteen feet across; he filled the inner one (which was on low-lying ground in the plain) with water diverted from the river. Behind them he constructed an earthwork with a rampart on top, twelve feet high; to this he attached a parapet and battlements, with large pointed stakes projecting at the joints where the parapet attached to the earthwork. This would slow down an enemy ascent. He placed towers all round the siege-works at intervals of eighty feet.

(73) Our forces were obliged to find timber and corn and to construct these extensive fortifications simultaneously. Because they regularly advanced considerable distances from the camp, their numbers were depleted as a result. Sometimes the Gauls would try to test our defensive works by making a sortie in strength from several of the town's gates. For this reason Caesar deemed it necessary to add to the works, to facilitate manning of the fortifications by a smaller number of soldiers. Tree-trunks and thick branches were cut down, stripped of their bark, and sharpened at the end: ditches five feet deep were dug, and the stakes inserted into them and fastened firmly at the bottom so that they could not be torn up. The branches were left projecting. There were five rows of stakes to a ditch, all joined and interlinked: anyone who

made his way into them would be impaled on the extremely
sharp spikes—the men called them 'gravestones'. In front of
them, set out in the diagonal rows of a quincunx pattern, pits
were dug three feet deep sloping slightly inwards from top to
bottom. Smooth stakes, as thick as a man's thigh and sharpened and tempered at the end were sunk into the pits; they
projected no more than three inches from the ground. For
strength and stability, earth was trodden in around them to
a depth of one foot, and the rest of the pit was then covered
with twigs and brushwood to camouflage the trap. Eight
rows of such pits were dug at three-foot intervals. From the
resemblance to a flower the men called these 'lilies'. In front
of them logs were dug into the earth: each of them was a
foot long and covered with iron hooks. These were scattered
everywhere a little way apart. The men called them 'spurs'.*

(74) Once these measures were completed Caesar constructed similar fortifications following the flattest line that
the terrain allowed. These encompassed a fourteen-mile cir-
cuit, facing in the opposite direction against the enemy outside.
This ensured that the garrisons on the defences could not be
overcome even by a great host, should the occasion arise.*
To avoid being forced to take the risk of leaving camp, he
ordered everyone to see that corn and forage for thirty days
was gathered.

(75) While this was going on at Alesia, the Gauls called a
meeting of their leaders. They decided not to follow Vercingetorix's proposal that all men able to bear arms should be called
up, but rather to levy a certain number from each state. This
would prevent their creating so large and ill-assorted an army
that it would be impossible to exercise control or pick out
their own people, or provide enough corn. From the Aedui
and their dependants—the Segusiavi, Ambluareti, Aulerci
Brannovices, and Blannovii—they demanded 35,000, and an
equal number from the Arverni together with the Eleuteti,
Cadurci, Gabali, and Vellavii (all of these peoples are usually
under Arvernian rule). From the Sequani, Senones, Bituriges,
Santoni, Ruteni, and Carnutes they demanded 12,000 each,
and 10,000 each from the Bellovaci and Lemovices, 8,000
each from the Pictones, Turoni, Parisii, and Helvetii, 5,000

each from the Suessiones, Ambiani, Mediomatrici, Petrocorii, Nervii, Morini, and Nitiobriges, the same from the Aulerci Cenomani, 4,000 from the Atrebates, 3,000 from the Velio-cassi, Lexovii, and Aulerci Eburovices, 2,000 from the Raurici and Boii, 30,000 in total from the maritime states which call themselves Aremoric—including the Curiosolites, Redones, Ambibarii, Caletes, Osismi, Veneti, and Venelli.* Of these states the Bellovaci did not complete their quota, because they declared that they were going to fight the Romans inde-pendently and in their own name and so would not bow to anyone else's command. At the request of Commius, however, they did send 2,000 men along with the rest, for the sake of their friendship with him.

(76) Caesar had enjoyed the loyalty and good offices of this Commius* in Britain in previous years. In return for these services, Caesar had declared that his state was to be exempt from taxation. He had restored its rights and laws, and made the Morini pay it tribute. In spite of this, the whole of Gaul was united in the desire of restoring liberty and their former reputation for warfare, to such an extent that neither services rendered nor the remembrance of friend-ship moved them, and they all concentrated all their efforts of will and resources on the war. Once 8,000 cavalry and about 240,000 infantry were mustered, a review and reckon-ing of numbers was held in Aeduan territory; then officers were assigned. The chief commands went to Commius the Atrebatian, the Aeduans Viridomarus and Eporedorix, and the Arvernian Vercassivellaunus, who was a cousin of Vercin-getorix. Subordinates from the Gallic states were assigned to them to advise on the conduct of the campaign.

They all set out for Alesia eager and full of confidence. Not a single one of them believed it would be possible to withstand even the sight of such a mighty host, especially as the battle would be fought on two fronts—for at the moment when this vast army of horse and foot came into view from outside, there was to be a sortie from the town.

(77) As for those who were trapped inside Alesia, the day when they had expected their reinforcements to arrive was past. Their corn was all gone, and they knew nothing of

what was happening among the Aedui. So they called a meeting to debate the outcome of their situation. Various opinions were declared, some advising surrender, others urging a sortie while they still had the strength for it. The speech of Critognatus, vile and remarkable for its cruelty, should not be passed over here.

Critognatus was an Arvernian of noble birth and considered to be a man of great influence. 'Not one word shall I speak', he said, 'concerning the opinion of those men who call shameful slavery by the name of "surrender"; nor do I think they should be treated as citizens of Gaul* or called to our assemblies. My concern is with those who are proposing a sortie. For this advice of theirs seems, through your support for it, to preserve some remembrance of former courage. Yet it is not courage, but a weak spirit, which is unable to endure such trifling hardship. It is easier to find men ready and willing to face death than men prepared to endure suffering with forbearance.

'Even so, I might have approved their advice—such is the force of their prestige—if I expected no loss from it beyond that of our lives. Yet we must look to the whole of Gaul in forming our plans, for it is the whole of Gaul that we have summoned to our assistance. If 80,000 men are killed in this one place, what do you think the state of mind of our relations and kinsmen will be when they are forced to give battle practically on top of the corpses? Do not rob them of your help, when they have ignored the danger threatening them to save you—and do not bring the whole of Gaul to ruin, or commit it to endless slavery because of your reckless lack of judgement or weakness of purpose.

'Or do you doubt their loyalty and determination because they have not arrived on the exact day? What then? Do you think that the Romans are hard at work on those outer defences every day for their own amusement? If you cannot find encouragement from their messengers because every approach is blockaded, let the Romans be your witnesses that they are drawing near. For it is fear of that event which keeps them busy day and night on the fortifications.

'So now, what do I advise? Do what our ancestors did in

the war (a much less important one) with the Cimbri and
Teutoni. When they were forced into the towns, under the
strain of a deprivation like our own, they sustained their
existence on the bodies of those who were too old to be of
use in the campaign: and as a result they did avoid surrendering to their enemies. Even if we had no precedent for such
a practice, I would still judge it a fine policy to establish for
the sake of liberty, and to hand down to our descendants.
After all, what resemblance was there between that war and
the present one? Certainly, once Gaul was devastated and
destruction widespread, the Cimbri did finally depart from
our land and go in search of other territories. They left us
our own laws and rights, our lands and liberty. In contrast,
what do the Romans seek, what do they desire, if not to
follow envy's prompting? To become established in the lands
and states of people whose distinguished reputation and
military strength they acknowledge, and to inflict perpetual
slavery upon them? Never have they waged a war on terms
other than these. But if you are ignorant of what happens
among far-off peoples, look at the part of Gaul which borders
our land: reduced to the status of a province, its rights and
laws changed, subjected to Roman dominion, it is oppressed
by perpetual slavery.'

(78) After everyone's opinions were expressed they decided
that all those whose age or infirmity made them useless in the
war should leave the town, and resolved to try every course
of action before resorting to Critognatus' proposal—but if
circumstances were pressing and the reinforcements were
delayed, then that was the time to put his advice into practice, rather than submitting to terms of peace and surrender.

The Mandubii, who had received them into the town, were
forced to take their wives and children and depart from it.
When they came to the Roman fortifications, in tears they
begged and pleaded to be accepted as slaves and given food.
Caesar, however, set guards on the rampart and refused to
admit them.*

(79) Meanwhile Commius and the other leaders entrusted
with the supreme command reached Alesia with all their
forces. They occupied a hill outside, less than a mile from

our fortifications, and took up position there. The next day they brought their cavalry out of camp and filled the whole of the plain which we described earlier as being three miles across. They withdrew their infantry force a short distance and halted it on high ground. From the town of Alesia there was a clear view on to the plain. Once the reinforcements were sighted the besieged inhabitants hurried together and began to congratulate one another—everyone was stirred to a state of rejoicing. So they led their army out and took up position in front of the camp. They covered the nearest trench with wicker hurdles* and filled it in with earth, then made ready for a sortie and any eventuality.

(80) Caesar arranged his entire army along the two lines of defence so that, if the occasion arose, each man would know his own station and stick to it. Then he ordered the cavalry to be led out of camp and engaged in battle. There was a clear view from the camps located all around the top of the ridge, so every soldier was watching intently for the outcome. The Gauls had interspersed a few archers and light-armed skirmishers among their horsemen to offer assistance if their own side gave ground, and to resist the charge of our cavalry: a number of our soldiers were unexpectedly wounded by these men, and began to leave the fighting.

The Gauls were now convinced that their men were the better fighters, and could see that ours were hard pressed by their weight of numbers. From all directions shouting and howling went up from the Gauls within the defences and from those who had come to their aid, strengthening the resolve of their men. The action took place in full view of all, and it was impossible for any deed, be it courageous or cowardly, to be concealed. Thus the desire for praise and the fear of failure roused both sides to acts of bravery.

The fighting continued without a definite outcome from midday almost until sunset. Then in one part of the battle the Germans massed their squadrons, charged the enemy, and routed them. Once the Gallic cavalry was put to flight the archers were surrounded and killed. Likewise, elsewhere our men pursued the Gallic fugitives right up to their camp, giving them no chance to re-form. Those who had advanced from

Alesia almost gave up hope of victory, and returned to the town in dejection.

(81) A day went by, during which time the Gauls manufactured a large quantity of wicker hurdles, ladders, and grappling-hooks.* At dead of night they quietly left their camp and approached the lines of defence in the plain. Suddenly a cry went up, which signalled their arrival to those who were besieged in the town. Then the Gauls began to throw down the hurdles and use slings, arrows, and stones to dislodge our men from the rampart; and they got ready everything they needed for an attack. At the moment when the shout was heard Vercingetorix had the trumpet sound the signal to his men, and led them out of the town. Our men took up the positions which they had previously been assigned on the defences, and by the use of slings firing large stones, stakes earlier set out along the defences, and missiles, they frightened off the Gauls. Darkness decreased visibility, with the result that both sides incurred many casualties. The artillery machines kept up a hail of missiles. The defence of these sectors had been allotted to the legates Mark Antony and Gaius Trebonius: they took men from towers further away and sent them to assist as reinforcements where they realized that our men were under pressure.

(82) While the Gauls were some distance from the defences they had the advantage in number of missiles, but when they came up closer they were impaled on the 'spurs' or fell into the pits and were transfixed, or they were killed by pikes thrown from the rampart and towers. Casualties were heavy on both sides, but there was no breach in the defences. As dawn approached, therefore, the Gauls were afraid of encirclement on their exposed flank from the Roman camp higher up, and retreated to their comrades. While this was happening those inside the town fetched out the equipment Vercingetorix had had made ready for a sortie, and filled in the first set of trenches:* but they took too long over their arrangements, and before they reached the defences learned that their comrades had withdrawn. So they returned to the town without accomplishing their purpose.

(83) The Gauls had now suffered serious set-backs on two

occasions, and began to discuss what to do. They summoned men who knew the area well, and from them found out about the site and defences of the Roman camp on the higher ground. There was a hill to the north which our men had been unable to include in the siege-works because of its large circumference; they had been obliged to set up the camp on ground which, because of a gradual slope, was slightly disadvantageous. In charge of it were the legates Gaius Antistius Reginus and Gaius Caninius Rebilus, with two legions. Once their scouts had reconnoitred the area, the Gallic leaders chose 60,000 of their men, from the states which had the greatest reputation for courage. They decided among themselves in secret what must be done, and in what manner, then fixed the time for the attack, at midday.

In charge of this force was an Arvernian called Vercassivellaunus. He was one of the four Gallic leaders, and a kinsman of Vercingetorix. During the first watch he left camp—after nearly completing his march by daybreak he concealed himself beyond the mountain and ordered his soldiers to rest and recover from their efforts of the previous night. When noon drew near he set out against the camp we described above. At the same time the cavalry began to ride up to the defences in the plain, and the rest of the force appeared in front of the camp.

(84) Vercingetorix saw his men from the citadel of Alesia and marched out of the town, taking the wicker hurdles, poles, shelters,* siege-hooks, and the rest of the equipment he had had made ready for the sortie. At one and the same moment there was fighting on every side, and every expedient was put to the test. Wherever a hint of weakness appeared, there they flocked to the attack. The Roman force was strung out along its extensive fortifications and found rallying to the defence difficult in many places. The shouting which arose behind them was effective in frightening our men as they fought, for they realized that the risk to themselves depended on the courage shown by others: after all, it is usually the case that what is unseen is more effective in disturbing men's minds.*

(85) Caesar took over a suitable spot and found out what

was happening in every quarter; he sent help to those who were in difficulties. Both sides realized that this was the very moment for putting their utmost effort into the fight—the Gauls must despair of saving themselves unless they broke through the Roman defences, and the Romans, if they held firm, were looking forward to the end of all their labours. The struggle was hardest on the upper defences where, as we explained, Vercassivellaunus had been sent. The unfavourable downward slope of the site played a crucial part. Some of the enemy threw missiles, others formed a 'tortoise' and moved up close; exhausted troops were continually being replaced by fresh. They all threw earth on to the defences, which gave the Gauls a means of ascent as well as covering over the devices which the Romans had hidden in the ground. Our men were now running out of weapons and of strength.

(86) When he realized what was happening Caesar sent Labienus with six cohorts to help the men in trouble. He told him that if it was impossible to hold his ground he should withdraw his forces and then launch a counter-attack—but this was only to be done in an emergency. Caesar then approached the rest of the men in person, and urged them not to give up the struggle. He explained how the fruits of all their previous battles depended on that day, that hour. Inside the Roman lines the enemy abandoned hope of success on the level ground because of the size of the defences; so they tried to climb one of the steep ascents to take it, and had all the equipment they had prepared conveyed there. A hail of missiles from the defenders on the towers scattered them, but they filled in the ditches with earth and hurdles, and started to tear down the rampart and parapet with grappling-hooks.

(87) Caesar sent first the young Brutus with some cohorts, then his legate Gaius Fabius with more. Finally, when the fighting grew more fierce, he came in person, leading fresh troops for reinforcements. The battle was renewed and the enemy forced back. Then Caesar made for the place where he had sent Labienus. He withdrew four cohorts from the nearest fort and ordered one section of the cavalry to follow him, the rest to move round the outer defences and attack the enemy from the rear. Once Labienus had found

that neither earthworks nor ditches could stand up to the enemy attack, he gathered eleven cohorts,* which happened to be available after their withdrawal from the nearby guard-posts. He then sent word to Caesar of what he thought needed to be done.

Caesar hurried to join in the fighting. (88) The conspicuous colour of the cloak* he habitually wore in battle proclaimed his arrival. Because the downward slopes were in clear view from the heights above, the enemy spotted the cavalry squad-rons and cohorts he had ordered to follow him and joined battle. A shout went up from both sides, and was answered by another from the rampart and defence-works. Our men threw their spears, then fought with swords. Suddenly the cavalry was glimpsed in the rear: more cohorts were advanc-ing. The enemy turned tail and the cavalry charged them as they fled. Massive slaughter followed. Sedulius, the com-mander and leader of the Lemovices, was killed. The Arvernian Vercassivellaunus was taken alive as he fled. Seventy-four military standards were brought back to Caesar. Only a few of the vast enemy host made their way safely back to camp. Those in the town viewed the slaughter and the flight of their comrades: abandoning hope, they withdrew their forces from the defences.

As soon as the news broke, the Gauls fled from their camp. If our men had not been exhausted after numerous relief efforts and all the struggles of the day they would have been able to wipe out the entire enemy army. The cavalry was sent out at around midnight and caught up with the enemy rear-guard. Many of the enemy were taken and killed, and the rest fled to their home states.

(89) The following day Vercingetorix called a council and argued that he had undertaken this war not in his own in-terests but for the liberty of all. Since they were forced to yield to fortune, he went on, he was putting himself in their hands, ready for either outcome, whether they wanted to make reparation to the Romans by putting him to death, or to hand him over alive.

They sent envoys to Caesar to discuss these options, and he ordered them to give up their weapons and bring out the ringleaders. Then he took his seat within the fortifications in front of his camp, and the ringleaders were brought to him there. Vercingetorix was handed over, and weapons were thrown down.* Caesar had the Aedui and Arverni kept back, in case he could use them to win back their states' allegiance, and the rest of the prisoners he shared out as booty, one apiece, to his entire army.

(90) Once this business was settled he set out for the territory of the Aedui and won back their nation. The Arvernian envoys who had been sent there pledged to carry out whatever he told them to do. He demanded a large number of hostages. Then he sent the legions to winter quarters. He returned about 20,000 prisoners to the Aedui and Arverni. He ordered Titus Labienus to take two legions and the cavalry and set out for the land of the Sequani, assigning to him Marcus Sempronius Rutilus. He posted his legates Gaius Fabius and Lucius Minucius Basilus with two legions among the Remi, to prevent any defeat being inflicted by the neighbouring Bellovaci. He sent Gaius Antistius Reginus to the Ambibareti, Titus Sextius to the Bituriges, and Gaius Caninius Rebilus to the Ruteni, each with a single legion. He stationed Quintus Tullius Cicero and Publius Sulpicius at Cabillonum and Matisco (Aeduan settlements near the Saône) to arrange a supply of corn. He himself decided to winter at Bibracte.

When dispatches arrived at Rome giving news of these events a thanksgiving of twenty days was decreed.*

The Eighth Book, by Aulus Hirtius:

51 BC

(AUC 703: Consuls, Servius Sulpicius Rufus,
Marcus Claudius Marcellus)

The Final Pacification of Gaul:
Preparations for Civil War

Preface

Dear Balbus: to prevent my daily refusal appearing more like an excuse for avoiding effort than a plea for pardon on grounds of difficulty, I have—at your continual prompting—undertaken an extremely difficult task. Because of the gap which existed between his earlier and later writings, I have composed a continuation of our friend Caesar's commentaries on his campaigns in Gaul. His latter work, which was unfinished, I have completed from the operations at Alexandria right up to the end—not the end of civil strife, for the conclusion of *that* is not in sight, but the end of Caesar's life. I am anxious that any who read my work should understand how reluctantly I undertook to write it: this will absolve me more effectively of the charge of arrogant folly in intruding myself into the midst of Caesar's writings. After all, there is general agreement that however carefully other writers have completed their work, the refinement of these commentaries is by far superior. They were published to prevent writers from lacking accurate information on such important events; but they have won such universal acclaim that, rather than gaining a subject, the same writers seem to have been robbed of one.

Even so, my admiration of this achievement is greater than others': for everyone else knows how well and faultlessly he composed, but I also know how easily and swiftly he completed the commentaries. For Caesar possessed not only considerable fluency and refinement in his writing but also extremely precise expertise in setting out his own intentions. As for me, it never chanced that I was involved in the

Alexandrian and African wars. I learned something of these campaigns from conversation with Caesar; but we listen in one way to events which strike us as remarkable or unprecedented, and in quite another to facts we must then set down as evidence.

Doubtless, as I am amassing all these reasons and excuses to avoid being compared with Caesar, I am subject to accusations of arrogance all the same on the grounds that I think anyone could consider me on a level with Caesar. Farewell.

(1) The whole of Gaul was now conquered. There had been no break in campaigning since the previous summer, and Caesar wanted the soldiers to have a time of rest and refreshment in winter quarters after their strenuous efforts—but at the same time a number of Gallic states were reported to be renewing hostilities and hatching plots. The most likely reason suggested for this was that the Gauls had realized it was impossible for them all to stand together against the Romans in one place; but if a number of states went on the offensive at the same time in different places, the army of the Roman people would not have sufficient reinforcements or time or men to respond to them all. It would be wrong for any state to refuse to incur harm, if the respite afforded by its fate enabled the rest to win back their liberty.

(2) To prevent the Gauls being confirmed in this belief, Caesar put his quaestor Mark Antony in charge of his own winter camp while he himself set out from Bibracte on 31 December. Together with a cavalry guard he made his way to the Thirteenth legion, which he had posted close to Aeduan territory in the land of the Bituriges. To it he added the Eleventh, which had been stationed close by.

He left two cohorts to protect the heavy baggage and led the rest of the army to the country of the Bituriges, which is extremely fertile. With their wide territories and numerous towns, the Bituriges had proved too much for a single legion in winter quarters to control and prevent from starting war or hatching plots.

(3) What happened when Caesar suddenly arrived was inevitable, given that the Bituriges were scattered and unprepared. Free from any apprehension they were working in the

fields, and the cavalry attacked them before they could flee to the towns for refuge. For Caesar had given orders that the usual signal of enemy invasion—generally marked by the burning of buildings—was to be omitted: this would prevent shortages of corn and fodder if he wished to advance further, and would also stop the enemy being panicked by the burning. Many thousands were taken prisoner, and the Bituriges were so frightened that those who had managed to evade the Romans on their arrival had fled to neighbouring states. These refugees were depending on individual friendships or on their common partnership strategy. To no avail. For Caesar arrived everywhere by forced marches, and gave none of the states an opportunity to take thought for another's safety rather than its own. This speed of action ensured that friendly peoples remained so, and it frightened waverers into coming to terms. The Bituriges realized that Caesar's clemency* opened up a way for them to return to his friendship, and that the neighbouring states had given hostages and been received back into friendship without suffering punishment: when offered the same terms, they did likewise.

(4) The soldiers had eagerly persisted with their duties during the winter-time, enduring extremely difficult marches and unbearable cold. As a reward for their toil and endurance Caesar promised to each man 200 sesterces, and as many thousand* to the centurions, instead of booty. He sent the legions back to their winter camp and himself returned to Bibracte on the fortieth day. While he was there dispensing justice the Bituriges sent him envoys to seek reinforcements against the Carnutes who, they complained, had launched an attack upon them. Caesar had spent no more than eighteen days in camp, but on hearing this he took the Fourteenth and Sixth legions out of their winter quarters on the Saône (it was explained* in the previous commentary that he had posted them there to arrange a supply of corn). So he set out to pursue the Carnutes with two legions.

(5) When the news of this force reached the Carnutes they remembered the disaster which had befallen others; so they abandoned their villages and towns, where they were living in inadequate shelters built to meet their immediate need by making the winter bearable (after their recent defeat, they

had left a number of their towns). Then they fled in all directions. Caesar did not want his soldiers exposed to the storms which were breaking out with particular ferocity at that time, so he pitched camp at Cenabum, a town of the Carnutes. He housed the soldiers partly in Gallic dwellings, partly in shelters made from tents hastily covered with thatch. Even so, he sent out cavalry and auxiliaries in every direction where the enemy was rumoured to have gone, and with good results—for most of our men returned loaded with booty they had seized. Because of the severe winter and their fear of imminent threat, the Carnutes were under pressure, driven from their homes, no longer daring to remain in one place for any length of time, unable to conceal themselves under the protection of the forest (because of the fierce storms). They dispersed and scattered to neighbouring states, with the loss of a large part of their population.

(6) This was the hardest time of year. Caesar therefore thought it sufficient to break up the forces which were assembling in order to prevent any outbreak of hostilities. As far as he could judge it seemed improbable that there would be any opportunity now for a war of much importance. He posted Gaius Trebonius and two legions, which he had with him, to winter quarters at Cenabum. He himself learned from numerous embassies of the Remi that the Bellovaci—a people outstanding among all the Gauls and Belgic peoples for their excellent record in war—and their neighbours were preparing an army for muster at a single location, under the leadership of Correus of the Bellovaci and Commius the Atrebatian. Their intention was to launch an attack in full force on the borders of the Suessiones, a people who paid tribute to the Remi. Caesar judged it crucial not only to his prestige* but also to his safety to prevent any harm being done to allies who had served the Republic well. So he recalled the Eleventh legion from winter quarters and sent a letter to Gaius Fabius, telling him to bring his two legions to the territory of the Suessiones. He also summoned one of Titus Labienus' two legions. In this way, as far as the arrangement of winter quarters and the strategic demands of war allowed, with unremitting effort on his part, Caesar imposed the burden of operations on different legions in turn.

(7) Once he had gathered his army he set out against the Bellovaci. He pitched camp in their territory and sent out cavalry squadrons in all directions to take prisoners from whom he could find out the enemy's strategy. The cavalry carried out their orders, and reported back that they had found very few men in the buildings, and even these had not remained behind to farm the land (for everywhere the evacuation had been thorough) but had been sent back as spies. When Caesar asked these prisoners where the host of the Bellovaci was, and what were their intentions, he discovered that all the Bellovaci capable of bearing arms had met in a single place, and with them the Ambiani, Aulerci, Caleti, Veliocasses, and Atrebates; also that they had selected a spot on high wooded ground surrounded by a marsh for their camp, and had transferred all their heavy baggage into the depths of the forest. Their campaign had a number of ringleaders, but the army gave special place to Correus, realizing that his hatred of the name of the Roman people was fiercest. A few days before, the prisoners went on, Commius the Atrebatian had departed from the camp to win reinforcements from the Germans, who were not only close at hand but also possessed of immense numbers of men. With the unanimous agreement of the leaders and eager assent from the people, the Bellovaci had decided that if—as was rumoured—Caesar was advancing with three legions, they should offer battle. This would avoid their being forced to fight under harsher and more difficult conditions with the entire Roman army at a later date. If Caesar brought up larger forces they would remain in the position they had already selected, and by means of traps would cut the Romans off from forage, which because of the time of year was both scanty and widely dispersed, and from corn and other supplies as well.

(8) Most of the prisoners were in agreement as to the facts, and after hearing them Caesar judged that the strategy being proposed was very cautious and far removed from the rash haste characteristic of barbarians. So he decided to attend to every matter which would tempt the enemy to despise his small numbers of men and thus give battle. He had the Seventh, Eighth, and Ninth, all veteran legions of outstanding courage; also the Eleventh, a select legion of young men

which showed great promise. The latter was now on its eighth campaign, but when compared with the others had yet to win a similar reputation for mature courage.

Caesar called a council and explained all the facts which had been laid before him. Then he spoke words of encouragement to the men. To see if he could persuade the enemy to engage, in the belief that he had only three legions, he arranged the column so that the Seventh, Eighth, and Ninth marched ahead of all the heavy baggage. The Eleventh were to bring up the rear of the baggage column, which was of moderate size, as was Caesar's custom on active operations. This would stop the enemy catching sight of an army larger than the one they had wanted. This ploy meant that his army was in virtual battle formation,* and he marched it to within sight of the enemy more quickly than they had expected.

(9) When the Gauls (whose confident plans had been reported to Caesar) suddenly caught sight of the legions approaching steadily as if ready for battle, they drew up their forces in front of the camp but did not move from the higher ground. Perhaps this was because of the risks involved in engaging, or because Caesar's arrival was so sudden, or because they were waiting to see what our plan was. Caesar had been keen to engage, but was surprised by the enemy's numbers; he pitched his camp opposite that of the enemy, with a valley more deep than broad in-between. He gave orders for the camp to be fortified with a twelve-foot rampart, and had a parapet constructed in proportion to the rampart's height. A double ditch was dug, fifteen feet wide and with perpendicular sides. Three-storey towers were erected at frequent intervals, and linked by covered gangways in between. The open faces of these were protected by wicker parapets. This meant that they could ward off the enemy by means of the double ditch and a double line of defenders, the first of which could launch missiles from the gangways where height offered a greater degree of safety. The second line, stationed on the rampart and hence closer to the enemy, was protected from falling missiles by the gangways. He placed doorways and higher towers at the gates.

(10) The strategy behind this defence was twofold. First,

he was hopeful that the extensive defence-works and his own apparent fear would instil confidence in the enemy; secondly, when it became necessary to go further afield in search of forage and corn, he saw that the camp could, with a small force, be protected by its own defences.

In the meantime small numbers of men from both sides were frequently running forward between the two camps and coming into conflict across the marsh. On occasions either our Gallic and German auxiliaries would cross the marsh and pursue the enemy fiercely, or in turn the enemy would cross instead and force our men to give way for a distance. It was inevitable, given that they were seeking it from a few scattered farms, that during the daily foraging expeditions forage parties spread out and were surrounded in difficult locations. This inflicted insignificant losses of pack animals and slaves on our men, but it inflamed the foolish hopes of the barbarians, all the more so because Commius (who, as I explained, had set out to win reinforcements from the Germans) had arrived with some cavalry. Although these numbered no more than 500, the barbarians were still relying on the arrival of the Germans.

(11) Caesar noticed that on several successive days the enemy remained in their camp, which was protected by the marsh and by the nature of its site; and he saw that the camp could not be attacked without a bloody conflict, while he would need a larger force if he was to surround the site with siege-works. So he sent a letter to Trebonius telling him to summon the Thirteenth legion, which was wintering among the Bituriges under his legate Titus Sextius, and thus to join him with three legions in all, after making his way by forced marches. Caesar himself had in turn called up a large force of cavalry from the Remi and Lingones and other Gallic states: these he sent out to escort the forage-parties, so that they could withstand sudden enemy attacks.

(12) Because this took place every day and had the force of habit, the Bellovaci grew careless: this is the usual result of routine activities. After ascertaining our cavalry's daily positions and selecting a force of horsemen, they laid a trap in the woods. Next day they sent their horsemen there, first

to lure our men on, then to surround them and attack. This evil fate befell the Remi, whose turn it was to carry out forage duty that day. On suddenly catching sight of the enemy cavalry, they reacted with contempt to such a small force (their own numbers being greater), pursued too eagerly, and found themselves encircled. This threw them into a panic more quickly than is usual in cavalry battles; they retreated after losing Vertiscus, who was the leader of their nation and a cavalry commander. Because of his age this Vertiscus was scarcely able to sit astride a horse, yet in keeping with Gallic custom he had neither used his age as an excuse for avoiding the command nor wanted the fight to go ahead without him.

The enemy were fired and roused by this successful engagement, and by the death of a leading citizen and commander of the Remi; but the defeat acted as a warning to our men to make their troop dispositions only after a more careful reconnaissance—and to be less hasty in pursuing the enemy.

(13) Daily engagements continued within sight of both camps. These took place at the fords and shallows of the marsh. Once during these skirmishes the Germans, whom Caesar had brought across the Rhine to fight amongst his cavalry, with great determination crossed the marsh in a body, killed a few of the enemy who stood their ground, and pursued the rest of their army vigorously. The result was panic: not just among those who were attacked at close quarters or wounded by missiles, but even among the reserves who were some way off. They fled like cowards, and did not stop running—more than once missing the chance of a better position—until they were back in their camp. In some cases they were driven by such shame that they ran even further still. The whole force was in such a state of fear because of this danger that it was virtually impossible to judge which was the more disproportionate: their arrogance following an insignificant success, or their panic after a slight defeat.

(14) Several days had gone by in these same camps when the leaders of the Bellovaci learned that Gaius Trebonius and his legions were advancing. In fear of such a siege as had taken place at Alesia, by night they sent away all the men who were too old or weak, or who had no weapons, and the

rest of the heavy baggage with them. They were getting the column into order: it was in a confused muddle, for a horde of waggons usually follows the Gauls even when they are supposed to be unencumbered and ready for action. Dawn caught them unawares, however, so they drew up their armed forces in front of their camp in case the Romans should start to pursue them before the baggage train could move a significant distance forward. Because of the steepness of the climb, however, Caesar judged that they were not to be attacked if they stood their ground. At the same time he decided that he must move up his legions to make it impossible for the barbarians to effect a safe withdrawal from their position without coming under pressure from his soldiers. He could see that the camps were separated by a marsh which would be difficult to cross, and that this would slow them down if they tried to pursue the enemy; but he noticed also that across the marsh there was a ridge reaching almost to the enemy camp, with only a shallow valley between. So he had gangways laid over the marsh, took his legions over, and quickly reached the top of the plateau on the ridge, which was protected on two sides by a downward slope. There he re-formed the legions and made his way to the far end of the ridge, where he formed his battle line. From here it was possible to discharge missiles from artillery machines into the thick of the enemy.

(15) Relying on the natural strength of their position, the barbarians were not averse to giving battle if the Romans should happen to attempt climbing the hill. On the other hand, they were unable to divide their forces up and send them away gradually in case they were scattered and routed: so they remained in battle formation. Caesar recognized their determination. Drawing up twenty cohorts, he measured out a camp on the spot and gave orders for its fortification. Once the works were completed he posted the legions he had drawn up in front of the rampart and stationed his cavalry on guard-posts with their horses ready bridled.

The Bellovaci saw that the Romans were prepared for pursuit and that they could not themselves pass the night where they were without serious risk, so they settled on the following plan for withdrawal. As usual, they had an abundance of bundles of straw and twigs in camp, and they passed them from hand to hand and put them in front of their battle line. At sunset the signal was given and all the bundles were set alight together. The sudden blaze of fire hid their entire army from the Romans' sight, at which moment the barbarians ran away with all possible speed.

(16) Although the fire blocked his view of the enemy withdrawal, Caesar was none the less suspicious that it was a ruse to aid their flight. So he moved his legions up and sent out cavalry squadrons in pursuit. But he was anxious about a possible ambush, in case the enemy were holding their position to entice our men on to unfavourable ground, and so he advanced with considerable caution. The cavalry were afraid to pass through the thick smoke and flame, and any who did venture forward with some eagerness could scarcely make out their own horses' heads. Their fear of a trap gave the Bellovaci an unrestricted opportunity of withdrawal. The enemy's flight was marked by fear and cunning in equal measure, and marred by no losses; they marched for less than ten miles and then pitched camp in a place with strong defences. From there they repeatedly set ambushes consisting of infantry and cavalry and inflicted serious casualties on the Roman forage-parties.

(17) This began to happen too frequently. Caesar discovered from a prisoner that Correus, the leader of the Bellovaci, had picked out 6,000 of his best soldiers and 1,000 from his cavalry. These he was using to set a trap at the place where he suspected the Romans would be going because of the store of corn and forage there. Once he knew of the plan Caesar led out more of the legions than usual. He sent the cavalry on ahead, which as usual acted as a guard for the forage-parties, and included light-armed auxiliaries among the horsemen. He himself approached as near as possible with his legions.

(18) The enemy were arranged in ambush. They had selected for this action a plain which extended for no more than a mile in any direction. It was protected on every side either by woodland or by a river which would be extremely

difficult to cross, and like a cordon of huntsmen they encircled it with ambushes.

But the enemy's strategy was exposed, while our men had
both weapons and spirits ready for the fight. With the legions
in support, moreover, they did not refuse to engage, but
advanced to the place squadron by squadron. Once they had
arrived Correus judged that he had been given his opportunity for battle; at first he appeared with a few men and
charged against the nearest squadrons. Our men held out
firmly against his attack, not too many of them rushing
together—for it commonly happens in cavalry battles that
because of some panic the very number of men involved
causes casualties.

(19) Now the squadrons were posted, it was the turn of
the men to engage in small groups. To prevent their comrades
being encircled on the flanks, as Correus was battling the rest
of the enemy burst out of the woods. The fighting was fierce
in every quarter, but when it continued inconclusively* for
too long a force of infantry which was standing ready gradually emerged from the woods and forced our cavalry to give
ground. Our light-armed troops, however, who, as I explained,
were sent ahead of the legions, swiftly came to their support:
they took up positions amongst our squadrons and fought
resolutely. For some time the fight was equal on both sides,
but then the nature of the combat made it inevitable that
those of our men who had held off the first attack began to
get the upper hand in the battle. This was because they had
not been so rash as to incur losses at the hands of the enemy
who were lying in wait for them.

Meanwhile the legions were drawing nearer, and a flurry
of reports reached both our men and the enemy simultaneously that the commander was at hand with all his forces at
the ready. When they heard this our men put their trust in
the protection of the cohorts and fought more eagerly than
ever, to prevent the battle going on too long so that they
would have to share the glory of victory with the legions.
The enemy lost heart and tried to flee in all directions. To no
avail. In the end they were themselves trapped by the same
natural barriers which they had hoped would cut off the

Romans. They were overcome and beaten and fled in confusion with the loss of more than half their force. Some made for the forest, some the river—and even these were despatched by our men, who pursued them keenly.

Correus, meanwhile, was far from crushed by this disaster, and could not be persuaded to leave the battle or take refuge in the woods, nor to take up the opportunity of surrender which we were offering. Rather, he fought with great courage and wounded many, thus provoking the anger of his conquerors and forcing them to cast their weapons against him.

(20) Such was the character of the fighting; Caesar came upon the traces of battle while they were still fresh, and expected that after news of this disastrous defeat arrived the enemy would abandon the site of their camp, which was said to be no further than about seven miles from the scene of slaughter. He saw that the river hindered his advance, but none the less took his army across and continued his march.

The Bellovaci, however, and the other Gallic peoples now suddenly had to welcome back the few fugitives—and wounded men at that—who had used the woods to advantage and managed to avoid their fate. Everything was against them: they learned of the defeat, the death of Correus, and the loss of both their cavalry and the best of the infantry. When they realized that the Romans were approaching they blew a trumpet to summon an assembly at once, and sent envoys and hostages to Caesar.

(21) This plan was universally approved. Commius the Atrebatian fled to the Germans from whom he had obtained reinforcements for this campaign. The rest immediately sent envoys to Caesar and requested that he be satisfied with the punishment his enemy had suffered—a punishment which, had he been in a position to inflict it on them without a fight and while they were still unscathed, he surely would never have done so, on account of his clemency and kindness. The cavalry battle, they said, had impaired the strength of the Bellovaci, and many thousands of their finest infantry had perished: hardly anyone had survived to bring news of the slaughter. Despite the magnitude of this disaster, however, the Bellovaci had obtained one great advantage from the

battle, namely, that Correus, the rabble-rousing instigator of the war, had been killed. For while he lived the senate had always been less in control of the state than the ignorant common people.

(22) As they made their pleas Caesar reminded the envoys of the following facts: during the previous year the Bellovaci had undertaken the war at the same time as the other Gallic nations. They had clung to their policy more obstinately than all the rest, and had not come to their senses when all the rest surrendered. He was quite aware that it was easy to lay the blame on dead men—no one man, however, could be so powerful as to urge a war, and wage it, with a feeble crowd of ordinary citizens if the leaders of the state opposed it, the senate resisted the move, and all right-thinking men obstructed it. Even so, he would be satisfied with the punishment which they had inflicted upon themselves.

(23) The following night the envoys reported his reply to their people, and collected the hostages. The envoys of the other nations, which were awaiting the fate of the Bellovaci, hastily assembled. Except for Commius, who was too afraid to entrust his own safety to anyone's good faith, they gave hostages and obeyed Caesar's orders. The previous year, while Caesar was dispensing justice in Nearer Gaul, Titus Labienus had caught Commius in the act of inciting revolt among the Gallic nations and plotting against Caesar; but he had judged that Commius' treachery could be suppressed without any breach of a safe conduct. Labienus did not believe, however, that Commius would come to his camp if summoned, and was unwilling to put him on his guard by attempting it. So he sent Gaius Volusenus Quadratus to feign interest in holding talks, and have him killed; and assigned to him a picked group of centurions well fitted for the task. When the parley took place and Volusenus seized Commius by the hand as arranged, a centurion—troubled by the unusual nature of the task, perhaps, or quickly obstructed by Commius' friends—failed to finish him off. Nevertheless, he did inflict a serious wound to Commius' head with a first stroke of his sword. Then swords were drawn on both sides, but each party was more intent on flight than fight—our men in the belief that

Commius had been dealt a mortal blow, and the Gauls because they saw this was a trap and were afraid that more perils awaited them than those which were apparent. After this it was said that Commius had resolved never to come within sight of a Roman again.

(24) The most warlike nations were now completely subdued, and it was evident to Caesar that there were no longer any peoples making ready for war for him to combat; rather, a number of people were leaving the towns and fleeing their lands to avoid the power now descending upon them. He therefore decided to send the army out to different areas. He kept his quaestor Mark Antony and the Twelfth legion at his side. He sent his legate Gaius Fabius with twenty-five cohorts to the remotest area of Gaul, because he was receiving reports that certain peoples in that region were in arms and he thought that the two legions commanded by his legate Gaius Caninius Rebilus (who was present in that area) were below full strength. He summoned Titus Labienus, but sent the Fifteenth legion, which had been with Labienus in winter quarters, to Cisalpine Gaul to guard the colonies of Roman citizens there. This would prevent a similar set-back to that inflicted the previous summer, when the people of Tergeste had suffered a sudden assault and raid from an invasion of barbarians.*

Caesar himself set out to ravage and sack the territory of Ambiorix. He had given up hope of bringing Ambiorix, who was a frightened fugitive, under his control, and he considered it the next best thing for his prestige to despoil his land of its citizens, buildings, and cattle so completely that Ambiorix would come to be hated by any of his people who might chance to have survived, and would be unable to return to his state because of these devastating disasters.

(25) Caesar sent out legions or auxiliary forces to every part of Ambiorix's territory, and inflicted devastation by slaughter, fire, and pillage. Large numbers of men were captured or killed. He then sent Labienus with two legions against the Treveri, a people who, because of their proximity to the Germans, had daily practice in warfare; they were little different from Germans in their barbarian way of life, and never followed orders unless forced to do so by an army.

(26) In the meantime the legate Gaius Caninius learned from a dispatch and messages sent by Duratius (who, despite the revolt of some of his people, had always remained a faithful friend to Romans) that a large enemy army had mustered in the territory of the Pictones. So he set out for the town of Lemonum. When he drew near to the town he received firm reports from prisoners that Lemonum was under attack from Dumnacus, the leader of the Andes, with many thousands of men, and that Duratius was under siege. Caninius did not want to risk setting weakened legions against this enemy, but pitched camp in a secure location. When Dumnacus heard that Caninius was at hand he shifted his entire force to face the legions and began an assault upon the Roman camp. After he had spent several days on this assault and, despite losing many of his men, had failed to undermine any part of the defences, he returned to the siege of Lemonum.

(27) At the same time the legate Gaius Fabius was receiving several nations back under Rome's protection and confirming the arrangement by a handover of hostages. He was informed by a letter from Gaius Caninius Rebilus of what was happening among the Pictones. On receipt of this information he set out to the assistance of Duratius. When Dumnacus heard of Fabius' approach, however, he feared for his life if forced both to withstand an external Roman enemy and at the same time to keep a nervous watch on the townspeople. So he suddenly withdrew from the place, together with his forces, and did not believe himself to be safe until he had got his army over the Loire, which is so wide that it must be crossed by means of a bridge. Fabius was not yet in sight of the enemy, nor had he joined forces with Caninius: none the less, he received information from men who knew the area, and so the spot which he thought the enemy would most probably make for was indeed where they were headed.

Fabius marched towards the same bridge with his army, and ordered the cavalry to make their way in front of the legionary column—as far ahead as possible without making the horses tired when returning to the same camp at the end of the march. In accordance with these instructions our cavalry set off in pursuit and attacked Dumnacus' column. The men they attacked on the march fled in panic, encumbered by their heavy packs. Many of them were killed, and a large amount of booty seized. After this successful engagement the cavalry returned to camp.

(28) The following night Fabius sent the cavalry on ahead in readiness to engage and block the progress of the entire column until he caught up. In order to carry out this action according to Fabius' orders the cavalry officer Quintus Atius Varus, a man of exceptional courage and sound judgement, urged on his men and caught up with the enemy column. Some of his cavalry squadrons he posted at appropriate points, and with the rest he engaged in a cavalry battle. The enemy cavalry fought the more boldly because their infantry was coming up in support, halting the entire column and offering the cavalry reinforcement against our men. A fierce battle ensued. Our men despised the enemy they had beaten only the day before, and recalled that the legions were on their way in support: both the shame of retreat and the desire to make an end of the fight all by themselves led them to battle bravely against the enemy infantry. The enemy, on the other hand, were convinced that, as they had been informed the previous day, no more of our forces were on their way—and they seemed to have a chance of wiping out our cavalry.

(29) The struggle continued for some time. Dumnacus drew up his battle line to give protection in turn to his cavalry. Then suddenly the legions came into enemy view, marching in close order. The barbarian squadrons were thrown into confusion at the sight of them, the enemy line panicked, and the baggage-column was in dismay—amid shouting and disorder they all fled. Our cavalry, however, who a moment before had been struggling against fierce resistance, were now full of elation at their success. A great shout went up on all sides and they surrounded the enemy in retreat. In the course of the battle they killed as many of the enemy as the stamina of their horses for the pursuit—and the strength of their hands for the slaughter—would allow. More than 12,000 were killed—either armed men or men who through fear had thrown their arms away. The whole baggage train was captured.

(30) After this it became apparent that one of the Senones, a man called Drappes, had mustered no more than 2,000 men from the rout and was making for the Province. Ever since Gaul first revolted he had gathered desperate men from all around, called slaves to liberty, summoned exiles from every state, and welcomed brigands. Thus he had been able to cut off the Romans' baggage and supplies. It was also evident that Lucterius the Cadurcan, who was known from the previous commentary to have wanted to attack the Province when Gaul first revolted,* was making common counsel with Drappes. The legate Caninius set out to pursue them with two legions, to prevent harm or panic in the Province causing deep disgrace because of the depredations of these outlaws.

(31) Gaius Fabius set out with the rest of the army against the Carnutes and the other states whose armies he knew had been destroyed in the battle against Dumnacus. For he was in no doubt that they would prove to be more amenable because of this recent defeat, although given time they could be incited if Dumnacus roused them. In the event Fabius had extreme good luck and made good speed in recovering these states. For the Carnutes, though often under attack, had never sued for peace, but they came to surrender and give up hostages; while when Fabius and the legions arrived the other states in the very farthest reaches of Gallic territory beside the Ocean (the ones known as Aremoric) at the Carnutes' instigation immediately bowed to his commands. Dumnacus was expelled from his own land: skulking and wandering alone, he was forced to make for the remotest regions of Gaul.

(32) When Drappes and Lucterius realized that Caninius and the legions were at hand, however, they were sure that they could not enter the Province with an army in pursuit without certain destruction. Also they had no opportunity of ranging freely and acting as outlaws. So they halted in the territory of the Cadurci. Formerly, when circumstances were favourable, Lucterius had exercised considerable power among his fellow-citizens—and an instigator of sedition was always influential among barbarians. With his and Drappes' armies

he seized control of Uxellodunum, a town which had once been a dependency of his* and had strong natural defences; and he joined forces with the townspeople.

(33) Gaius Caninius speedily arrived there, and observed that all areas of the town were protected by sheer rock faces. Indeed it would be difficult to climb up even with no one defending the town. On the other hand, he could see that the townspeople had large quantities of baggage: if, therefore, they tried to run away secretly taking it with them, they would find it impossible to escape not only the cavalry but even the legions. So he divided his cohorts into three sections and constructed a triple camp on very high ground. From this camp he began gradually—as much as his strength of numbers allowed—to build a rampart around the town.

(34) When the townspeople saw this they were much troubled by dreadful recollections of Alesia, and feared a similar outcome to this siege. In particular Lucterius, who had already suffered that fate, warned them to devise some strategy for the corn supply. It was unanimously decided to leave part of their army in the town, and to take light-armed troops and set out to bring in corn.

Now that this plan was approved, the following night Drappes and Lucterius left 2,000 armed men behind and led the rest out of the town. After a few days they collected a large quantity of corn from the land of the Cadurci, some of whom were happy to help supply corn, while others could not prevent their taking it. On more than one occasion, however, they made night-time raids to attack our forts. Because of this Gaius Caninius put off completing the encirclement of the town, in case he was either unable to defend the works when complete, or obliged to post weak garrisons at too frequent intervals.

(35) Now that they had plenty of corn, Drappes and Lucterius took up position no more than ten miles from the town. From here they could convey corn to the town a little at a time. They divided up the duties between them—Drappes remained with part of their army to guard the camp, while Lucterius took the train of pack animals to the town. He set guard-posts at various points, and at around the tenth hour

of the night he began to take corn into the town along narrow woodland paths.

Our camp sentries heard the noise they made, and scouts were sent out who returned to report what was going on. With the armed cohorts from the nearest forts Caninius made a swift dawn attack upon the Gauls who were transporting the corn. This sudden calamity threw them into a panic and they fled to their guard-posts; when our men caught sight of these, they were yet more fiercely roused against the enemy soldiers, and allowed none of them to be taken alive. Lucterius fled the place with a few men and did not return to his camp.

(36) Following this successful operation Caninius learned from prisoners that part of the enemy army was encamped with Drappes, not much more than eleven miles off. Several people informed him of this fact. When he realized that one of their leaders had been routed, and that the rest of their men were terrified and could easily be subdued, he thought it a stroke of luck that no one had survived the slaughter to return to camp and bring news of the defeat to Drappes. He foresaw no danger in what he was to attempt, but still he sent on ahead all the cavalry and the German infantry, who move with great speed, to the enemy camp. Then he assigned one legion to the triple camp and led the other out without its heavy kit.

When he drew near to the enemy he learned from the scouts he had sent on ahead that they had given up the higher ground and that their camp—as is practically habitual among barbarians—was down by the river-bank. He also heard that the cavalry and the Germans had swept down and caught them off guard and unawares, and had joined battle. On receipt of this information he led out his legion, armed and in battle order. So it was that the signal suddenly went up from every side and the high ground was taken. Once this took place, the Germans and the cavalry battled with renewed vigour on catching sight of the legionary standards. At once the cohorts launched an assault from all quarters: the enemy were all either killed or captured, and much plunder was taken. Drappes was taken prisoner in the battle.

(37) Caninius had brought this engagement to a successful

conclusion, and his own soldiers were virtually unscathed. He then went back to continue besieging the townspeople. The enemy outside had been destroyed: it was in fear of them that Caninius had been prevented from dividing up his garrisons and encircling the townspeople, so now he gave orders for the work to be set in train at every point. Next day Gaius Fabius arrived with his army and took part of the town to blockade it.

(38) In the meantime Caesar left his quaestor Mark Antony with fifteen cohorts in the land of the Bellovaci so that the Belgae would not have an opportunity of planning some fresh revolt. He himself approached the other peoples; he demanded more hostages, and as they were all in a panic he gave them reassurance. When he came to the Carnutes—the people among whom the war began, as Caesar explained in the previous commentary*—he could see that their guilt was making them particularly nervous. So as to allay their fears the more swiftly he demanded for punishment Gutruater, the ringleader in the plot and instigator of the war. Although Gutruater did not entrust his safety even to his fellow-citizens, nevertheless they all did their best to seek him out, and he was taken to Caesar's camp. Strong pressure from his soldiers forced Caesar to punish Gutruater, against the bias of his own inclination: they blamed him for all the dangers and losses they had suffered in the war. So he was beaten to death and then decapitated.

(39) A number of dispatches from Caninius then informed Caesar of what had happened to Drappes and Lucterius, and of the resolution with which the townspeople were holding out. Even though he scorned them because of their small numbers, he judged it necessary to punish their obstinacy severely: he had to prevent the whole of Gaul thinking it was resolution, rather than sufficient strength, that it lacked for resisting the Romans, and he must also stop other peoples following this example and making the most of their advantageous positions to win their liberty. He was aware that all the Gauls knew that his command* was due to last for only one more campaign season: if they could endure this, they would have no more threat to fear. For this reason Caesar

left his legate Quintus Calenus with two legions to follow
him by regular marches. He himself set out at top speed with
all the cavalry to join Caninius.

(40) Contrary to everyone's expectation Caesar arrived at
Uxellodunum. He observed that the town was enclosed by
siege-works and that it was impossible to draw back from
the siege under any circumstances. He also learned from
deserters that the townspeople had plentiful supplies of corn,
so he began to try and cut off the enemy's water. A river ran
along the bottom of the valley which almost surrounded the
hill on which the town of Uxellodunum, with its sheer sides,
was situated. The nature of the ground meant that diverting
the stream was impossible, for the way it flowed at the foot
of the hill meant that its course could not be deflected by
digging channels. On the other hand, for the townspeople the
way down to the river was steep and difficult: if our soldiers
stood in their way they could not reach the river and make
their way back up the steep climb unscathed, without risk-
ing their lives. Caesar perceived their difficulty and posted
archers and slingers; he also set up artillery at certain points
to face the easiest downward paths. In this way he deprived
the townspeople of water.

(41) All the townspeople in a body came together to get
water at a single point beneath the town wall—there a large
spring gushed out and there was a space of about 300 feet
where the river did not encircle the town. Although everyone
else was hopeful that the townspeople could be cut off from
this spring, Caesar alone saw how to bring it about: he began
to bring up movable shelters facing the place and opposite
the hill, and constructed an earthwork with great effort and
amid constant fighting. The townspeople ran down from their
vantage-point, engaging at long range and at no risk to themselves, and wounding many of our men as they doggedly made
their way up. Yet our men were not deterred from bringing
the shelters forward, and their struggles and hard work overcame the difficulties of their position. At the same time they
were bringing mine tunnels forward to the water channels and
the head of the spring—and this action was able to proceed
without risk, and without arousing the enemy's suspicions.

The earthwork was built up to a height of sixty feet, and a ten-storey tower placed upon it. This was not intended to equal the height of the wall (an aim impossible to achieve) but rather to reach above the height of the spring. Catapults discharged missiles at the approach to the spring, and the townspeople could not fetch water safely. The result was that not only the cattle and pack animals but also all the enemy were consumed by thirst.

(42) This affliction threw the townspeople into a panic. They filled casks with tallow, pitch, and shingle, which they set alight and poured on to the siege-works. At the same time they fought with extreme ferocity, so that the threat posed by battle would deter the Romans from putting out the fire. Suddenly a blaze broke out on the siege-works—for every missile discharged down the steep incline stuck fast in the shelters and the earthwork and ignited whatever stood in its way. On the other hand, although our soldiers were under pressure because of this dangerous style of fighting and their difficult position, they none the less stood their ground with exceptional courage. This action took place on high ground and in sight of our army, and a loud shout went up on both sides. Thus each man tried his best to be noticed, and to have his courage marked and witnessed, by exposing himself to the missiles and fires of the enemy.

(43) Caesar saw that a number of his men were wounded. He ordered the cohorts to climb the hill on every side of the town and, while pretending to attack the walls, to raise a shout all round. This action terrified the townspeople. As they were in doubt as to what was happening elsewhere, they recalled their soldiers from the attack on the siege-works and stationed them on the walls. In this way our men ended the battle and either put out the fires on the siege-works or cut away the parts which were burning. The townspeople continued to put up strong resistance and, despite the fact that many of them had died of thirst, they persisted in their intention; yet in the end the mines enabled us to cut off and divert the channels of the spring. This act caused the spring, which had never yet failed, to dry up; the townspeople now lost all hope of saving themselves, and believed that this had happened

not through human stratagem but by the will of the gods. Thus they were forced of necessity to surrender.

(44) Caesar knew that his leniency was universally known, and so he was not afraid that if he acted somewhat harshly he would appear to have done so out of any innate cruelty; nor, indeed, could he foresee any successful outcome of his strategies if more of the enemy in other areas acted similarly in adopting such a course. For this reason he decided upon making an example of the townspeople in punishing them, so as to deter the rest. He allowed them to live, therefore, but cut off the hands of all those who had carried arms against him. This made the punishment for wrongdoers plain to see.

Drappes (who, as I explained, had been captured by Caninius) refused food for a number of days and so died—either because of the shame and grief of being held in chains or in fear of a more severe punishment. At the same time Lucterius who, as I described, had escaped from the battle, fell into the power of an Arvernian called Epasnactus. Lucterius was unable to spend too long in any one place and, frequently changing location, was obliged to entrust his personal safety to the good faith of many—for he was aware of what an enemy he must have in Caesar. This Arvernian Epasnactus, who was a loyal friend of the Roman people, bound Lucterius in chains and sent him to Caesar without hesitation.

(45) Meanwhile Labienus fought a successful cavalry engagement in the land of the Treveri, and killed some of the Treveri and a number of Germans—who never refuse to help anyone fighting the Romans. Their leaders he took alive and subdued. Among them was an Aeduan called Surus, a man of distinction in both courage and lineage, who alone of the Aedui had still remained ready to fight.

(46) On learning of this, Caesar observed that operations in every part of Gaul were going well, and he judged that Gaul had now been conquered and humbled by the campaigns of previous seasons. He had, however, never been to Aquitania in person, but had conquered part of it through Publius Crassus. He therefore set out for that region, to spend the final part of his campaign season there. This action was

as swiftly and successfully completed as all the rest had been, for all the Aquitanian peoples sent Caesar envoys and surrendered hostages to him. After this he set out for Narbo with the cavalry as escort.

He had his legates settle the army in its winter quarters. Four legions he posted in Belgium under his legates Mark Antony, Gaius Trebonius, and Publius Vatinius. Two he sent to the Aedui, whose influence in all Gaul he knew to be pre-eminent. Two he posted among the Turones, on the Carnutes' borders, to exercise control over the whole of the region which borders the Ocean. The remaining two went to the lands of the Lemovices, close to the Arverni. Thus no area of Gaul was free from his army's presence.

He lingered in the Province for a few days, hastening through all the assize towns, hearing public disputes and distributing rewards to those who deserved them: for he had an excellent opportunity of learning what had been each person's attitude to the Gallic revolt, a revolt which he had withstood because of the loyal assistance given by the Province. These affairs settled, he withdrew to his legions in Belgium and wintered at Nemetocenna.

(47) There he learned how Commius the Atrebatian had clashed in battle with the Roman cavalry. Antony had reached winter quarters and found the Atrebates staying loyal, but Commius, after being wounded as I related earlier, had habitually kept himself in readiness for any disturbance among his fellow-citizens so that when they looked for a plan of campaign a leader and commander would not be lacking. Now that the Atrebates were in subjection to the Romans he supported himself and his followers by using his cavalry for raids. By lying in wait along the roads he intercepted a number of supply convoys which were on their way to the Romans' winter camp.

(48) Gaius Volusenus Quadratus had been assigned to Antony as cavalry officer, to winter with him. Antony sent him in pursuit of the enemy cavalry. Volusenus combined with his exceptional courage a great hatred of Commius, so he was all the more glad to carry out these orders. He set up ambushes, attacked Commius' cavalry, and won his engagements. At

last, in an encounter somewhat fiercer than usual, his eagerness to intercept Commius himself enticed Volusenus into
pursuing him too tenaciously with only a few men. In his
impetuous flight his enemy Commius had drawn Volusenus
on too far, and now suddenly called upon the loyal assistance of his men not to allow the wounds treacherously*
inflicted on him to stay unpunished. Leaving the rest behind,
Commius turned his horse and recklessly charged towards
Volusenus. All his cavalry followed, turning our small force
and chasing after it. Commius spurred on his horse and drew
level with Volusenus' mount, then pointed his spear and thrust
it with all his might through Volusenus' thigh.

Now that the Roman commander had been wounded, our
men did not hesitate—they stood their ground, then turned
their horses and routed the enemy. When this happened several of the enemy were struck and wounded by the force of
our attack—some were trampled as they fled, others trapped.
Commius escaped this fate thanks to the speed of his horse,
but despite winning the battle Volusenus was badly hurt, and
was taken back to camp apparently in danger of his life.
Perhaps Commius' sense of grievance was now satisfied, or
perhaps he had lost too many men: but he now sent envoys
to Antony and surrendered hostages, promising to remain
where he was told to stay and to do as he was ordered. He
begged for one concession to his fear—not to be obliged to
come within sight of any Roman. Antony judged that his
request sprang from a legitimate fear, so he pardoned him as
requested and accepted the hostages.

I am well aware that Caesar composed a separate commentary
for each year, but I have decided not to follow his example,
because in the following year, the consulship of Lucius Paulus
and Gaius Marcellus,* no action of any significance took
place in Gaul. Nevertheless, to avoid anyone remaining ignorant of where Caesar and his army were at that time, I have
decided to write a brief addition to this commentary.

(49) When Caesar was wintering in Belgium his one intention
was to maintain friendly relations with the peoples there and

to give no one a hope or motive for starting hostilities. There was nothing he wanted less than to find himself obliged to fight another war just as he was about to depart from his province: there was a danger that if the army had to with-draw it would leave behind a war which the whole of Gaul could join in without immediate risk. So he addressed the peoples with respect, made generous payments to their leaders, and imposed no new burdens; and by these means he easily kept the Gauls subdued and more obedient, for they were exhausted by their many defeats.

(50) Once winter was past, in a change from his usual practice Caesar set out at top speed for Italy, to address the communities and colonies—he had already recommended to them the candidature of his quaestor Mark Antony for a priesthood.* On behalf of so close a friend, whom he had sent on ahead to pursue his candidature, he exercised his influence gladly, and also eagerly, to combat the factional power of a few men* who wanted to defeat Antony in order to overthrow Caesar's influence when he left his province.

Although Caesar heard in the course of his march that Antony had been made augur before he reached Italy, he thought there was still good reason for visiting the commun-ities and colonies to thank them for offering Antony their full support. He also wanted to commend his own candidature for office* in the following year; his enemies were gloating arrogantly at the election of Lucius Lentulus and Gaius Marcellus as consuls, for they would strip Caesar of his office and prestige*—the office of consul had been wrested from Servius Galba, despite his greater popularity and larger number of votes, because he was a friend of Caesar and one of his legates.

(51) Caesar's arrival was greeted by all the communities and colonies with incredible respect and affection, for he was visiting for the first time following the war against the whole of Gaul. In decorating gates, roads, and all the places Caesar was to pass through, nothing they could think of was left undone. All the people came with their children to see him, animals were sacrificed everywhere; the market places and temples were full of dining couches,* as it were in anticipation

of the happiness of a triumph so long expected. Such was the splendid generosity of the richer people, and the eager enthusiasm of the more humble.

(52) When Caesar had sped through all the districts of Cisalpine Gaul he quickly returned to his army at Nemetocenna, summoned the legions from winter quarters to the lands of the Treveri, then set out for the same place himself. On arrival he conducted a review of his army.* He put Titus Labienus in charge of Cisalpine Gaul, so that his recommendation could reinforce their support for his candidature for the consulship. He himself undertook as much marching as he judged—by effecting a change of location—necessary for the health and well-being of his men.

During these marches Caesar was receiving frequent reports that his personal enemies were trying to win Labienus over; and he was informed that this was being done on the advice of a few men, with the intention of using a resolution of the Senate* to deprive him of part of his army. But Caesar did not believe any of the rumours about Labienus, nor could he be induced to do anything to oppose a resolution of the Senate. For he judged that his cause would easily prevail among the senators if they declared their opinions freely. For when Gaius Curio, who was a tribune of the people, had undertaken to defend Caesar's cause and his prestige, he had often made a promise to the Senate: since Pompey's armed tyranny was inflicting no small degree of panic in the Forum, if anyone was troubled by fear of Caesar's arms, Curio proposed that both men should give up their arms and disband their armies. Such an act would make the Roman state free and autonomous.

This was no empty promise, for Curio even tried to obtain a decree of the Senate by bringing it to a vote. The consuls and Pompey's friends prevented this happening.* By delaying the matter they ensured its failure.

(53) This was a strong indicator of the attitude of the Senate as a whole, and accorded with its earlier action. For the previous year, when Marcellus was attacking Caesar's prestige, he had brought the matter of Caesar's provinces before the Senate prematurely, in contravention of a law of

Pompey and Crassus.* After the senators' opinions were expressed Marcellus brought it to a vote. He was looking for any prestige to be won from envy of Caesar, but the whole Senate together voted against his motion. Caesar's enemies were not discouraged by these set-backs, but they were made aware of the need for more favourable circumstances in which the Senate could be forced to give its approval to their decisions.

(54) A decree of the Senate then followed, to the effect that Pompey and Caesar should each send one legion for the Parthian war.* Evidently one man was to be deprived of two legions—for Pompey had sent him the First legion, a legion levied in Caesar's own province, and had handed it over to be, in effect, Caesar's own. Although there was scarcely a doubt of his enemies' intentions, nevertheless Caesar sent the legion back to Pompey. For his own part, he ordered the Fifteenth, which he had kept in Nearer Gaul, to be handed over in accordance with the senatorial decree. He sent the Thirteenth legion to Italy in its place to maintain the garrisons from which the Fifteenth was being withdrawn. He arranged winter quarters for the army, posting Gaius Trebonius to Belgium with four legions, and sending Gaius Fabius with the same number to the Aedui. This, he believed, would ensure that Gaul was as secure as possible—if the Belgae, pre-eminent in courage, and the Aedui, pre-eminent in influence, were under the control of armies.

Caesar then set out for Italy. (55) When he arrived, he found that thanks to the consul Gaius Marcellus the two legions which he had sent back, and which were destined—in accordance with a senatorial decree—for the Parthian war, had been handed over to Pompey and were being kept back in Italy. After this there was no doubt of what was being planned against Caesar. Yet Caesar decided that he must endure it all, so long as he still had some hope of deciding the issue according to law, rather than by fighting it out.

EXPLANATORY NOTES

Numbers refer to books and paragraphs:

1.2   *the consulship . . . Piso*: 61 BC—the usual Roman method of dating by the names of the two consuls elected for that year.

    our Province: ambiguous. It means both 'my (i.e. Caesar's) sphere of command' and 'our (i.e. the Romans') subject territory'. Cf. 'our soldiers'.

    miles: the Roman *milia passuum*, literally 'a thousand paces', is 95 yards short of a modern mile (0.918 miles: 1.45 km). So 220 English miles is about 240 *milia passuum*.

1.6   *Allobroges . . . pacified*: by the praetor Gaius Pomptinus in 61 BC.

    the consulship . . . Gabinius: 58 BC.

1.7   *Caesar*: the first time he names himself in the third person.

    only one legion: the Tenth, Caesar's favourite legion. See e.g. 1.40–1.

    Lucius Cassius . . . under the yoke: in ancient warfare, an act of ritual humiliation and token of submission. A defeated army was made to pass under a low arch made of two vertical spears with a horizontal one on top. Cassius was defeated by the Tigurini (one of the tribal groups of the Helvetii: see 1.12) in 107 BC.

1.9   *hostages*: the exchange of hostages was a regular way to seal an alliance: also subject states could be made to supply hostages as guarantees for good behaviour. Typically, such hostages would be children of leading citizens.

1.12 *the third watch*: for Roman soldiers, the time between sunset and sunrise was divided into four watches of equal length. Thus the third watch would begin at around midnight.

    the grandfather . . . Cassius: in 59 BC Caesar married his third wife, Calpurnia—daughter of Lucius Calpurnius Piso.

1.16 *'Vergobret'*: a Gallic word meaning 'dispenser of judgement'.

1.18 *collection rights . . . bid against him*: the usual Roman method of raising taxes was for magistrates to auction off collection rights to individuals or companies (who had to extract enough to ensure a profit as well).

1.21 *second-in-command*: as 'legatus pro praetore', Titus Labienus would be in command of the army during the winter (when Caesar would be in Italy) and also acting governor of the Province.

1.21 *Publius Considius ... Marcus Crassus*: Lucius Cornelius Sulla ('Felix') was dictator (the title of a long-obsolete emergency magistracy which he revived) at Rome from 81 to ?79 BC, and a bitter enemy of Gaius Marius (c.157–86 BC), a *novus homo* and renowned military leader who was also Caesar's uncle. Marcus Licinius Crassus was Pompey's consular colleague in 70 and 55 BC, and with Pompey and Caesar formed the so-called 'first Triumvirate' in 60 BC.

1.24 *triple battle line*: the regular battle formation. In an emergency the army could march in three parallel columns which could then be quickly redeployed in a battle line.

formed a phalanx: i.e. a compact mass of infantry, formed up in depth: the front rank held its shields overlapping, those behind held them over their heads (Livy 10.29.6). Thus it was possible for Roman javelins to pierce the shields and pin them together (see 1.25).

1.25 *his own horse ... flight*: i.e. the horses of his officers, not the cavalry horses.

exposed side: the right side, which was not covered by the shield each soldier carried with his left arm.

1.26 *the seventh hour*: the time between sunrise and sunset was divided into twelve hours, the length of which varied according to the time of year; hence the seventh hour would always be the period just after noon—about one o'clock. See 3.15 n.

1.28 *treated them as enemies*: probably a euphemism for putting them to death.

1.33 *Brothers and Kinsmen*: the terminology of formal alliance, first made between the Aedui and Rome in 123 BC.

Cimbri and Teutoni: their migration at the end of the second century BC caused panic at Rome, until they were finally defeated at Aquae Sextiae by Gaius Marius (1.21 n.) in 102.

1.34 *made his own ... in war*: Caesar puts into Ariovistus' mouth a deliberately provocative statement, to which he must then respond firmly.

1.35 *Messalla ... Piso*: see 1.2 n.

1.39 *The panic began . . . friendship*: Caesar blames the panic (*sic*) on his officers, not his men. Military tribunes had once commanded legions, but in this period the post was administrative, or used as an opportunity to gain military experience. Legates (*legati*), like Labienus, could command legions, under a magistrate or promagistrate (Caesar was a proconsul). Prefects were officers in charge of an auxiliary corps of archers or slingers. The 'other men' referred to could be youths attached for training to Caesar's staff (*contubernales*) or hangers-on in search of booty. The third-century AD historian Cassius Dio gives a very different account of the so-called 'mutiny at Vesontio' (38.35.1–47.2).

1.40 *slave revolt in Italy*: the uprising (73–71 BC) led by a former gladiator, Spartacus.

the Tenth legion . . . bodyguard: see 1.7 n. The Tenth is often important at moral cruces in the narrative. The bodyguard (*praetoria cohors*) was first instituted by Scipio Aemilianus in 133 BC, and consisted of men hand-picked for bravery (rather than a permanent regiment) to attend the general in the field. Under the Principate, it eventually became the emperor's personal bodyguard.

1.42 *enrolling . . . equites*: the aristocratic cavalry (*equites*, i.e. knights) of early Rome had long since abandoned any military function and had turned into a social rank just below the Senators: the actual battle cavalry (also *equites*) by now consisted of allies, i.e. non-Romans of inferior status to citizen legionaries. So by transferring the men of the Tenth to the *equites*, jokes this soldier, they are not being *de*moted but *pro*moted.

1.45 *defeated . . . Maximus*: 121 BC.

1.47 *Gaius Valerius Procillus*: see 1.19; a Gaul who took his Roman patron's name, and acted as interpreter.

1.52 *legates . . . quaestor*: the quaestor would be Caesar's principal staff officer. Legates were men of senatorial rank nominated by Caesar and acting as staff officers. Labienus was pre-eminent among his legates (see e.g. 1.21, 1.54, 1.39 n.).

2.2 *two new legions*: bringing the total up to eight (each of about 5,000 men), plus perhaps 20,000 auxiliaries.

2.4 *Diviciacus*: not to be confused with the Aeduan.

2.6 *'tortoise'*: *testudo*, the Latin word for the shell of a tortoise, a term used to describe a formation in which soldiers lock shields over their heads to cover an advance. It can also mean (like *vinea*, 2.12 n.) a sloping-roofed structure, used to shelter men working on undermining walls or filling ditches: see 5.42 and Caesar, *The Civil War* (CW) 2.2.

2.8 *Once he realized . . . his own men*: a problematic passage. If a camp discovered to the NE of Berry-au-Bac, between the Aisne (Axona) and the Miette, is the one referred to here, then the two ditches run parallel, in opposite directions from the height (NW–SE), each towards one of the waterways, and at right angles to the line of march.

2.12 *Noviodunum*: i.e. marching west, along the left bank of the Aisne.

movable shelters: Lat. *vineae*, screens to protect siege-workers, probably named after the resemblance of their structure to rows of trellised vines.

earthworks . . . set up: Lat. *agger*. In a siege, the construction of an *agger*, made of wood, stones, and earth, in front of a stronghold, was a primary operation. It was an embankment wide enough to support at least one siege-tower (*turris*), from which the attacking army could force the besieged from their walls. See e.g. Caesar, *CW* 2.8 (the siege of Massilia); Sallust, *Jugurtha* 76; Lucan, *Civil War* 3.396.

2.14 *Britain*: this first mention of the island gives Caesar a preparatory justification for the invasion in Books Four and Five.

clemency: this word (*clementia*) became associated with Caesar's policy of pardoning enemies, especially Roman enemies after the civil wars. He himself only applies it to his treatment of foreign foes. See 8.3 n.

2.21 *fit on their emblems*: the exact reference is unclear. The Latin (*insignia*) may perhaps refer to the crests on their helmets, or to some other symbol by which they could be quickly identified as Romans.

2.24 *I mentioned earlier*: it is very rare for Caesar to refer to himself thus in the first person singular (see also 4.27).

main entrance gate: the *porta decumana* was placed farthest from the enemy, at the end of the street which bisected the camp.

2.29 *The Aduatuci . . . Teutoni*: an improbable connection.

2.30 *a rampart . . . length*: the text says either 'a rampart 14 miles long', which is most improbable, or 'a rampart 15,000 feet long', which is not Caesar's usual way of recording distance. To correct a numeral (they are easily corrupted in MSS) from 'XV' to 'V' seems a plausible solution.

2.32 *sold everything . . . people*: the usual fate of the inhabitants of a captured town was to be sold into slavery. A great part of Roman war profits came from the sale of people, as well as of property.

2.35 *a thanksgiving . . . anyone before*: a thanksgiving (*supplicatio*) was granted by a resolution of the Senate (Livy 10.21, 22.10), and usually (but not always: see Cato's letter in Cicero, *Letters to Friends* 15.5) followed by a triumph. Further *supplicationes* were decreed later (see 4.38 and n., 7.90).

3.4 *javelins*: not the usual Roman javelins (*pila*), but native ones (*gaesa*: cf. Old Irish *gaë*, Old High German *gēr*).

3.9 *some distance away*: according to Plutarch (*Caesar* 21.3; *Pompey* 51.3; *Crassus* 14.5) and Suetonius (*DJ* 24), before he set out for Transalpine Gaul Caesar was at Luca (the southernmost town in Cisalpine Gaul) for a conference with Pompey and Crassus, as a result of which his term of office as proconsul was extended from 1 March 54 (when it was due to expire) for five more years.

landlocked waters: Caesar means the Mediterranean.

they made alliance . . . those regions: Caesar apparently thinks that the Gallic coast from the Rhine to the Pyrenees was parallel with the south coast of Britain. The involvement of the Menapii and Morini (who lived some 400 miles from Brittany) is significant, as their territory will have to be the base for Caesar's expedition to Britain.

3.11 *Aquitania . . . forces*: Aquitania reaches from the Garonne to the Pyrenees. Mommsen rightly remarked (*pace* Rice Holmes) that Caesar fails to persuade of the invasion as a necessary defensive measure.

3.12 *every twelve hours*: nonsense. Some emend the MSS (exchanging 'XXIV' for 'XII'), but it is hard to see how the error could have crept into the text. Others delete the word 'twice' (*bis*), or exchange it for a less specific one, 'here' (*hic*). Yet the Mediterranean is hardly tidal at all: perhaps Caesar mistook what he saw, or was misinformed by others. Or maybe the details did not matter for readers in Rome.

3.14 *set out . . . fleet*: the location of the sea-battle between the Veneti and Decimus Brutus is probably, as Napoleon III suggested,

Quiberon. The 'hills and heights' from which the Roman army watched would then be at Saint-Gildas, and the River Auray the place from which the Veneti's fleet set out.

3.15 *fourth ... sunset*: the time represented by 'the fourth hour' cannot be calculated exactly, because it depends on both the latitude of the battle-site (which is disputed, 3.14 n.) and the date on which it took place. From 3.12 the latter may be estimated at around the end of August, when each daylight 'hour' would last approximately 1 hour and 9 minutes (1.26 n.); this gives a probable time of approximately 10 a.m. for 'the fourth hour'.

3.20 *Lucius Valerius Praeconinus ... baggage*: in 78 BC Mallius (or Manlius: praetor in 79?) was defeated by Hirtuleius, a subordinate of the rebel Roman commander Sertorius (Plutarch, *Sertorius* 12; cf. Livy, *Periochae* 90). Plutarch makes no mention of a legate called Valerius Praeconinus.

3.22 *'soldurii'*: the meaning is not certain, though the context suggests an élite force of warriors or perhaps cavalry.

3.23 *Nearer Spain*: this Roman province reached from the Pyrenees to the Ebro.

Quintus Sertorius: see 3.20 n. Plutarch's *Sertorius* is the main source for his career.

3.24 *double line*: instead of the triple-line formation, giving his small force a wider front to face the enemy.

4.1 *farming their land*: this passage qualifies Caesar's statement in 6.22 that the Germans do not practise agriculture.

4.3 *somewhat more civilized ... race*: there is a problem with the text here: an odd word-order and words left out or interpolated. But the sense is clear enough.

4.4 *the Germans*: i.e. the Usipetes and Tencteri.

4.10 *The Meuse ... Vosges*: in fact it springs from the Langres plateau.

is joined ... the Ocean: the geography of the Netherlands has changed since Caesar's account was written. He describes the Meuse (Mosa) and Rhine (Rhenus) having (at this point) parallel courses on their way to the North Sea, with the Waal (Vacalus) flowing from the latter into the former and cutting off a section of land to form an island delta.

4.12 *Piso . . . Senate*: the Roman name of this dead Gaul points to Roman influence in Aquitanian Gaul well before the time of Caesar's arrival.

4.13 *quaestor*: this is the title both of the most junior senatorial magistracy in Rome, and of an official responsible for handling the financial affairs of the army in the field.

4.14 *women and children . . . hunt them down*: such ruthlessness was in itself acceptable in Roman warfare, but Plutarch claims (citing Tanusius) that Cato both condemned the senatorial vote of an official thanksgiving for this victory (on the grounds that Caesar had broken the truce) and urged that Caesar be given up to the Germans (*Caesar* 22). Characteristically, Caesar leaves the text to justify him: as a direct result of this slaughter, the Germans are panicked into flight (4.15).

4.15 *military standards*: the importance attached by the Romans to defending the standards is clear from e.g. 4.25. According to Pliny the Elder (*Natural History* 10.16), Marius (see 1.21 n.) ruled that the eagle (*aquila*) was the only animal to be represented on a standard. Before his reorganization many totemic animals—wolf, minotaur, horse, and boar as well as eagle—had figured on standards, and they continued to do so on Gallic and German standards in the first century.

4.16 *a number of reasons*: these are given in full at 4.19.

4.17 *cross the Rhine . . . dignity*: the site of Caesar's bridge over the Rhine has been disputed. Napoleon III suggested Bonn, others have proposed Cologne, and (more plausibly) Andernach or Koblenz. The fact that at the latter city the Rhine is nowadays more than 350 metres (390 yards) wide gives some indication of the magnitude of the achievement of Caesar's engineers. The bridge makes a claim for, as well as a statement about, his dignity (*dignitas*), a word which suggests prestige, worth, rank, status—matters of crucial importance to the Roman politician. When Caesar crossed the Rubicon and entered Italy in 49 BC, he claimed he was acting in defence of his *dignitas*.

Twin braces . . . apart: the precise meaning of this sentence is disputed.

planks . . . lengthways: i.e. to form the road surface on which the army was to cross.

4.21 *Commius . . . them*: the Atrebates had been allies of the Nervii and were defeated with them, but Caesar made no mention of Commius in his account of 57 BC: see 2.16, 23.

4.23 *the third watch ... fourth hour*: the third watch always begins at midnight, and the date, reckoning from the full moon mentioned at 4.29 (31 August), was 26 August, 55 BC. At this latitude and season the day began *c*.5 a.m., so Caesar reached Britain (at Dover) at about 8 or 9 o'clock.

he landed ... shore: at a point 7 Roman miles west of Dover, variously identified as Lympne in Romney Marsh, or between Walmer Castle and Deal.

4.24 *carried the Eagle ... Commander*: probably by Caesar's day the eagle-bearer (*aquilifer*) carried the standard of the *primus pilus* or senior centurion of the *triarii* (the other two main standards belonged to the chief centurions of the divisions known as *hastati* and *principes*). The intervention of this un-named *aquilifer* is the first instance of direct speech in *GW*: it marks the importance of the moment as well as the intensity of the threat. Caesar had two legions in Britain: the other was the Seventh (see 4.32).

4.27 *I have already described ... Britain*: see 2.24 and note.

4.28 *eighteen ships ... port*: see 4.23. Only now does the cavalry leave Gaul to join Caesar.

4.33 *Their method ... as follows*: Caesar makes no mention of scythes on British chariot wheels.

4.36 *the autumnal equinox*: on 24 September. Caesar had been in Britain for almost a month.

4.37 *marshes ... previous year*: see 3.28.

thanksgiving of twenty days ... achievements: greater than the fifteen of which Caesar was so proud (see 2.35), though no battles of similar stature had been fought. The achievement lay rather in the breaching of a frontier ('revealing Britain, rather than actually passing it down', as Tacitus puts it in *Agricola* 13). Cassius Dio remarks of the thanksgiving that Caesar and the Romans made much of the British expedition because they hoped for great material gain from it, but he also notes that the expedition won neither Caesar nor Rome anything but glory (*doxai*): glory, however, is itself a valuable commodity in Roman politics.

5.1 *winter quarters for Italy*: see 1.54. Caesar was delayed in Gaul so that he did not reach Italy to hold assizes until the new year, i.e. the fifth year of the war.

the waves there ... tidal changes: he means in the Channel, where waves do not match the size of ocean swells, but are very choppy. In fact the waves are small because the water is shallow and narrowly confined.

5.2   *Portus Itius*: or 'the Itian harbour'. Generally assumed to be Boulogne.

5.3   *Indutiomarus and Cingetorix*: both names, and hence presumably the Treveri also, are Celtic, not Germanic. Cingetorix was Indutiomarus' son-in-law (see 5.56).

5.6   *Dumnorix ... before*: see 1.18–20.

5.8   *carried too far ... previous summer*: the Channel tide carried him east-north-east, past Dover and Deal, so that he had to row back to find the beaches. A hundred years later the emperor Claudius' expedition was to land at Richborough, but there is no reason to suppose that—even if Caesar had known of it—this harbour would then have proved suitable for the ships of his day.

private vessels ... convenience: these individuals were probably traders who dealt with the army, or men attracted by rumours of British wealth. In June of 54, just before the second expedition, Caesar wrote to Cicero (as did his brother Quintus Cicero, prominent at 5.38–41), who then told Atticus, 'there is not a speck of silver in this island nor any hope of booty except from the sale of captives—and I reckon you do not anticipate any of them being very musical or lettered' (*Letters to Atticus* 4.16.7).

5.9   *a river*: probably the Stour.

       'tortoise': see 2.6 n.

5.11 *Thames ... sea*: from 4.13 it is evident that Caesar had no clear picture of Britain's geography, and thought that the Thames (eventually) flowed north towards the third side of the triangular island (see 5.13). The distance given here must refer to his march from the sea to the place where he crossed the Thames.

5.12 *The inland regions ... winters milder*: this first section of Caesar's ethnography of Britain—once suspected by editors to be an interpolation in the narrative—reveals the limitations of his account. Any tin would have come from Cornwall, not midland regions, and not all bronze was imported: perhaps because he assumed a lack of native copper, he inferred the latter point. Both beech and silver fir are native to Britain, though Caesar may well not have observed either for himself.

5.13 *The island . . . circumference*: this section too is a mixture of observation, information, and inference. The coastal dimensions he gives are an underestimate, but no one is known to have circumnavigated the island before the first century AD (see Tacitus, *Agricola* 38). The idea that Spain lay to the west, in the same direction as Ireland (Hibernia), is an error Caesar may have adopted from Pytheas of Massilia (Marseilles), who sailed to Britain in Alexander's time (see Pliny, *Natural History* 2.77). Mona is either a wrongly located Anglesey or, more likely, the Isle of Man. The smaller islands, off the west coast of Scotland, have been assumed, perhaps also originally by Pytheas, to lie within the Arctic circle.

5.14 *way of life . . . brought first*: archaeology shows that corn was grown in inland Britain long before Caesar arrived: woollen and linen cloth was also made there. Woad (*vitrum* or *isatis tinctoria*) is a plant from the leaves of which a blue dye was pressed. It is not clear whether Caesar means that each group of ten men had one wife between them or one wife each: but the custom of polyandry is not otherwise attested among Celts, though one commentator has defended it as a control measure necessitated by the high population density mentioned at 4.12.

5.18 *a single spot*: unidentified, but probably above where the river ceases to be tidal. Bede (*Ecclesiastical History* 1.2) wrote that the stakes referred to here were still visible in his day, 'as thick as a man's thigh and covered with lead', but there is no evidence that either these or the remains of stakes discovered at Brentford were put there by the Britons Caesar faces here.

5.19 *about 4,000 . . . remained*: this number, suspiciously large, may be corrupt in the MSS.

5.20 *Trinobantes*: or Trinovantes, a people of Essex, centred on Camulodunum, modern Colchester (see Tacitus, *Annals* 14.31).

5.21 *Cenimagni . . . Cassi*: these peoples must all be from southeastern Britain but cannot securely be located more closely. Cassivellaunus' stronghold (*oppidum*) has been identified by some with Verulamium (St Albans): Caesar intends to contrast it here with 'real' strongholds, properly fortified (*oppidum* can also be translated 'town').

5.23 *To avoid . . . destination*: i.e. Caesar arrived in Britain in early July and left at the end of September.

5.24 *assembly ... Samarobriva*: i.e. at Amiens. Caesar seems to have held such assemblies regularly (see 4.6, 5.2, 5.24, 6.3).

5.27 *Roman knight*: i.e. an *eques*, or member of the social rank below the senatorial aristocracy. See 1.42 n.

5.30 *Cotta ... reinforcements*: the style of the arguments prepares the reader for disaster. Cotta has the support of the tribunes and centurions, which marks his as the right opinion, reinforced by his mentioning the need to do what Caesar orders. Sabinus is shown to be at fault, not only misrepresenting events among the Carnutes (see 5.25) and using direct speech (he must be as persuasive as possible), but also manipulating the men into rejecting Cotta's opinion.

5.34 *commander*: Sabinus, not Caesar.

5.35 *open flank*: see 1.25 n.

the eighth hour: about 2 p.m.

5.36 *Gnaeus Pompeius*: another Gaul who had taken the name of his Roman patron: see 1.47 n.

5.38 *the Nervii*: at 2.28 Caesar stated that their fighting strength was wiped out. See also 7.75, where they send 5,000 men to Alesia.

5.40 *The towers ... attached*: if the circumference of the camp was about 1,400 metres, then the 120 towers would be about 12 metres apart. The whole length of the walls could then be covered by defensive missiles from the towers, while protecting the men better than a simple rampart could do.

5.41 *pointed to Ambiorix ... their point*: because his presence proved that Sabinus and Cotta had been defeated, and because his previous loyalty to Rome (like that of other Gallic peoples) was now overcome.

5.42 *fortification ... all round*: there is a problem with the text here. The MSS suggest a circumvallation of 15 or 10 Roman miles, both of which distances are absurdly out of proportion for a camp of about a mile in circumference. '3 miles' is a plausible conjecture.

5.46 *the eleventh hour ... day*: about four o'clock.

come ... to him: Caesar was at Samarobriva.

5.47 *the third hour*: nine o'clock.

5.48 *Greek*: some scholars argue that *Graecis litteris* must mean 'Greek characters', rather than 'the Greek language': but see

1.29, 6.14. Perhaps the Nervii, further from the Province than the Helvetii (1.29) were less likely to know Greek: but at 6.14 Caesar states that 'Greek' (the same letters/language ambiguity is present) was widespread among the Gauls.

5.54 *I do not know . . . Roman people*: a rare first-person authorial comment on the narrative.

6.1 *proconsul Pompey . . .* : in 55 BC he was granted a proconsulship of Spain (with six legions) to balance Caesar's second five-year term in Gaul, but remained near the city and governed through legates. This reference to Pompey is far from neutral—staying at Rome while in possession of proconsular *imperium* (technically the right to enrol troops, this excluded him from staying in the city itself) is not evidence of impressive generalship. More important, this legion was to become the subject of one of Caesar's strongest grudges against Pompey: with civil war looming, he was forced to return it (see 8.54: *CW* 1.4 [where Caesar claims Pompey knew he was wrong to demand the legion's return], 32). It is pointed out here that Pompey had raised these troops within an area under Caesar's jurisdiction.

6.1 *to him in Gaul*: see 5.53 (the first time Caesar had wintered there).

6.2 *kinsmen . . . money*: at 5.4 they were Caesar's hostages, so he must have set them free on his return from Britain (for Indutiomarus to be able to revolt without bringing about their deaths).

6.4 *dependants*: Lat. *in clientela*. The *patronus–cliens* or 'patronage' relationship was an institutionalized form of dependence inherent in Roman society (see Cicero, *On the Republic* 2.16), but its terminology is readily transferred both to Gallic society (e.g. 7.4) and to relationships between peoples (e.g. 6.12).

6.11 *factions*: Lat. *factiones*. *Factio* is a politically loaded and negative term in late-Republican politics. As applied by *popularis* politicians to the wealthy *nobiles* or aristocracy in particular, it implies a division of interest contrary to the common good (*res publica*), and a source of potential weakness and fragmentation.

6.14 *Druids . . . immortal gods*: the word Caesar uses for this priestly class, *druides*, is of Celtic origin, but its etymology is disputed. Caesar is the earliest extant source to describe them in detail, but Strabo (64/3 BC–AD 21: *Geography* 4.4) differentiates the picture further to include *vates* (concerned with practical aspects of religious sacrifice) and *bardi* (poets and singers).

Augustus, Tiberius, and Claudius all attempted measures of repression. See further Tacitus, *Annals* 14.29–30, *Agricola* 14 (Suetonius Paulinus and the attack on Anglesey); Suetonius, *The Divine Claudius* 25; Pliny, *Natural History* 16.249 (on the place of oaks and mistletoe in druidic practice).

6.15 *retainers*: see 3.22 (the Aquitani and their *soldurii*). Here the word is *ambacti*, again Celtic in origin. *Soldurii* and *ambacti* are probably of higher status than the *clientes* or dependants.

6.16 *images of the gods*: the Latin word here, *simulacra*, can simply mean an image, but is frequently used of images of gods in human form, such as statues.

6.17 *Mercury ... and Minerva*: not surprisingly Caesar concentrates on features which he and his Roman readers would have recognized as familiar, giving a corresponding Roman name to each Gallic divinity: Mercury for Teutates, Apollo for Belon, Mars for Hesus, Jupiter for Taranis (Minerva's Gallic parallel is not certain, though the moon-goddess Belisana has been suggested). There is no sign of the animal totemism (in which the boar was especially sacred) once so prominent in Gallic religion.

6.18 *one father, Dis*: the Roman name for Pluto, god of the underworld (see Cicero, *On the Nature of the Gods* 2.26). This suggests a Gallic claim to autochthony: to being an aboriginal rather than an immigrant people.

the passage of time ... after night: this is obscurely put, but suggests that because the Gauls were sprung from the god of earth and darkness, they begin the reckoning of time with darkness, calling a period of time a number of nights (just as in the English expression 'a fortnight'). So too did the Germans, according to Tacitus (*Germania* 11).

6.19 *head of a noble family ... slaves*: the Latin term for head of a family is *paterfamilias*, which indicates the male head of a Roman household with power of life and death over its members. Caesar does not state that the Gauls practised polygamy, but this is what the plural 'wives' (*de uxoribus*) implies. Interrogation 'like slaves' means under torture.

6.20 *The states ... anyone else*: see 4.5.

6.21 *Vulcan*: i.e. fire.

6.24 *they sent colonies ... Orcynian forest*: Caesar's mention of colonies is corroborated by Livy (5.34) and Tacitus (*Germania*

28). Eratosthenes (*c.*275–194 BC) was an Alexandrian critic, geographer, mathematician, philosopher, and poet: the 'certain ... Greeks' may include Timosthenes and Posidonius.

6.25 *It takes ... described below*: some scholars excise sections 25–8 of Book 6 as an interpolation.

6.26 *There is an ox ... and size*: probably the reindeer, which of course has twin antlers.

6.27 *elks*: see Pliny, *Natural History* 8.15. Both he and Caesar describe (erroneously) the lack of joints, which may derive from another source or from misinterpretation of native information.

6.28 *wild ox*: or auroch, *bos primigenius*.

6.29 *Once Caesar ... further*: this section resumes the narrative thread broken off at the end of 6.10.

6.29 *the Ardennes forest ... 460 miles across*: its size is exaggerated.

6.30 *Fortune*: Caesar often remarks on the importance of *fortuna* (*tychē* in Greek), which, from the Latin, could refer to either a quality or a divinity. Plutarch (*Caesar* 38) and others make *fortuna* a special adjunct of Caesar: see 1.40, where he claims the relationship (there also called *felicitas*) himself.

6.33 *Scheldt*: Lat. *Scaldis*. This river does not, and perhaps never did, flow into the Meuse.

6.34 *maniples*: see Introduction, *Caesar's Army*. A maniple consisted of two centuries, or one-third of a cohort, perhaps equivalent to the English 'company.'

6.37 *main gate*: the *porta decumana*.

6.38 *we mentioned*: see 2.25, 3.5.

6.44 *ancestral custom*: Lat. *more maiorum*. Probably Acco was flogged to death and then beheaded (see 8.38).

outlawed: literally 'he forbade them the use of water and fire', a standard formula for banishment.

7.1 *Publius Clodius ... his province*: Publius Clodius Pulcher (*c.*92–52 BC) was a *popularis* politician, tribune in 59, and agent of Cicero's exile (see Introduction, p. xiv). He was killed during factional violence involving his enemy Milo in January, 52 BC (see Cicero's speech *In Defence of Milo*). Here 'his province' must refer only to Cisalpine Gaul.

Acco: see 6.4, 44.

... from their ancestors: Caesar marks this meeting as the start of a sinister new trend in Gallic affairs, with the Gauls uniting

under the banner of common Gallic freedom, motivated by a threateningly Roman preference for death over dishonour, and liberty instead of subjection. See also 7.20, 25, 29, 64 (a suggestive coupling of *imperium* and *libertas*), 66, 71, 76–7, 89.

7.3 *end . . . Arvernian territory*: the third watch ended about 8 p.m. The Arverni were mentioned as important at 1.31, but this is their first involvement in the action.

7.4 *an Arvernian called Vercingetorix*: Caesar's greatest Gallic adversary, and in later times a symbol of Gallic resistance to the threat of invasion. For the Gallic historian Camille Jullian he had the stature of a Hannibal or a Mithridates: he became a romantic national icon to the French in the twentieth century, symbolizing the struggle of the Resistance against Hitler, the imperialist aggressor. Montaigne was not the last to question his wisdom in seeking refuge in Alesia (*Essais* 2.24). Following his defeat at Alesia, he surrendered and was put to death in 46 BC after being paraded in Caesar's unprecedented quadruple triumph (see Cassius Dio, 43.19.4).

7.5 *As to whether . . . Arverni*: here Caesar indicates his awareness that this is the moment when the loyalty of the previously dependable Aedui is first brought into question. The fact that the Aedui's claim that the Bituriges were turning traitor is at once substantiated helps to dissipate any sense that Caesar was at fault for continuing to trust them.

7.6 *the resolution of Pompey*: a deliberate irony, with Caesar, writing in late 50, maintaining the fiction of reliance on Pompey's friendship. Rioting after the death of Clodius on 18 January led directly to Pompey's election as *consul sine collega*, and to calls that he be made dictator: so both were by now locked in a struggle for security and supremacy.

7.9 *the young Brutus*: Decimus Junius Brutus, like Trebonius (7.11), one of Caesar's assassins in 44. See CW 1.36, 56–7.

Vienna: now Vienne, south of Lyons (Lugdunum).

the rest of the legions: see 6.44. As well as these two, there were six quartered at Agedincum and two on the Treveri's borders.

. . . the Arverni: an oblique rebuttal of the hopes expressed by the Gallic leaders at 7.1. The sequence of events in 7.7–9 is complicated: Vercingetorix had planned, through Lucterius, to rouse the peoples bordering the Province so as to expose it to an invasion force. Caesar prevents this, first by forcing him

back on to the defensive, then by concealing his own departure and by gathering his army together safely.

7.11 *Cenabum ... as quickly as possible*: problematic, because Cenabum is not on a direct route to Gorgobina from the probable site of Vellaunodunum. Perhaps Caesar takes the need to punish Cenabum for granted, as an unavoidable part of his march.

7.12 *Noviodunum ... on his route*: this cannot refer to Noviodunum of the Aedui (Nevers), which was not on his route. It must be some other settlement, between Cenabum and Avaricum.

7.13 *from the beginning*: presumably of the seventh campaign.

7.14 *the time of year ... favour*: it was March, and there would be no forage in the fields before June.

7.15 *pity for the people*: because they would lose their homes in winter.

7.18 *pile up their packs*: see 1.24. Before a battle the soldiers' packs were put in a pile out of the way.

7.19 *As a result ... Avaricum*: 'equal battle conditions' is *aequo Marte*—Mars, the god of war, is a common Latin metonym for battle. Caesar is careful here to explain why the Gauls only *appear* to be brave, and to counter their specious courage with the genuine enthusiasm of the Romans in a way which reflects well upon himself also.

7.20 *practically defended itself*: the text is defective here but the sense clear enough.

So that you understand ... starved: the shift to direct speech, unexpected after such a long indirect speech, is characterized by irony, as Vercingetorix claims to be telling the truth (*sincere*) at the very points when he deceives his own men, passing off slaves as Roman soldiers.

7.21 *as is their custom ... proposal*: see also Livy 28.29, Tacitus, *Germania* 11.

Bituriges ... credit: Lat. *penes eos*. Caesar indicates that the Gallic position is being undermined by internal rivalries. Many editors adopt the inferior reading *paene in eo*, and thus the meaning that the Gauls expected the outcome of the war to depend on their holding Avaricum.

7.22 *... of the town*: much of the precise detail in 7.22 is disputed. For the use of siege-hooks, see 3.14: nearly four centuries before Thucydides had described how nooses were used (at the siege of Plataea), first to break the blow of battering rams by turning them aside, then, drawn tight, to drag a ram from its position. The Roman earthwork (*agger*) would have been made of earth and stones, but with plenty of wood as well, which made it vulnerable to fire (see 2.12 n.): the siege-towers were mounted on wheels (Livy 32.17). It is not clear why the Gauls built towers all along their walls, as Caesar was not encircling the town (7.17). By countermining the Roman mines (*cuniculi*) from above, the Gauls could make openings through which to push stakes or pour pitch and stones, thus blocking enemy progress.

7.25 *dart . . . machine*: the Latin, *scorpio*, here indicates the machine, but can also refer to the small, sharp darts which it discharged at close range (see Livy 26.47).

7.28 *neither . . . children*: Caesar uses triple anaphora of *non* to highlight this fierce vengeance, rather than attempting to conceal it. Killing people who might have been sold into slavery for profit is meant to show the disinterested nature of the soldiers' revenge.

7.32 *dependent supporters*: Lat. *clientela*.

7.36 *Opposite . . . a hill*: the Roche Blanche, about a mile to the south of the town.

7.40 *make the camp smaller*: because there were only two legions left to defend it.

7.44 *. . . along the ridge*: there is a difficulty here in the precise reference of the word *collis* ('hill', 'high ground'). At first, *collis* refers to a hill south-west of the Gergovia plateau: the 'smaller camp' is on a hill south of the Gergovia plateau (7.36), so the second hill is to the north-west of this first. The 'crest along the ridge of high ground' (*dorsum iugi*) joins the second hill directly to the Gergovia plateau, and offers Caesar a chance of access. The words translated 'one hill . . . another high point' are also both *collis*, however: *collis* must here refer to the 'crest along the ridge', since Caesar's puzzlement is because the 'second hill' is empty now all the Gauls are defending what must be the ridge. There remains a doubt whether Vercingetorix's drawing his men off from the hill in order to defend the adjoining ridge is either a plausible or a probable military strategy: the confusion may be explained by Caesar's need to justify himself in anticipation of his most serious defeat in Gaul.

7.45 *emblems*: see 2.21 n.

Aedui . . . on the right: the Aedui were to march from the east while the legions attacked from the south.

7.47 *Caesar ... intended*: a controversial claim, which many scholars have seen as an attempt to disguise the failure of his manœuvre. The question is whether 'what he intended' implies the completion of the entire manœuvre, or its successful progress *up to that point*. Thus far, nothing of military significance has been achieved, so it is more likely that Caesar wants the reader to assume he is about to regroup half-way through a planned manœuvre. He does not explain, however, what he would have done next if discipline had not broken down at this point; and he is careful to distance himself from blame by inserting at an earlier point the information that he warned his officers not to let this happen (7.45). This is then picked up in the aftermath of battle (7.52).

the Tenth legion ... halted at once: the text is corrupt, and reads 'legionique [or "legionisque"] decimae, quacum erat concionatus, signa constituit'. The reading adopted here as the least unsatisfactory on grounds of sense is 'legionisque decimae quacum erat continuo signa constiterunt', but it is hard to see how such a corruption could have come about.

7.48 *above*: at 7.44.

7.50 *agreed sign*: Heller's conjecture *pactum* is read here instead of the MS *pacatum*, which would mean 'the token of peace'.

Marcus Petronius ... saviour of his men: surely for the Roman reader one of the most emotive and appealing *exempla virtutis* in *GW*. The manner of his self-sacrifice, enhanced by the attribution of direct speech, underlines the moral superiority of the Romans at the time of their most serious defeat.

7.52 *an assembly ... courage and daring*: the assembly (*contio*) is a masterpiece of rhetoric, in which criticism of the soldiers' failure is offset against stylistically highlighted evocations of their bravery (e.g. by triple anaphora of *non*; or casting in the form of a quasi-*praeteritio*: 'However admirable . . .').

7.53 *Vercingetorix ... back to camp*: some scholars are puzzled that Caesar did not engage with Vercingetorix (and even emend the text to state that the latter did *not* come down on to level ground, to explain this 'failure'). It is clear, however, that Caesar's intention was merely to restore his troops' morale and 'face', rather than attempt a final resolution at such an unpropitious moment.

7.55 *[or ... province]*: the words in square brackets have been excised from the text by a number of editors.

7.57 *supplementary levy*: see 7.7.

7.60 *Roman knight*: see 1.42 n.

7.63 *commander*: Lat. *imperator*—a title with official Roman connotations, much more ominous than the title of 'leader' (*dux*) given to e.g. Camulogenus (7.62).

7.64 *named . . . effected*: the text, 'denique ei rei constituit diem; huc . . .' is clearly corrupt. This translation adopts the emendation, 'diemque ei rei constituit'.

7.65 *veterans*: the Latin is *evocati*, which strictly refers to soldiers who had completed their time of obligatory service and were invited to re-enlist with better pay and terms of service; Caesar also refers to *veteres milites*, 'long-serving soldiers', as well as to *milites veterani*, which has a sense of 'retired' about it. See e.g. CW 3.4 (also for *legiones veterani*: cf. 1.25); 3.24.

7.67 *withdrew . . . midst*: during the march baggage was carried between the legions, but if attack threatened, they formed up in a square and placed it in their midst.

7.68 *circumvallation*: the construction of siege-works by a besieging army was standard practice—see e.g. 7.11, 17. The scale of the circumvallation at Alesia, however, was so astonishing as to become the classic proof of Caesar's mastery of the art of generalship and command. The first, inner, line of siege-works stretched for more than 10 miles (Vercingetorix got his cavalry out just in time to fetch help): a second line, even longer, was then constructed to guard the Romans from Gallic attack in the rear (see also 7.4 n.).

7.69 *actual . . . Alesia*: the most popular identification (illustrated in this translation) is that of Napoleon III—Alise-Sainte-Reine, but others have been suggested. The size of the forces on both sides is disputed: 50,000 has been suggested for Caesar's entire force, both cavalry and infantry, and 80,000 for the Gallic force inside Alesia.

7.73 *the siege-works . . . 'spurs'*: Caesar's secondary defence measures are clearly innovative. His men give ironic or humorous names to them—'gravestones' (the Latin, *cippus*, means both 'boundary marker' and 'gravestone'), 'lilies' (presumably because each pit with its projecting stake looked like such a bloom), and 'spurs' (i.e. metal objects designed to increase speed rather than, as here, forcing a halt). A 'quincunx' is a pattern of five points arranged as on the face of a die.

7.74 *This ensured . . . occasion arise*: the MSS include the words 'eius discessu', which are either a senseless reference to Caesar or a hopelessly corrupt one to Vercingetorix and his cavalry. They may be a gloss on the preceding phrase, also awkward in the context ('si ita accidat': 'should the occasion arise'), but are not translated here.

7.75 *Aedui and their dependants . . . Veneti and Venelli*: the orthography of some of the Gallic states here, and their placing within the list, are disputed.

7.76 *Commius*: at 4.21, 35; 5.22.

7.77 *citizens of Gaul*: see 7.1 n. The Latin word, *cives*, usually indicates membership of an individual state or nation (*civitas*), but in this context must imply association with something more general and universal.

7.78 *The Mandubii . . . admit them*: Caesar, brief and blunt, gives no hint of their fate. But Cassius Dio (*c.*AD 150–235: 40.40) states that Caesar refused to admit them both because he was short of supplies and because, expecting them to be received back into the town, he intended to increase the pressure on Alesia; instead, they died wretchedly between camp and city. Caesar's decision was later criticized, by Macaulay (*History of England*, vol. iii) and Arnold (*Lectures on Modern History*), among others.

7.79 *wicker hurdles*: see 7.72.

7.81 *grappling-hooks*: hooks fixed to long poles, used for tearing down walls and ramparts.

7.82 *first . . . trenches*: see 7.72.

7.84 *shelters*: Lat. *musculi*. Caesar gives a detailed description of their construction at *CW* 2.10.

after all . . . minds: another rare general observation from Caesar.

7.88 *eleven cohorts*: the figures given in the MSS are corrupt, but 'XI' is a relatively plausible conjecture.

conspicuous colour of the cloak: a reference to the scarlet *paludamentum* worn by the *imperator* (see Pliny, *Nat. Hist.* 22.3).

7.89 *he took his seat . . . thrown down*: a very restrained portrait of the final victory. Plutarch improves the drama with a tale of Vercingetorix putting on his finest armour and galloping to where Caesar was seated, then leaping from his horse to fall at Caesar's feet. For his execution, see 7.4 n.

7.90 *a thanksgiving . . . was decreed*: on the thanksgiving, see 2.35, 4.37, and nn.

8.3 *Caesar's clemency*: a word Caesar uses with caution, preferring *lenitas* or *beneficium*. It underlines the shift in portrayal of Caesar which took place both during his time of supremacy and following his assassination. See 2.14 n.

8.4 *as many thousand*: the text is corrupt here.

it was explained: at 7.90.

8.6 *prestige*: the notorious *dignitas*. See also 8.24, 50, 52, 53; 4.17 n.

8.8 *virtual battle formation*: i.e. *agmen quadratum*, with baggage in the middle and troops at four corners.

8.19 *inconclusively*: Lat. *pari Marte*—see 7.19 n.

8.24 *the people . . . barbarians*: reading *illorum* instead of *incolae illorum*.

8.30 *who was known . . . revolted*: see 7.7.

8.32 *a dependency of his*: Lat. *in clientela . . . eius*.

8.38 *the people . . . commentary*: see 7.2.

8.39 *his command*: Lat. *provincia*. The terminal date of Caesar's Gallic command was disputed at the time and still is: his final campaign season, however, was the summer of 50 BC.

8.48 *treacherously*: reading *perfidia* instead of *per fidem*. The reference is to events related at 8.23.

Consulship . . . Marcellus: 50 BC.

8.50 *communities and colonies . . . priesthood*: Lat. *municipia* (these communities had citizen rights under the Lex Julia of 90 BC) and *coloniae* (settlements of citizens from Rome). Their citizen votes were needed for Antony's election to the College of Augurs.

factional power . . . men: literally, 'the faction and power of a few men' (*factio et potentia paucorum*). This is the language of late Republican political strife.

office: the consulship.

office and prestige: Lat. *honor et dignitas*. Lentulus and Marcellus were elected consuls for 49.

8.51 *dining couches*: Lat. *triclinia*, couches for three people to lie on at dinner. There is a reference here to the rite of *lectisternium*, or 'strewing of couches', at which a banquet was placed before images of the gods set upon the couches.

8.52 *review of his army*: the *lustrum* was a purification ceremony (such as that performed by the censors every five years): it is appropriate to mark the end of the war.

resolution of the Senate: Lat. *senatus auctoritas*. A decision of the Senate *not* vetoed by a tribune of the people was called a decree, *senatus consultum*.

The consuls ... happening: the text here is slightly confused, but the sense clear.

8.53 *a law ... Crassus*: so-called because they were consuls in 55 BC, but in fact it was the Lex Trebonia, which gave Caesar his second five-year term in Gaul.

8.54 *Parthian war*: Cassius Dio affirms that the war (which had been conducted by Caesar's erstwhile consular colleague Bibulus) was already over, and hence was a pretext for depriving Caesar of the two legions (40.65–6): the issue is followed up in *CW*.

GLOSSARY

ACCO (6.4, 44; 7.1): a leader of the Senones.

ADIATUNNUS (3.22): a leader of the Sotiates.

ADMAGETOBRIGA (1.31): a town in the territory of the Sequani, location unknown. Site of a battle between Ariovistus and the Gauls.

ADUATUCA (6.32, 35): a stronghold of the Eburones, site unknown.

ADUATUCI or ATUATUCI (2.4, 16, 29, 31; 5.27, 38–9, 56; 6.2, 33): a tribe of German origin, on the W bank of the Meuse.

AEDUI (1.10 and *passim*; 2.5, 10, 14–15; 5.6, 7, 54; 7 *passim*; 8.45–6, 54): powerful and influential Gallic people, important Roman allies, sited between the Loire and Saône around Lyons.

Lucius AEMILIUS (1.23): a cavalry officer (*decurio*).

Lucius AEMILIUS Paulus (8.48): consul in 50 BC.

AGEDINCUM (6.44; 7.10, 57, 59, 62): chief town of the Senones.

AISNE (2.5, 9): Lat. *Axona*. A tributary of the Oise.

ALESIA (7.68–84; 8.14, 34): a stronghold of the Mandubii, site of Caesar's great victory over Vercingetorix.

ALLIER (7.34–5, 53): Lat. *Elaver*. A tributary of the Loire, rising in the Cevennes.

ALLOBROGES (1.6, 10, 11, 14, 28, 44; 3.1, 6; 7.64–5): a powerful people sited between the Rhône and Isère (Isara).

ALPS (1.10; 3.1, 2, 7; 4.10): the natural frontier between the two Gauls (Trans-alpine and Cis-alpine).

AMBARRI (1.11, 14): a people sited between the Rhône and Saône, dependants (*clientes*) of the Aedui.

AMBIANI (2.4, 15; 7.75; 8.7): a Belgic people centred on Samarobriva.

AMBIBARETI or AMBIVARETI (7.75, 90): dependants of the Aedui.

AMBIBARII (7.75): one of the Aremoric peoples sited between the Seine and Loire.

AMBILIATI (3.9): site unknown. Allies of the Veneti.

AMBIORIX (5.24–41; 6.2–9, 29–43; 8.24–5): a leader of the Eburones, who revolted in 54 BC and treacherously betrayed Cotta and Sabinus. He was never captured.

AMBIVARITI (4.9): a Belgic people.

ANARTES (6.25): a Dacian people.

ANCALITES (6.21): a British people.

ANDECOMBORIUS (2.3): a leading citizen of the Remi.

ANDES (2.35; 3.7; 7.4, 75; 8.26): a Gallic people N of the Loire.

ANGLESEY (5.13): Lat. *Mona*.

Gaius ANTISTIUS Reginus (6.1; 7.83, 90): one of Caesar's legates.

Mark ANTONY (7.81; 8.2, 24, 38, 46–50): Lat. *Marcus Antonius*. Born *c.*83 BC, he served under Caesar in Gaul until the end of 50. Tribune in 49, he fled to join Caesar and took part in the ensuing civil war, including Pompey's defeat at Pharsalus. In 43 he formed the 'second' triumvirate with Lepidus and Octavian (Caesar's great-nephew, adopted son and heir, later the emperor Augustus).

APOLLO (6.17): a Greek deity whose principal roles at Rome were healing and prophecy. The name Belon (or Belenus/Belenis) is usually given as his equivalent.

AQUILEIA (1.10): a town in Cisalpine Gaul, at the N end of the Adriatic.

AQUITANI (1.1; 3.21): peoples of Iberian origin, living in SW Gaul.

AQUITANIA (1.1; 3.11, 20–7; 7.31; 8.46): one of the three ethnic and geographical divisions of Gaul.

ARDENNES (5.3; 6.29, 31, 33): Caesar (or his source) exaggerated the extent of this forest in the territory of the Belgae.

ARECOMICI: *see* VOLCAE.

AREMORIC STATES (5.53; 7.75; 8.31): the coastal peoples between the Loire and Seine in Brittany and Normandy (Aremoric = 'maritime').

ARIOVISTUS (1.31–53; 4.16; 5.29, 55; 6.12): king of the Suebi, he had invaded Gaul at the invitation of the Sequani some years before Caesar came to Gaul, and defeated a combined Gallic force at Admagetobriga: he was given the title of Friend of the Roman people before he clashed with Caesar, who mentions his death only in passing (5.29).

Marcus ARISTIUS (7.42–3): a military tribune.

Gaius ARPINEIUS (5.27–8): a Roman knight (*eques*) and friend of Sabinus.

ARVERNI (1.31, 45; 7.3, 5, 9, 34–8, 64–90; 8.46): a Gallic people sited in modern Auvergne, who had previously controlled much more extensive territories (so Strabo 4.2.3).

ATIUS

 (i) Quintus ATIUS Varus (8.28): a cavalry commander (*praefectus equitum*).

 (ii) Quintus ATIUS Labienus (1.10, 21–2, 54; 2.1, 11, 26; 3.11; 4.38; 5.8, 11, 23–4, 27, 37, 46–58; 6.5, 7–8, 33; 7.34, 56–62, 86–7, 90; 8.6, 23–5, 45–52): in 63 he prosecuted Gaius Rabirius as part of an attack on the Senate's power, thus marking an association with Caesar, whose principal subordinate commander he was throughout the Gallic war. He held commands against the Treveri in 54–3 and the Parisii in 52 BC.

It has been suggested that he had always been an adherent of Pompey, to whom he deserted in 49. He died at Munda in 45 BC.

ATREBATES (2.4, 16, 23; 4.21; 5.46; 7.75; 8.7, 47): a Belgic people defeated in 57 BC, who revolted again in 51.

Quintus ATRIUS (5.9–10): one of Caesar's officers.

AULERCI (2.34; 3.29; 7.4; 8.7): a numerous people, including the Aulerci Brannovices, Diablintes, and Eburovices.

Lucius AURUNCULEIUS Cotta (2.11; 4.22, 38; 5.24–37, 52; 6.32, 37): one of Caesar's legates, killed by the Eburones.

AUSCI (3.27): an Aquitanian people.

AVARICUM (7.13, 18, 29–32, 47, 52): now *Bourges*, principal stronghold of the Bituriges.

BACENIS FOREST (6.10): a forest in Bavaria.

BACULUS: *see* SEXTIUS.

BALBUS: *see* CORNELIUS.

BALEARIC: (2.7): specialist slingers from the Balearic Islands (Majorca and Minorca).

Titus BALVENTIUS (5.35): a leading centurion.

BASILUS: *see* MINUCIUS.

BATAVI (4.10): a people sited between the Waal and the Rhine.

BELGAE (1.1; 2.1–6, 14–19; 3.7, 11; 4.38; 5.24; 8.6, 38; 54): one of Gaul's three ethnic divisions.

BELGIUM (5.12, 25; 8.46, 49, 54): the territory occupied by the Belgic peoples.

BELLOVACI (2.4–5, 10, 13–14; 5.46; 7.59, 75, 90): a Belgic people.

BIBRACTE (1.23; 7.55, 63, 90; 8.2, 4): on *Mont Beuvray*. The main city of the Aedui.

BIBRAX (2.6): either *Beaurieux* or *Vieux Laon*. A town of the Remi.

BIBROCI (5.21): a British people.

BIGERRIONES (3.27): an Aquitanian people.

BITURIGES (1.18; 7.5, 8–15, 21, 29, 75, 90; 8.2–4, 11): a Gallic people centred around Avaricum and Noviodunum.

BLANNOVII (7.75): a Gallic people, dependants (*clientes*) of the Aedui.

BODUOGNATUS (2.23): supreme commander of the Nervii.

BOII (1.5, 25, 28–9; 7.9, 10, 17, 75): a powerful Gallic people, centred on Gorgobina.

BRANNOVICES (7.75): *see* AULERCI.

BRATUSPANTIUM (2.13): a stronghold of the Bellovaci, site uncertain.

BRITONS (4.21; 5.11, 14, 21): the peoples of Britain had much in common with those of mainland Gaul. Chief among them were the Trinobantes.

BRITAIN (2.4, 14; 3.8–9; 4.20, 30, 37–8; 5.2, 6, 8, 12–13, 22; 6.13;

7.76): Lat. *Britannia*. Though Caesar penetrated only the SE region in his expeditions of 55 and 54 BC, he was aware that it was an island.

BRUTUS: *see* JUNIUS.

CABILLONUM (7.42, 90): now *Chalons-sur-Saône*, a stronghold in Aeduan territory.

CABURUS: *see* VALERIUS (i).

CADURCI (7.4, 64, 75; 8.32, 34): a people of SW Gaul.

CAEROESI (2.4): a German people sited in Belgium.

CAESAR: *see* JULIUS.

CALENUS: *see* FUFIUS.

CALETES (2.4; 7.75; 8.7): one of the Aremoric peoples.

CALPURNIUS

(i) Lucius CALPURNIUS Piso (1.12): consul in 112 BC. He was killed by the Tigurini in 107 BC, in the same battle as Lucius Cassius.

(ii) Lucius CALPURNIUS Piso Caesoninus (1.6, 12): consul in 58 BC, grandson of the above and father of Caesar's third wife Calpurnia.

CAMULOGENUS (7.57, 59, 62): a leader of the Aulerci.

Gaius CANINIUS Rebilus (7.83, 90; 8.24-39, 44): one of Caesar's legates in 52 BC, he was sent by Caesar to negotiate with Pompey in 49, and then to serve with Curio in Africa, and at Thapsus and Munda.

CANTABRI (3.26): a people of N Spain (Hispania Tarraconensis).

CANTIUM (5.13-14, 22): now Kent.

CARNUTES (2.35; 5.25, 29, 56; 6.2-4, 13, 44; 7.2-3, 11, 75; 8.4-5, 31, 38, 46): a Gallic people centred on Cenabum, supporters of Vercingetorix.

CARVILIUS (5.22): a king of part of Cantium.

CASSI (5.21): a British people.

Lucius CASSIUS (1.7, 12): consul in 107 BC, killed by the Tigurini.

CASSIVELLAUNUS (5.11, 18-22): chief commander of the British resistance to Caesar's second invasion.

CASTICUS (1.3): a leader of the Sequani.

CATAMANTALOEDIS (1.3): king of the Sequani and father of Casticus.

CATURIGES (1.10): a people of the Province.

CATUVOLCUS (5.24, 26; 6.31): joint ruler of the Eburones with Ambiorix.

CAVARILLUS (7.67): Aeduan infantry commander.

CAVARINUS (5.54; 6.5): king of the Senones.

CELTS (1.1): usually referred to as 'Gauls', one of the three ethnic divisions of Gaul.

CELTILLUS (7.4): father of Vercingetorix.

CENABUM (7.3, 11, 14, 17, 28; 8.5–6): now *Orléans*, chief stronghold of the Carnutes.

CENIMAGNI (5.21): a British people.

CENOMANI (7.75): *see* AULERCI.

CEUTRONES

   (i) (1.10): a people of the Province.

   (ii) (5.39): a Belgic people.

CEVENNES (7.8, 56): a mountain range in S Gaul, part of the frontier of the Province.

CHERUSCI (6.10): a German people.

CIMBERIUS (1.37): brother of Nasua, joint leader of the Suebi.

CIMBRI (1.33, 40; 2.4, 29; 7.77): a German people, who migrated with the Teutoni at the end of the second century, defeating a Roman army in 113 BC. In 110 they defeated another under Marcus Junius Silanus, but were eventually conquered by Gaius Marius in 101.

CINGETORIX

   (i) (5.22): a king of part of Cantium.

   (ii) (5.3–4, 56–7): a leader of the Treveri.

CISALPINE GAUL: *see* GAUL.

CLAUDIUS

   (i) Appius CLAUDIUS Pulcher (6.1): consul for 54 BC.

   (ii) Gaius CLAUDIUS Marcellus (8.48, 55): consul for 50 BC.

   (iii) Gaius CLAUDIUS Marcellus (8.50): consul for 49 BC.

   (iv) Marcus CLAUDIUS Marcellus (8.53): consul for 51 BC, he tried to rescind the Lex Trebonia which gave Caesar his second five-year term in Gaul.

Publius CLODIUS Pulcher (7.1): brother of Claudius (i). In 59 BC he transferred from the patricians to the plebs with Caesar's support. An enemy of Cicero, his tribunate in 58 was notorious for the 'popular' measures it enacted. He was murdered in 52.

COCOSATES (3.27): an Aquitanian people.

COMMIUS (4.21, 27, 35; 5.22; 6.6; 7.75–6, 79; 8.6–7, 10, 21, 23, 47–8): appointed king of the Atrebates through Caesar in 57 BC, he acted as Caesar's agent in Britain. He joined the revolt of 52 and later settled in Britain.

CONCONNETODUMNUS (7.3): a leader of the Carnutes.

CONDRUSI (2.4; 4.6; 6.32): a German people sited in Belgium.

Publius CONSIDIUS (1.21–2): a Roman officer.

CONVICTOLITAVIS (7.32–3, 37, 39, 42, 55, 67): a magistrate of the Aedui.

CORNELIUS

   (i) Lucius CORNELIUS Balbus (8.*preface*): a native of Gades (*Cádiz*) granted citizenship through Pompey in 72. He later became an adherent first of Caesar and then of Octavian. Hirtius claimed to have written GW 8 at his request.

(ii) Lucius CORNELIUS Lentulus Crus (8.50): consul for 49 BC, and enemy of Caesar.

(iii) Lucius CORNELIUS Sulla [Felix] (1.21): the dictator (82–80 BC), who died in 78. Though a legislator in the senatorial interest at the people's expense, his legislative and military activities set precedents for Caesar to follow.

CORREUS (8.6–7, 17–21): a leader of the Bellovaci.

COTUATUS (7.3): a leader of the Carnutes, identified by some with Gutruater.

COTUS (7.32): an Aeduan aristocrat.

CRETANS (2.7): Crete was famed for her archers.

CRITOGNATUS (7.77–8): an Arvernian aristocrat who proposed cannibalism at the siege of Alesia.

CURIOSOLITES (2.34; 3.7, 11; 7.75): an Aremoric people.

CURIO: see SCRIBONIUS.

DACI (6.25): a people living in modern Romania.

DANUBE (6.25): Lat. Danuvius.

DECETIA (7.33): now Decize. A town of the Aedui.

DIABLINTES (3.9): see AULERCI.

DIS (6.18): in Roman religion the ruler of the Underworld.

DIVICO (1.13–14): a leader of the Helvetii.

DIVICIACUS

(i) (1.3, 16–20, 31–2, 41; 2.5, 10, 14–15; 6.12; 7.39): the Aeduan, a supporter of Rome and brother of Dumnorix.

(ii) (2.4): a king of the Suessiones who controlled parts of Belgium and Britain.

DONNOTAURUS: see VALERIUS (ii).

Lucius DOMITIUS Ahenobarbus (5.1): consul for 54 BC and an enemy of Caesar. At the start of the civil war he was forced to surrender at Corfinium. He died at Pharsalus.

DRAPPES (8.30, 32, 35–6, 39, 44): a leader of the Senones.

DOUBS (1.38): Lat. Dubis. A tributary of the Saône, rising in the Jura mountain range.

DUMNACUS (8.26–31): a leader of the Andes.

DUMNORIX (1.3, 9, 18–20; 5.6–7): an Aeduan, brother of Diviciacus and hostile to Rome.

DURATIUS (8.26–7): a leader of the Pictones and supporter of Rome.

DUROCORTORUM (6.44): now Rheims. Principal stronghold of the Remi.

EBURONES (2.4; 4.6; 5.24, 28–9, 39, 47, 58; 6.5, 31–5): a Belgic people, dependants (clientes) of the Treveri. In 54 BC they destroyed a Roman army, for which Caesar punished them in 53.

EBUROVICES (3.17; 7.75): *see* AULERCI.

ELEUTETI (7.75): a people under Arvernian control.

ELUSATES (3.27): an Aquitanian people.

EPASNACTUS (8.44): an Arvernian supporter of Rome.

EPOREDORIX

(i) (7.67): the leader of the Aedui in a war against the Sequani, captured by Caesar in 52 BC.

(ii) (7.38–40, 54–5, 63–4, 76): an aristocratic young Aeduan who served in Caesar's cavalry.

ERATOSTHENES (6.24): *c.*275–194 BC. A polymath whose interests included geography, chronology, and mathematics.

ESUBII (2.34; 3.7; 5.24): a Gallic people sited in modern Normandy.

FABIUS

(i) Gaius FABIUS Maximus (5.24, 46–7, 53; 6.6; 7.40–1, 87, 90; 8.6, 24, 27–8, 31, 37, 54): one of Caesar's legates.

(ii) Lucius FABIUS (7.47, 50): a centurion of the Eighth legion, killed at Gergovia in 52 BC.

(iii) Quintus FABIUS Maximus Allobrogicus (1.45): consul in 121 BC, he was active in Transalpine Gaul against the Arverni and Ruteni.

FUFIUS

(i) Quintus FUFIUS Calenus (8.39): an adherent of Caesar in the 50s, then one of his legates in Gaul and a supporter in the civil war, consul in 47 BC. Later a follower of Mark Antony, he became a governor of Gaul and died there in 40.

(ii) Gaius FUFIUS Cita (7.3): a Roman knight (*eques*) and superintendent of the corn supply, killed at Cenabum in 52 BC.

FURTHER GAUL: *see* GAUL.

GABALI (7.7, 64, 75): a Gallic people, dependants (*clientes*) of the Arverni.

Aulus GABINIUS (1.6): a supporter of Pompey before his consulship in 58 BC, later on Caesar's side.

GALBA (2.4, 13): king of the Suessiones.

GAULS (*passim*): Lat. *Galli*, more precisely (1.1) *Celtae*. One of the three ethnic divisions of Gaul.

GAUL

(i) NEARER [*Citerior*] or CISALPINE (1.10, 24, 54; 2.1–2; 5.1–2; 6.1; 8.23–4, 52, 54): N Italy, divided by the Po into Cispadane and Transpadane.

(ii) FURTHER [*Ulterior*] or TRANSALPINE (1.7, 10; 7.1, 6): a territory bounded by the Alps, Rhine, Pyrenees, and Atlantic.

GARONNE (1.1): Lat. *Garumnus*.

GARUMNI (3.27): an Aquitanian people.

GATES (3.27): an Aquitanian people.

GEIDUMNI (5.39): a Belgic people under the sway of the Nervii.

GENAVA (1.6–7): now *Geneva*. A stronghold of the Allobroges.

GERGOVIA (7.4, 34–45, 59): a stronghold of the Arverni on the Auvergnes range, 4 miles S of Clermont. Site of Caesar's most serious defeat in Gaul.

GERMANS (1.1, 27–52; 2.1–4; 3.7–11; 4.1–7, 13–19; 5.2, 27–9, 55; 6.2–12, 21–42; 7.63–70, 80; 8.7, 10, 13, 25, 36, 45): a warlike nation described by Caesar as semi-nomadic. Caesar makes mention of the Suebi, Cherusci, Ubii, Sugambri, Marcomani, Usipetes and Tencteri, Harudes, Nemetes, Triboces, Vangiones, Latovici, Tulingi, Sedusii, Cimbri, and Teutoni.

GERMANY (4.4; 5.13; 6.11, 24–5, 31): in Caesar's time, the territory E of the Rhine, but later defined more closely as bounded by the Rhine, Danube, Weichsel, and Ocean.

GOBANNITIO (7.4): uncle of Vercingetorix.

GORGOBINA (7.9): a stronghold of the Boii, site uncertain.

GRAIOCELI (1.10): an Alpine people.

GRUDII (5.39): a Belgic people under the sway of the Nervii.

GUTRUATER/GUTRUATUS (8.38): a leader of revolt among the Carnutes, identified by some with Cotuatus (7.3).

HARUDES (1.31, 37, 51): a German people.

HELVETII (1.1–30, 40; 4.10; 6.25; 7.75): a Gallic people grouped into four districts (*pagi*), of which Caesar mentions two, *Verbigenus* and *Tigurinus*.

HELVII (7.7–8, 64–5): a people of the Province.

HERCYNIAN FOREST (6.24–5): apparently sixty days' journey in length and nine in width, in central Europe.

ICCIUS (2.3, 6, 7): a leader of the Remi.

ILLYRICUM (2.35; 3.7; 5.1): part of Caesar's sphere of command (*provincia*), on the NE of the Adriatic.

INDUTIOMARUS (5.3–4, 26, 53–8; 6.2, 8): a leading citizen of the Treveri, and rival of Cingetorix (ii).

ITALY (1.10, 33, 40; 2.29, 35; 3.1; 5.1, 29; 6.1, 32, 44; 7.1, 6–7, 55, 57, 65; 8.50, 54–5): usually refers to the province of Cisalpine Gaul.

IRELAND (5.13): Lat. *Hibernia*.

ITIUS PORTUS (5.2, 5): now *Boulogne*. The harbour whence Caesar's second expedition to Britain set sail.

Lucius JULIUS Caesar (7.65): consul in 64 BC, he became Caesar's legate in 52.

JUNIUS

(i) Decimus JUNIUS Brutus Albinus (3.11, 14; 7.9, 87): commanded Caesar's fleet against the Veneti in 56 BC, and later at Massilia in 49, following which he was made governor of Transalpine Gaul. One of Caesar's assassins. He took command of the Senate's troops after the deaths of Hirtius and Pansa in 43, but was eventually executed on Mark Antony's orders.

(ii) Marcus JUNIUS Silanus (6.1): one of Caesar's legates.

(iii) Quintus JUNIUS (5.27–8): a Spanish envoy in Caesar's employ.

JUPITER (6.17): an Italian sky-god with some political and military functions. His Gallic equivalent is Taranis.

JURA (1.2, 6, 8): a mountain range on the France–Switzerland border.

Quintus LABERIUS Durus (5.15): a military tribune killed during the second invasion of Britain.

LABIENUS: *see* ATIUS.

LATOVICI (1.5, 28–9): a German people.

LAKE LEMANNUS (1.2, 8): now Lake Geneva.

LEMONUM (8.26): now *Poitiers*. A stronghold of the Pictones.

LEMOVICES (7.4, 75, 88; 8.46): a Gallic people.

LENTULUS: *see* CORNELIUS (ii).

LEPONTII (4.10): an Alpine people.

LEUCI (1.40): a Gallic people.

LEVACI (5.39): a Belgic people.

LEXOVII (3.9, 11, 17, 29; 7.75): one of the Aremoric peoples of Normandy.

LICINIUS

(i) Marcus LICINIUS Crassus (1.21; 4.1; 8.53): consul I, 70 BC, II, 55. Member of the 'first triumvirate' with Pompey and Caesar. In 55 went to Syria but was killed at Carrhae in 53.

(ii) Marcus LICINIUS Crassus (5.24, 46–7; 6.6): elder son of (i). Quaestor in 54 BC, he served under Caesar in Gaul.

(iii) Publius LICINIUS Crassus (1.52; 2.34; 3.7–11, 20–7; 8.46): younger son of (i). First a cavalry officer (*praefectus equitum*) of Caesar, then a legate. He died at Carrhae with his father.

LINGONES (1.26, 40; 4.10; 6.44; 7.9, 63, 66; 8.11): a Gallic people separated by the Saône from the Sequani.

LISCUS (1.16–18): a principal magistrate of the Aedui.

LITAVICCUS (7.37–43, 54–5, 67): an aristocratic young Aeduan.

LOIRE (3.9; 7.5, 11, 55–6; 8.27): Lat. *Liger*.

Quintus LUCANIUS (5.35): a leading centurion.

LUCTERIUS (7.5, 7–8): a leader of the Cadurci.

LUGOTORIX (5.22): an aristocratic Kentish commander.

LUTETIA (6.3; 7.57–8): a stronghold of the Parisii on an island in the Seine near Paris.

Lucius MALLIUS (3.20): or Manlius. Governor of Transalpine Gaul in 78 BC.

MANDUBII (7.68, 71, 78): a Gallic people, centred on Alesia.

MANDUBRACIUS (5.20, 22): a leader of the Trinobantes.

MARCELLUS: *see* CLAUDIUS.

MARCOMANI (1.51): a German people.

Gaius MARIUS (1.40): (*c.*157–86 BC) uncle of Caesar by marriage. Of his seven consulships (107, 104–100, 86), five were held in continuous succession, enabling him to counter the Cimbri at Vercellae and Teutoni at Aquae Sextiae.

Mark ANTONY: *see* ANTONY.

MARNE (1.1): Lat. *Matrona.*

MARS (6.17): a principal Italian god with agricultural and military functions. His Gallic equivalent is Aesus/Hesus.

MATISCO (7.90): now *Mâcon.* A stronghold of the Aedui on the Saône.

MEDIOMATRICES or MEDIOMATRICI (4.10; 7.75): a Gallic people W of the Rhine.

MEDITERRANEAN (5.1): Lat. *nostrum mare* ('our sea').

MELDI (5.5): a Gallic people on the Marne.

MENAPII (2.4; 3.9, 28; 4.4, 22, 38; 6.2, 5–6, 9, 33): a Belgic people sited between the Scheldt and Meuse, ejected from their former territory on the Rhine by the Usipetes and Tencteri.

MERCURY (6.17): a god of Greek origin (Hermes), associated with trade and commerce. His Gallic equivalent is Teutates.

MESSALLA: *see* VALERIUS (vi).

METIOSEDUM (7.58, 60–1): a stronghold of the Senones on an island in the Seine.

METTIUS (1.47, 53): an envoy sent by Caesar to Ariovistus.

MEUSE (4.9–10, 12, 15–16; 5.24; 6.33): Lat. *Mosa.*

MINERVA (6.17): an Italian goddess of crafts. Her Gallic equivalent is unclear.

Lucius MINUCIUS Basilus (6.29–30; 7.90): a Roman cavalry officer, possibly a legate. He was praetor in 45 BC.

MOON (6.21): a deity of the Germans.

MORINI (2.4; 3.9, 28; 4.21–2, 37–8; 5.24; 7.75–6): a Belgic people.

MORITASGUS (5.54): brother of Cavarinus (king of the Senones).

Lucius MUNATIUS Plancus (5.24–5): one of Caesar's legates. Proconsul of Transalpine Gaul in 44/3 BC, where he founded Lugdunum, now *Lyons.* He changed sides in 43, joining with Antony and Lepidus, and was made consul in 42. After supporting Antony, he went over to Octavian in 32, for whom he proposed the name Augustus in 27.

NAMMEIUS (1.7): a Helvetian envoy.

NAMNETES (3.9): a Gallic people N of the Loire.

NANTUATES (3.1, 6; 4.10): an Alpine people on the border of the Province. If the text at 4.10 is correct, some of them, or another people of the same name, lived in the upper valley of the Rhine.

NARBO (3.20; 7.7; 8.46): now *Narbonne*. A town of the Volcae Arecomici in the Province.

NASUA (1.37): brother of Cimberius, joint leader of the Suebi.

NEARER GAUL: *see* GAUL.

NEMETES (1.51): a German people.

NEMETOCENNA (8.46, 52): now *Arras*. A stronghold of the Atrebates.

NERVII (2.4, 15–19, 23, 28–32; 5.24, 38–48, 56, 58; 6.2–3, 29; 7.75): a powerful Belgic people.

NITIOBRIGES (7.7, 31, 46, 75): an Aquitanian people.

NOREIA (1.5): now *Neumarkt*.

NORICUM (1.5): a territory in the Alps, roughly equivalent to Austria.

NOVIODUNUM

   (i) of the Aedui (7.55): *Nevers*.

   (ii) of the Bituriges (7.12, 14): ?*Neuvy-sur-Barangeon*.

   (iii) of the Suessiones (2.12): near *Soissons*.

NUMIDIANS (2.7, 10, 24): African auxiliaries in Caesar's army.

OCEAN (1.1; 2.34; 3.7, 9, 13; 4.10, 29; 6.31, 33; 7.4, 75; 8.31, 46): the Atlantic.

OCELUM (1.10): now *Drubiaglio? Avigliana?*

OCTODURUS (3.1): now *Martigny*. A settlement of the Veragri.

OLLOVICO (7.31): the father of Teutomatus (king of the Nitiobriges).

ORCYNIAN FOREST (6.24): *see* HERCYNIAN FOREST.

ORGETORIX (1.2–4, 9, 26): an aristocrat of the Helvetii.

OSISMI (2.34; 3.9; 7.75): one of the Aremoric peoples of Brittany.

PAEMANI (2.4): a Belgic people.

PARISII (6.3; 7.4, 34, 57, 75): a Gallic people centred on Lutetia.

PAULUS: *see* AEMILIUS.

Quintus PEDIUS (2.2, 11): a nephew of Caesar and one of his legates. He supported Caesar in the civil war and became consul in 43.

PETROCORII (7.75): a Gallic people sited in what is now Périgord.

Marcus PETRONIUS (7.50): a centurion of the Eighth legion killed at Gergovia in 52 BC.

Lucius PETROSIDIUS (5.37): a standard-bearer (*aquilifer*) in the army led by Cotta and Sabinus.

PICTONES (3.11; 7.4, 75; 8.26–7): a Gallic people.

PIRUSTAE (6.1): an Illyrian people.

PISO

   (i) *see* CALPURNIUS; PUPIUS.

   (ii) PISO (4.12): an Aquitanian aristocrat.

PLANCUS: *see* MUNATIUS.

PLEUMOXII (5.39): a Belgic people under the sway of the Nervii.

PO (5.24): Lat. *Padus*.

POMPEIUS

(i) Gnaeus POMPEIUS Magnus [Pompey the Great] (4.1; 6.1; 7.6; 8.52–5): (106–48 BC) a supporter of Sulla, his early military success was spectacular. Consul in 70 with Crassus (i) as his colleague. At first Caesar's ally (in the 'first triumvirate'), he became a rival and enemy, mobilizing senatorial support against him. After his defeat at Pharsalus in 48 he fled to Egypt, where he was murdered.

(ii) Gnaeus POMPEIUS (5.36): an interpreter employed by Sabinus.

PRAECONINUS: *see* VALERIUS (v).

PROCILLUS: *see* VALERIUS (iv).

The PROVINCE (also TRANSALPINE GAUL, 1.6, 10, 19, 28, 35, 44, 53; 3.20; 7.1, 6, 77): now *Provence*. After 27 BC it was known as Gallia Narbonensis after its capital Narbo, hence separate from the rest of Transalpine Gaul which was divided into Gallia Lugdunensis (from Lugdunum [Lyons]), Belgica, and Aquitania.

PTIANII (3.27): an Aquitanian people.

Titus PULLO (5.44): a centurion.

Marcus PUPIUS Piso (1.2, 35): consul in 61 BC.

PYRENEES (1.1): Lat. *Pyrenaei montes*.

QUADRATUS: *see* VOLUSENUS.

RAURICI (1.5, 29; 6.25; 7.75): a Gallic people.

REBILUS: *see* CANINIUS.

REDONES (2.34; 7.75): one of the Aremoric people of Brittany.

REGINUS: *see* ANTISTIUS.

REMI (2.3–7, 9, 12; 3.11; 5.3, 24, 53–6; 6.4, 12, 44; 7.63, 90; 8.6, 11–12): a powerful Belgic people favoured by Caesar.

RHINE (1.1–2, 5, 27–8, 31–7, 43–4, 53–4; 2.3–4, 29, 35; 3.11; 4.1, 3–6, 10, 14, 19; 5.3, 24, 27, 29, 41, 55; 6.9, 24, 29, 32, 35, 41, 42; 7.65; 8.13): Lat. *Rhenus*. The frontier between the Gauls and Germans.

RHÔNE (1.1–2, 6, 8, 10–12, 33; 3.1; 7.65): Lat. *Rhodanus*.

ROME (1.7, 31, 39; 6.1, 12; 7.90): Lat. *Roma*.

Lucius ROSCIUS Fabatus (5.24, 53): one of Caesar's subordinate commanders. As praetor in 49 BC he secured the enfranchisement of the Transpadanes.

RUFUS: *see* SULPICIUS (i).

RUTENI (1.45; 7.5, 7, 64, 75, 90): a Gallic people.

RUTILUS: *see* SEMPRONIUS.

SABINUS: *see* TITURIUS.

SAMAROBRIVA (5.24, 47, 53): now *Amiens*. A stronghold of the Ambiani.

SAMBRE (2.16, 18): Lat. *Sabis.*

SANTONI (1.10–11; 3.11; 7.75): a Gallic people.

SAÔNE (1.12–13, 16; 7.90; 8.4): Lat. *Arar.*

SCHELDT (6.33): Lat. *Scaldis.*

Gaius SCRIBONIUS Curio (8.52): quaestor in 54 BC, tribune of the people in 50. Though previously numbered among the aristocratic opposition to Caesar he became a supporter in the civil war. He was killed in Africa (see *CW* 2.23–44).

SEDULIUS (7.88): a leader of the Lemovices.

SEDUNI (3.1, 2, 7): an Alpine people.

SEDUSII (1.51): a German people.

SEGNI (6.32): a Belgic people.

SEGONTIACI (5.21): a people of S Britain.

SEGOVAX (5.22): a king of part of Cantium.

SEGUSIAVI (1.10; 7.64, 75): a Gallic people, dependants (*clientes*) of the Aedui.

SEINE (1.1; 7.57–8): Lat. *Sequana.*

Marcus SEMPRONIUS Rutilus (7.90): one of Caesar's officers.

SENONES (2.2; 5.54, 56; 6.2–5, 44; 7.4, 11, 34, 56, 58, 75): a powerful Gallic people.

SEQUANI (1.1–12, 19, 31–5, 38, 40, 44, 48, 54; 4.10; 6.12; 7.66–7, 75, 90): a Gallic people centred on Vesontio on the Doubs.

Quintus SERTORIUS (3.23): a supporter of Marius in the war with Sulla, he was praetor in 83 BC with Spain as his province and remained there in defiance of Rome until he was murdered in 73 or 72.

SEXTIUS

(i) Publius SEXTIUS Baculus (2.25; 3.5; 6.38): a senior centurion of the Twelfth legion, given special mention for bravery by Caesar.

(ii) Titus SEXTIUS (6.1; 7.49, 51, 90; 8.11): one of Caesar's legates.

SIBUZATES (3.27): an Aquitanian people.

SILANUS: *see* JUNIUS.

Titus SILIUS (3.7–8): one of Caesar's officers.

SONTIATES (3.20, 21): a powerful Aquitanian people.

SPAIN (1.1; 3.23; 5.1, 13, 27; 7.55; see also 5.26): Lat. *Hispania.* Nearer Spain (Hispania Citerior) was a source of cavalry, horses, and rigging for ships.

SUEBI (1.37, 51, 54; 4.1, 3–4, 7–8, 16, 19; 6.9–10, 29): a German people.

SUESSIONES (2.3–4, 12–13; 8.6): a Belgic people.

SUGAMBRI (4.16, 18–19; 6.35): a German people.

SULLA: *see* CORNELIUS.

SUN (6.21): a deity of the Germans.

SULPICIUS

  (i) Publius SULPICIUS Rufus (4.22; 7.90): one of Caesar's legates.

  (ii) Servius SULPICIUS Galba (3.1–6; 8.50): one of Caesar's legates.

SURUS (8.45): an aristocratic Aeduan.

TARBELLI (3.27): an Aquitanian people.

TARUSATES (3.23, 27): an Aquitanian people.

TASGETIUS (5.25, 29): an aristocrat of the Carnutes.

TAXIMAGULUS (5.22): a king of part of Cantium.

TECTOSAGES (6.24): *see* VOLCAE.

TENCTERI (4.1, 4, 16, 18): a German people.

TERGESTE (8.24): now *Trieste*.

Titus TERRASIDIUS (3.7–8): an officer in Caesar's army.

TEUTOMATUS (7.31, 46): son of Ollovicus and king of the Nitiobriges.

TEUTONI (1.33, 40; 2.4, 29; 7.77): a German people. *See* CIMBRI.

THAMES (5.11, 18): Lat. *Tamesis*.

TIGURINI (1.12): inhabitants of one of the four Helvetian districts.

Quintus TITURIUS Sabinus (2.5, 9, 10; 3.11, 17–19; 4.22, 28; 5.24, 26–33, 36–41; 47, 52–3; 6.1, 32, 37): one of Caesar's legates, 57–54 BC. Despite success against the Venelli, he was betrayed and killed by Ambiorix and the Eburones in 54.

TOLOSA (3.20): now *Toulouse*.

TOLOSATES (1.10; 7.7): a people of the Province.

TRANSALPINE GAUL: *see* GAUL.

Marcus TREBIUS Gallus (3.7–8): an officer in Caesar's army.

TREBONIUS

  (i) Gaius TREBONIUS (6.40): one of Caesar's officers.

  (ii) Gaius TREBONIUS (5.17, 24; 6.33; 7.11, 81; 8.6, 11, 14, 46, 54): a tribune of the people in 55 BC who carried the Lex Trebonia which granted five-year commands to Pompey and Crassus. He served as Caesar's legate from 55 to 50 and conducted the siege of Massilia in 49, but changed sides to take part in the conspiracy to assassinate Caesar by keeping Antony from his side. He was murdered by Dolabella during his proconsulship of Asia in 43.

TREVERI (1.37; 2.24; 3.11; 4.6, 10; 5.2–4, 24, 47, 53, 55, 58; 6.2–9, 29, 32, 44; 7.63; 8.25, 45, 52): a powerful Gallic people of German origin.

TRIBOCES (1.51; 4.10): a German people.

TRINOBANTES or TRINOVANTES (5.20–2): a British people living in Essex. They surrendered to Caesar in 54 BC.

TULINGI (1.5, 25, 28–9): a German people.

Quintus TULLIUS Cicero (5.24, 27, 38, 41, 45, 48–9, 52–3; 6.32, 36; 7.90; 8.46): 102–43 BC. Younger brother of Marcus Cicero the orator and statesman. Governor of Asia from 61 to 59, a legate first of Pompey in 57/6, then of Caesar from 54 to 51 and in 51/50 of Marcus Cicero in Cilicia. He supported Pompey in the civil war but fell victim to the proscriptions of 43.

TULLUS: *see* VOLCATIUS.

TURONES or TURONI (2.35; 7.4, 75; 8.46): a Gallic people centred on the Loire.

UBII (1.54; 4.3, 8, 11, 16, 19; 6.9–10, 29): a German people.

USIPETES (4.1, 4, 16, 18; 6.35): a German people.

UXELLODUNUM (8.32, 40): now *Puy d'Issolou*? A stronghold of the Cadurci.

VALERIUS
  (i) Gaius VALERIUS Caburus (1.47; 7.65): a Gaul of the Helvii granted citizenship by Valerius (iii). Father of Valerii (ii) and (iv).
  (ii) Gaius VALERIUS Donnotaurus (7.65): son of Valerius (i).
  (iii) Gaius VALERIUS Flaccus (1.47): governor of Transalpine Gaul in 83 BC.
  (iv) Gaius VALERIUS Procillus (1.19, 47, 53): son of Valerius (i), acted as Caesar's interpreter.
  (v) Lucius VALERIUS Praeconinus (3.20): a Roman commander defeated and killed in Aquitania in 78 BC.
  (vi) Marcus VALERIUS Messalla Niger (1.2, 35): consul for 61 BC.

VALETIACUS (7.32): an Aeduan magistrate.

VANGIONES (7.51): a German people.

VARUS: *see* ATIUS.

Publius VATINIUS (8.46): one of Caesar's legates. As tribune of the people in 59 BC he carried a law giving Caesar Cisalpine Gaul and Illyricum as his province. Consul in 47.

Quintus VELANIUS (3.7–8): one of Caesar's officers.

VELIOCASSES (2.4; 7.75; 8.7): a Gallic people of Normandy on the Seine.

VELLAUNODUNUM (7.11, 14): site uncertain, perhaps *Montargis*. A stronghold of the Senones.

VELLAVII (7.75): a Gallic people, dependants (*clientes*) of the Arverni.

VENELLI (2.34; 3.11, 17; 7.75): one of the Aremoric peoples of Normandy.

VENETI (2.34; 3.7–11, 16–18; 7.75): a powerful Aremoric people of Brittany.

VENETIA (3.9): the land of the Veneti.

VERAGRI (3.1–2): a Gallic people of the Alps.

VERBIGENE (1.27): one of the four Helvetian districts.

VERCASSIVELLAUNUS (7.76, 83, 85, 88): cousin to Vercingetorix. A leader of the Arverni.

VERCINGETORIX (7.4, 8, 9 and *passim*): leader of the Arverni and commander of the Gallic rebellion. After success at Gergovia he was defeated at Alesia and taken prisoner, but was not executed until after Caesar's quadruple triumph in 46 BC.

VERTICO (5.45, 49): a well-born Nervian.

VERTISCUS (8.12): a cavalry commander and leading magistrate of the Remi.

VERUCLOETIUS (1.7): a Helvetian envoy.

VESONTIO (1.38–9): now *Besançon*. Site of unrest or perhaps even mutiny among Caesar's troops.

VIENNA (7.9): now *Vienne*. Chief stronghold of the Allobroges.

VIRIDOMARUS (7.38–40, 54–5, 63, 76): an aristocratic young Aeduan alleged to have been killed by the Romans.

VIRIDOVIX (3.17–18): leader of the Venelli, in command of the rebel peoples in 56 BC.

VIROMANDUI (2.4, 16, 23): a Belgic people centred on the Somme.

VOCATES (3.23, 27): an Aquitanian people sited on the Garonne.

VOCCIO (1.53): a king of Noricum, perhaps the same one who sent troops to Caesar's assistance in the civil war (*CW* 1.18).

VOCONTII (1.10): a Gallic people of the Province, E of the Rhône.

VOLCAE

(i) ARECOMICI (7.7, 64),

(ii) TECTOSAGES (6.24): powerful Gallic peoples of the Province extending from Aquitania to the Rhone. The Volcae Tectosages inhabited the region from the Pyrenees to Narbo (main stronghold Tolosa) and the Volcae Arecomici lived farther to the east (centred on Nemausus, now *Nîmes*).

Gaius VOLCATIUS Tullus (6.29): one of Caesar's officers.

Gaius VOLUSENUS Quadratus (3.5; 4.21, 23; 6.41; 8.23, 48): a military tribune and cavalry commander.

Lucius VORENUS (5.44): a centurion.

VOSGES (4.10): Lat. *Vosegus*. A mountain range in NE Gaul.

VULCAN (6.21): representing fire, a deity of the Germans.

WAAL (4.10): Lat. *Vacalus*.

TEXT VARIANTS

Oxford Classical Text	Variant Reading Adopted
1.24.2 *[ita uti supra]; sed*	delete
1.54.1 *Ubii*	*ubi*
2.1.1 *[in hibernis], ita uti supra demonstravimus*	delete
2.6.2 *portas succendunt*	*propius succedunt*
2.19.2 *†quod hostis†*	*quod hostibus*
2.30.2 *XV milium*	*V milium*
3.1.6 *[ad hiemandum]*	delete
3.13.6 *scopulis*	*copulis*
4.3.3 *paulo quam sunt eiusdem generis et ceteris humaniores*	*paulo sunt quam eiusdem generis ceteri humaniores*
5.25.3 *†inimicis*	*inimici*
et eis	delete
5.49.8 *valles*	*vallem*
6.22.2 *qui †cum† una*	*quique una*
7.38.4 *[multos]*	delete
7.45.2 *impedimentorum*	*iumentorum*
7.45.7 *qui*	*ne*
7.47.1 *legionique decimae quacum erat †concionatus† signa constituit*	*legionisque decimae quacum erat continuo signa constiterunt*
7.50.2 *†pacatum†*	*pactum*
7.64.1 *†denique† ei rei constituit †diem; huc†*	*diemque ei rei constituit*
7.65.5 *[sed et]*	delete
7.74.1 *†eius discessu†*	delete
7.84.5 *salute*	*virtute*
7.87.5 *XL*	*XI*
8.24.3 *†incolae illorum†*	*illorum*
8.29.4 *eo*	delete
8.48.4 *per fidem*	*perfidia*
8.52.5 *†iusserunt†*	*intercesserunt*

American Literature

British and Irish Literature

Children's Literature

Classics and Ancient Literature

Colonial Literature

Eastern Literature

European Literature

Gothic Literature

History

Medieval Literature

Oxford English Drama

Poetry

Philosophy

Politics

Religion

The Oxford Shakespeare

A complete list of Oxford World's Classics, including Authors in Context, Oxford English Drama, and the Oxford Shakespeare, is available in the UK from the Marketing Services Department, Oxford University Press, Great Clarendon Street, Oxford OX2 6DP, or visit the website at www.oup.com/uk/worldsclassics.

In the USA, visit www.oup.com/us/owc for a complete title list.

Oxford World's Classics are available from all good bookshops. In case of difficulty, customers in the UK should contact Oxford University Press Bookshop, 116 High Street, Oxford OX1 4BR.

A SELECTION OF **OXFORD WORLD'S CLASSICS**